From the Frozen Chosin to Churchill

From the Frozen Chosin to Churchill

The Biography of CSM Ray Hooker
Cottrell as told to Bob Brooks

Robert Brooks

Library of Congress Control Number:		2016920732
ISBN:	Hardcover	978-1-5245-6920-4
	Softcover	978-1-5245-6919-8
	eBook	978-1-5245-6918-1

Print information available on the last page.

Rev. date: 01/24/2017

To order additional copies of this book, contact:
Xlibris
1-888-795-4274
www.Xlibris.com
Orders@Xlibris.com
745928

CONTENTS

DEDICATION

To my wife Lovell, my daughter Brenda, and my Hero Ray Jr.
With Love, Hugs, and Prayers Forever
Plus One Day

INTRODUCTION

A S THE AUTHOR of Everything watches, mankind has always had a reason to fight. Our cities, states, and nations are formed by the ideas and wants of its people, usually driven by the voices of their leaders. Sometimes they are motivated by needs, such as farming land and resources. Sometimes they are motivated by greed and avarice. Sometimes they fight to prevent annihilation or genocide. When it is not over resources, it is usually over power or ideas.

When these states come into conflict, they look to their leaders to get the job done, to keep the citizens safe, and to take their warriors to victory. We call our leaders by different names such as pharaoh, king, czar, imam, prime minister, emperor, chancellor, or president. In the more modern times, we use terms like admiral, commander, general, colonel, and others. We give them stars or other symbols to wear on their hats, and shoulders so we can tell which one has more authority over the others. We want order to be recognized to prevent anarchy or loss of command and control. It is also a sign of their power and how much power they have. Man wants and needs order in the chaos of war.

For thousands of years it has been this way. For thousands of years, mankind has not learned that in the end measurement, of all the boots sent to battle, there is almost always boots left behind. The citizenry hears the numbers, but it is the individual families that feel the pain. History reports these conflicts in statistical statements and paint them in broad brushstrokes. It isn't until the power of communications that brought us instant news worldwide, that the citizenry was given the chance to see war from the eyes of the cameras. With that came embedded journalists on the fighting fields. With that came the court of public opinion. With that came the opportunity for the country to become divided or unified in its endeavors. History tells us that the United States has not won a major war since WWII. In the citizenry and military alike, there are some who hold that is because of the reporter. This book will not debate that issue. It is intended to tell the story of one soldier and to help the reader close the gap between what we as citizens understand about our armed services members and how the armed services see themselves. An education of time and events run parallel with the story of our soldier to give insight on some of the What's, and Why's in his history and our history as well.

Since 1778, the non commissioned officer (NCO) in the United States Military has been set along the side of their military leaders. They accomplish many goals for their officers. They could be called the glue that makes it all work out. From generals on down the commissioned officer corps to the platoon leader, it is the NCO that gets the bulk of the labor of the command and missions set before our forces. They have been called to train the new officers who have the textbook knowledge but lack personal experience on the battlefield. They have been called to be the go-between from the officer and the enlisted. They are used for advisors to their commanders and strategists in mission planning. From the Pentagon to the ditches and mud or sand of the battlefield, an NCO can be found.

Each level of the enlisted NCO brings with it unique challenges and tasks. Each individual works long hours and hectic schedules. Work levels are so cumbersome that a week might only allow a couple of hours of sleep a night before the next day begins. They are there when the recruits wake up and there to turn the lights out. When soldiers in the field are sleeping, they are usually working. There is very little rest for the NCO. As they go up in rank, the more their responsibilities pileup. When you come across a good one, you want to access their talents wherever possible.

This is the story of one such NCO. Equally versed in training and planning as he is in leading and fighting, and raised from the poverty of the Great Depression, our soldier enters the service at sixteen. Like many kids in WWII, he lies about his age to have the opportunity to do more than just survive. It has been argued that there was no such thing as a teenager until the '70s. When you left the house, you were considered an adult. You made decisions as an adult, you were treated as an adult, and you were respected as an adult. This soldier becomes that adult when his first experience in war comes at age seventeen in the frozen land of North Korea in 1950. From Inchon to Suwon, to the Chinese border of the Yalu, and the Chosin Reservoir, he travels and fights for his country 6,000 miles away from home. He is not old enough to drink or vote but old enough to die. He grows up in the military under the tutelage of his commanders and leaders. He couldn't read a compass before he was put in charge of a platoon of fighting men, all of whom older than him, some by a decade or more.

From the troubles in Germany in a post-WWII Europe, he continues his life on the front lines. Followed by a threat of WWIII in Cuba, to the jungles of Vietnam, he continues to put himself out there on the tip of the spear. He is an NCO that leads from the front. He grows to become geared for action. While well-versed in the requirements of desk work, he is called from within to be on the battlefield. He is geared to succeed.

He will continue with other careers when he retires. Lucky, and skilled enough to be a survivor of the battlefield, this warrior takes his honor and discipline into the working world of the civilian. Ever connected to the army for life, he will evolve into a highly successful individual that goes from used-car salesman to the sport of kings. He sees the world through two lenses: "The Mission" and protecting the ones that are to see that "Mission Completed." He lives for the challenge and fights for success. When others came home broken or beaten, he sticks to his training and overlays it on his new mission. Life. It keeps him going. To put on the breaks is to lay down. The NCO has no time for breaks. A man can wear many hats in his lifetime, but rare is the time when that same man can make the transition almost effortlessly.

In a world of instant messaging and satellite television, this combat veteran sticks to what works from the old world. For him, work is what defines him the most. His standards are high, but so are his morals. He fights to leave no one behind and works tirelessly to move forward, taking as many as he can with him to a better life. He holds that if the planning is done right, and the mission is followed through wisely, there is not much room for failure. Always planning for tomorrow. If self-discipline is the hardest lesson ever learned, he is the mentor that you would choose to teach it.

With so many distractions in the world, and a drop in respect for our men and women in the military as a whole, the gap between how the civilians see the military and how the military sees itself is noticeably widening. This book hopes to bridge that gap so that they will see a little better eye to eye. Our soldier's life within these pages hope to accomplish just that. Along with that challenge, it is hoped that current military and the military retiree or veteran can take away with them the hope and outline to become as successful in the service as they can become outside of it is obtainable.

With so many clicks of the clock, we lose veteran after veteran. The personal stories of these fighting men and women are hardly recorded. It is the hope of the author to capture the insights of this particular "brother-in-arms" and challenge the reader to gather all that they can of our other veterans before their knowledge and wisdoms are lost to the ages. History, once lost, can never be rediscovered to its highest possible value later.

CHAPTER 1

The Ray Hooker Cottrell Story

THE TEMPERING OF our souls is brought about through the test of the fires of our life. Few have walked harder or have been tested more than Ray Hooker Cottrell. This is the evolution of a warrior. From Cowboys and Indians and erector sets to battle, every so often a person is born into the world with a path that leads to the highest level of mastery of life. And even more so, a path that comes naturally. Their roads will take them through so many aspects of the world and to so many places that the mere experience generates a wisdom for the ages. It is even more valuable when that same person takes to it like a fish to water. Their purpose is easily identifiable to themselves even if they are not paying attention to the road signs. God lays before them the test and obstacles, and if the individual sticks to their moral compass, the results are exceedingly wondrous. It creates the type of human being that should not only be admired but also remembered and copied. Life presents no path that is easily walked. For that is not the lot for any man. It is for us to work with what we have and make the best of what we are given.

Ray is eighty-three and still has the mind of a warrior commander. At 5:00 a.m., before the alarm goes off, he will slip out of bed and start his day. He opens the shop hours before the rest are even expected to be there. Even if employees come in early, two pots of coffee are already hot. The newspaper is spread out and glanced over like Admiral Vanderbilt would do. The lights are warmed up, and the television is turned on to the news. The weather is checked. Any unfinished paperwork is signed and put into the outbox. A full day of work lies ahead of him, conversations with customers and credit managers. He oversees every aspect of the business to ensure no snags are accrued along the way. He does all the things that any good manger would do. He does not lead with an iron fist, but he does lead from the front. His management style would fall into the category of casual and family-like to anyone on the outside looking in. But to earn trust from him should be considered and honor. At closing time, he is there when the lights are turned out. At this age though, he might leave an hour before closing as long as he knows everything is going to close out smoothly. More often than not, he will be there himself. Then it is home for dinner. A nap in his recliner and up again to make a little family time with the wife. A quick check of the evening news maybe, and then it is off to bed for a good five hours of sleep to prepare to do it all over again. This is the routine seven days a week. Not bad for an octogenarian.

What sets Ray out from that pack goes even further. He could boast as having more valor medals than Audie Murphy, but he doesn't. He would say, *"I might have more than him, but they are not as high ranking as his."* [1] Then you would see a sheepish look come over his face almost as if he was embarrassed to even have to make that clarification. He always has a sense of humbleness in his voice and actions that is spattered with a sly sense of humor reminiscent of Hawkeye Pierce from the TV show *Mash*. Hardly what one would expect from a seasoned combat veteran, he seems uncomfortable to tout his own accolades, even for someone who is in his eighties. People of this age range don't typically show a sense of shyness.

In that same vein though, Ray has accomplishments that would make most people jealous. His philanthropy has allowed him to commit to so many causes that they are too numerous to express them all. Personal stories of his dealings with individuals and families are more than just a charity given but in his mind more so "just doing the right thing."

Ray does not throw his money out there wildly either. He has a very black-and-white concept of what and when to give his attention to in any given situation. As Mr. Kuster, a close friend who has followed in the same division and regiments as Ray was associated with, but ten years behind him, would say, *"Ray doesn't change. Work doesn't change him. Money doesn't change him. Prestige doesn't change him."*[2] On that note, as we did our interviews, you will always see his tie pin showing his admiration and affiliation with the U.S. Army. You will always see his work badge showing Ray's Ford with a hand-scribed "Ray" in blue marker underneath the logo. Kuster is right. Ray doesn't change. Ray would attribute this to one fact. One of his own personal standards is this: "You treat everyone the same." He truly believes in the saying "All men are created equal." This has the added bonus of not only keeping him from having to change who he is in any given situation but also offers a steadfast consistency for anyone that comes into his life. It helps make him the rock that he is.

Ray was raised in the Southern state of Virginia in the 1930s and 1940s, one of the original colonies and the eighth state to formally secede from the Union. He was born on May 11, 1933, in Richmond, the third child of seven siblings. He grew up in a racially segregated time, living in the central part of Virginia less than seventy years from the Civil War.

Children of that time were often born in their homes, and Ray was no different. Getting the mother to a hospital oftentimes proved dangerous, and it was good thing that the doctor made it to the house. This was a time of midwives, four years into the Great Depression. Ray was born to a Baptist family.

This is Ray's childhood home post-1933. The steps and handrail were added after he left the house. It originally had makeshift steps. [3]

As a child living in the Great Depression, he found life a bit of a struggle. It was a time when 25 percent of the country's population was unemployed. Water bowls and pitchers on nightstands was the form of cleaning up. Life was tough living on a farm or in a city. Hundreds of thousands of people were living on the road or migrating in search of work. This speaks volumes to the work ethic that the family must have had. Having seven children during the peak of the Depression was a daunting task for any family at that time, perhaps even more so in Richmond.

Ray was born to uniqueness and luck from the onset. It is as if he was born under a special star. Ray Cottrell was named after his family physician, Dr. Raymond Cottrell Hooker. His mother, probably at a loss for naming the child, called him Raymond Hooker Cottrell as a compliment to the doctor. When putting things into perspective regarding the time, location, and economics, it really is no great surprise at all. Women are still known to name their child after ambulance workers and doctors. This was not a time when ambulances and crack specialists in the medical field were abound though. The action of his mother is a sign of respect for the doctor's ability and commitment to the family.

Their home is small. Makeshift steps get you into their four-room house. A picture of his childhood home hangs on an opposite wall, just to the right of his desk. The house appears to be only twenty-five feet wide at the front. He tells me, *"One needed to get to bed before the others if you wanted a good place on the bed."[3] His* childhood consisted of three kids sleeping in one bed. Running water was an issue for most people of the town: a commodity in his childhood. Not all homes had running water. Natural gas in homes was not introduced until 1950. Shit on a shingle is a good meal for the day.

Ray with his pet on the road that leads to the backyard of his house. The road continues to Sugar Bottom and the watering spigots. [3]

His parents were on rocky ground in his preteen years. This was his life. He has few memories of his childhood now. His father was a truck driver for a meat company. His mother was an egg grader. His grandparents on his mother's side are only referenced to as Mother and Father.

This is a childhood memory that Ray still holds, and it serves as one of the many roots of the boy that would later be the man. It is hard to imagine in our time what it is like to not have clean running water in the house. But this is the time of outhouses and no TV. Radio and newspapers are the media outlets. His home is located on one side of the community water fountain. Its location is approximately a quarter mile down the dusty road that runs directly toward his backdoor. The water is only obtainable by carrying or carting it. At this location, if someone needed clean drinkable water, this was about the only place to get it. The water spigots are below ground level in a concrete walled area with stairs leading down to it. There are four spigots at this location: two for drinking and two for filling containers with. On the far side of the watering hole, and about a mile and a half further down the road, is the start of the black community of the town, often heard of as the other side of the tracks.

It is 1944 and segregation is in full swing in Virginia. While accompanying two of his friends, Ray was found playing in the area just outside of the neighborhood called Sugar Bottom. Lewis Taylor is one of these friends that is with him. Sugarbottom is a black neighborhood just down the road at the back of his house. He overhears a raucous taking place down at the watering hole. As they look over the retaining wall, looking down at the area of the spigots, they see a group of boys giving a young black girl a hard way to go. She is there doing the daily run of water for her family. She has pulled a wagon with two five-gallon containers in it. This is not a blazing red American Flyer type of wagon. This is a wagon built for chores, not for play.

In a post-1941 world, everyone is doing their part to support the war effort of World War II. Metal, rubber, and a host of other normal possessions have been usurped for the war effort. The task of obtaining water, as with many children of the time, is troublesome to say the least when you overlay this effort in comparison to the modern conveniences of our times. Roads are not well-kept. Sidewalks are either nonexistent or limited to certain upper areas of town.

As they look on, the bullies surrounded the young girl, spilling her water onto the ground. Name-calling and unwarranted nasty harassment of the racial kind takes place. They have called her names and told her that she was not allowed to draw water from this spot and should go somewhere else to get her jugs filled. They warned her to never come back there. As many young teens and preteens would show their angst and cluelessness of the things going on around them, they were not aware that they had been caught. Seeing the despair on the young girl's face, Ray's crew, the "Lucky" crew, moves down and goes into action.

As they confronted the boys face-to-face, the encounter turns violent. The boys are overcome by these would-be knights in shining armor. Ray adds to the equation with a stern scolding and a warning. Should these guys ever try to harass this girl again, they would ensure another ass-whooping of a greater proportion. From that point on, whenever the young girl's path would cross Ray's, she would make eye contact and wave to him as if to say thanks and that he had made a new friend. He says, *"It was not unusual for the girl to wait for me to come into view just to wave hi."* [1] A great reward for just doing the right thing. Even early on in his childhood, a sense of responsibility and respect could be found in young Ray, an attribute that would serve him well in his careers and life to come. Ray would say, *"I knew even then, that you treated everyone the same way."* [1] But anyone can see the warrior side and lack of fear coming out early in his life.

Young kids of that age were often left to their own devices in this era. There were creeks to walk, crawdads to find, fishing the James River, and the usual risk-taking that most parents would be aghast about if they knew what their children were up to. Ray has become a pretty street-savvy young boy at this age. When chores were done, he would be off like a rocket. He was quick to do things to make a dime or a quarter if he could find it. Cut some grass for a neighbor, move some boxes for a stranger, bag groceries for the local store. Basically he hustled for pocket change to do the things that a boy needed money for. Independent thinking might be an understatement. Having an allowance for him is unheard of.

At the age of eleven, Ray found himself on a bus to the other side of town. Bus riding was common for him as he would often ride to church with his grandmother and to watch movies at the local theater. He was no stranger to the streets, but this day would prove to be different.

Richmond is fairly big in the mid-1940s. The things for a young boy to do often took him away from the house to do it. Being street-savvy is not a thing to underestimate or disrespect, especially when thinking about all the things that come to the mind of a young boy wandering through Virginia. This is just the nature of things at the time. Ray learns and appreciates personal freedom, independence, and the responsibility that comes along with it.

After watching the 10-cent Saturday night flick, it was time to go home. Night had fallen, and it was getting late. Before boarding the bus, he discovers that he only has 13 cents on him. That would not seem like such a big deal, but the bus ride home was 14 cents. Thinking that he could slip one past the driver, Ray dropped his money into the glass-walled box that is used for taking fares. He remembers, *"I quickly went to the back of the bus as fast as I could, hoping that the driver wouldn't notice, or at least didn't care."*[1]

Unfortunately, he couldn't be more wrong. The driver did notice, and he was quick to inform the young rider to return to the front. When charged to come up with another penny to take the fare, he was unable to. The driver quickly put him off the bus. The bus driver did, however, send the money down the holding box. No returns, no refunds. After sundown on a summer evening on the far side of town from his home, Ray is forced to walk home.

Richmond in the late '30s to mid-'40s was experiencing record growth. It had a population of over 255,000 in 1936. The growth rate of businesses from 1935 to 1946 boomed by 250 percent. By 1945, it was sending 350 million pounds of material for the war effort. By 1946, it was the fastest-growing industrial city in the United States. This was the landscape of his journey. He sees the sights and sounds of an industrialized city as he treks his way back home in the late evening. A mother today would lose her mind in these modern times if she knew her youngster was hiking across town alone in the middle of the night.

One would think that this adventure was anything but lucky. As the story unfolds, he recalls, *"When I got home, I made it a personal note to never not have money in my pocket again. To this day, if I find a penny on the ground, I will pick it up. My grandfather gifted me a 1933 50-cent piece. I carry it with me every day so that I would always have money on me. I still have that coin and never go without it."* [1] That coin is well worn but still in his possession. At some point, that coin took on a greater value.

This is why to this day, if Ray sees a penny on the ground, he picks it up. This is a family tradition handed down until this day. If the old adage has any weight to it—*"When you see a penny pick it up, and all day you will have good luck"*—then one can only imagine the blessings and luck that the Cottrell family has enjoyed.

At age thirteen, the morning starts out with delivering newspapers, Monday through Sunday with no days off. Up before dawn, and down to the paper route drop off point. The only thing that slows him down is a little bad weather, but that would never stop him from getting the job done. It must be done because every penny counts.

Then it is off to the grocery store to bag groceries for 25 cents an hour. A good forty-hour week, if he could get it, would fetch him ten bucks. Because his mother was an egg grader, she had access to the product. There would be eggs for breakfast and even at times when it wasn't breakfast. His mother and father make do with what they have. Oftentimes, dinner would be chipped beef from a can. Added to water and bread instead of dumplings, this would make for a fine dinner. This was good eating and good times to the young lad trying to make it through. There is a difference between being a kid and eating, and being a kid and eating well, but when you are poor, it is never noticed. It is just another day.

Because of the war effort, everything counts. Everyone is pitching in. Ray takes advantage of this need for materials as a way to supplement his income. A one-pound can of bacon grease in a jar, if it could be collected, or tin cans crushed up, could gain access to things otherwise unavailable. Ten of these cans could allow admittance into the movie theater. Bacon grease in a jar would allow the same. Anything of value could be repurposed for the war effort. Taking advantage of this is just a common thing to do. For Ray, it is a necessity that must be followed. Just another day in Richmond.

Four years of running the paper route afforded him some other opportunities as well. On occasion, he picked out four or five customers to magically not receive their paper. He is careful to not pick customers that would be fast to complain. He learns this process the hard way. At the end of his route, if he had a few papers left over, he could head to the street corner and sell them for three cents. Oftentimes, these buyers would just give him a nickel and tell him to keep the change. That was always a lucky event.

Being a streetwise kid had its advantages. He is not getting rich, but he is affording himself opportunities that some other kids his age cannot or do not have. An occasional trip to the movies or the chance to pick up some fishing hooks to take down to the James River makes for a good day and a break from the trials and tribulations of being a kid.

Life running the streets also comes with some hurdles. Scrapping with young gangs of boys is somewhat commonplace. Ray is a fighter though. Backing down from such clashes can have long-term effects, while winning some of these clashes have beneficial results. They don't fight over territory grounds. They could fight just for the fact that one boy thought he was stronger than Ray or maybe didn't like the look on his face when something was said. Winning fights like these keeps the bullies at bay and thus prevents rehashing these petty squabbles later. Losing a fight would tend to mean that there would be a rematch at some unexpected, unannounced, and inopportune time. He is not prone to start a fight, but he is all in when there are no better choices. The young warrior must scratch out his place, and he has no tolerance for people who do stupid, aggressive, or just mean things to the innocent.

He understands what it takes to make it on the streets. This type of understanding would qualify him as a very young "wise guy" if he stayed this course. One becomes intuitive of others and insightful of what could happen next. This wisdom does not prevent the bad things that can happen from happening. But intuition is a requirement if one is to make it on the streets. Each new experience, good or bad, generates knowledge and molds the person going through the process.

Ray was raised by his grandparents after leaving his father's house. By the time he was a teenager, his parents have divorced. His father attempted to keep the boy, but the friction between Ray and his stepmother proved to be too much. At thirteen, Grandfather Cottrell insisted that the boy would stay with him from here on. By fifteen, he has saved enough money to buy a car.

He would often return to his maternal grandmother's house to visit. Still young, he would indulge himself with the distractions of the time: hunting, fishing, and swimming down at the watering hole. All the things that a scrapping boy would do at the time. While there, he would often make time for the next-door neighbor's daughter.

Her name was Lovell. She would go by the nickname of Tootie as a child. The two of them had befriended each other very early in life. This friendship would turn serious as time went on. Tootie, whom Ray affectionately calls Lovey, would one day become his wife. But not yet. Many things would have to happen first. There were classes to take, chores to do, friends to run around with, and trouble to get into. Lots and lots of trouble.

In his sixteenth year, while attending school, Ray was on the football team. From time to time, teachers would let athletes leave class early to prepare for practice. George Hatfield, the school's running back, and he are close friends. Both of them are in the hallway making their way down to the practice field. As they made their way out, they come across the most dreaded of students: the hall monitor. We will only refer to her as Mary. She is an attractive young lady with a sense of responsibility about her. She tells the boys that she will have to write the guys' names down for being in the hall during classes without a pass. George and Ray tell the girl that she can't do that, as they were let out early to go to football practice.

Both the boys knew her. She was a senior. George, not only being a well-accomplished halfback at an all-state level, was also a charmer. George starts flirting with the girl. The phrase "able to charm the pants off her" is exactly what happened. Ray is embarrassed about this story, but in the sake of full disclosure, the story goes on. George, elated by his conquest, starts running down the hall from the third floor shouting in a teasing juvenile voice, *"I've got Mary's panties, I've got Mary's panties."* What happens next is the launching point that would catapult Ray from adolescent teen to manhood. The next few weeks accelerated his life much like going from 0 to 200 mph on a skateboard.

George and Ray continue to football practice. George had secured the newfound item and made it not only through practice with them but all the way home. This is what starts the wheels in motion. Someone, perhaps Mary herself, had reported that George and Ray had this amazing accomplishment. Word reaches the girl's parents, who in turn relay the information on to the police. Ray and George are immediately called into the principal's office. Both claim their innocence. The school principal tells the boys, *"Come tomorrow morning. You two are to have that item returned to this office."[1]* Things look rather bleak for the two boys. Even worse for George.

Ray gave George a ride home that afternoon in his old Model A Ford. The car was purchased by his own endeavors. George's father was a boxer of some standing. As the two pulled onto the property, George's father was in the front of the house waiting on them. Ray recounts, "The man snatched George from my car and beat the shit out of him. I put the pedal to the metal and got the hell out of there." George would be seen the next day with two black eyes and a couple of bruises to boot. Ray got up that morning and came straight to school. *"I didn't want to go by and get George 'cause I didn't want to get my ass kicked."* [1] He thought it more prudent to just get to school and report to the principal's office.

As Ray sat in the chair outside the office, George appeared with a brown bag in hand. He thinks, *I am hoping that it was his lunch bag, but I know that it is not.* [1] Apprehensive of things to come, they both go into the office to meet with the principal. George approaches the desk and puts the bag on it. In a blink of an eye, they are both now suspended from school indefinitely.

This was not without other problems as well. The football team was set to play in the state championship game. As luck would have it, George, because of his all-state athletic ability, was let back in school and back on the team. Ray was not that fortunate. He recalls, *"I played football, but I wasn't that good."* [1] He was declined the opportunity to get back to classes, much less the football team.

Ray, now sixteen, has to make some choices. As with many young men in the Great Depression, the military is looking like a good idea. He falsifies his paperwork and signs up with the National Guard, effectively leaving George, his grandparents, family, and Lovey (Tootie) behind. Tootie, now his girlfriend, would communicate with him throughout his enlistment. She was not allowed to date, so when he spent time with her, it would be heavily watched over by her mother.

In need of money, and a place to stay, he is thought of as seventeen by the National Guard. He forges his papers and his parents' signatures. He does his basic training at Fort Indiantown Gap in Pennsylvania. A quick haircut and some new clothes that don't fit well, and off to boot camp he goes.

Private Ray Hooker Cottrell, U.S. Army, Fort Knox, Kentucky, 1950. Photo from personal library. [3]

CHAPTER 2

Getting Ready

I N HIS SEVENTEENTH year, Ray grew up in the army. While that might create several opportunities for a teen to evolve, it is always up to the individual to take the proper path. This early encounter with the military and the events of his past make it easy to understand that his natural predilections would be the building blocks that make the man.

Indiantown Gap National Guard Training Center

He is trained in artillery. His time there is short, and there are few recollections of his induction to the guard. Since June of 1949, Ray has been with the Pennsylvania National Guard. Indiantown Gap is a base of about 18,000 acres. Its population is eighty. The amount of military personnel, however, is in the thousands. Before the end of the next year, this base will be a major training ground for the United States for its efforts in Korea. His training is centered on artillery. In April of 1950, it is time to make a decision again. After all, the guard is just a part-time job. It is hard to make a living one weekend a month. That decision is easy for him. Ray decides to go full-time army. He enlists.

He knows he can handle it. One can't just lollygag around town until it is time to go back to guard duty. On July 13, 1950, he moved to Fort Knox, Kentucky. He was ahead of the issues of basic training this time. He had the haircut, the desire, the need, and the motivation. What is one more run through basic training? This second time would hold no surprises. Another couple of weeks of marching, cleaning, sleeping, marching, cleaning, sleeping. An education in tanks is ahead of him. This will serve to increase his level of knowledge in the ways of war as well. This time should prove to be much easier. It is never too early to start a career. Besides that, Lovey is waiting for him at home.

The Oath

The military always stresses its code of conduct and discipline. Its tenants have stretched from one generation of military personnel to the next. The oath goes like this:

I, (*NAME*), do solemnly swear (or affirm) that I will support and defend the Constitution of the United States and the State of (*STATE NAME*) against all enemies, foreign and domestic; that I will bear true faith and allegiance to the same; and that I will obey the orders of the President of the United States and the Governor of (*STATE NAME*) and the orders of the officers appointed over me, according to law and regulations. So help me God.

This current oath has been the standard since 1962. The original oath of the military, as it was performed at the forming of the country, was a little bit different. If you were committing to the Continental Army in 1775, your oath would be like this:

I (Name) have, this day, voluntarily enlisted myself, as a soldier, in the American continental army, for one year, unless sooner discharged: And I do bind myself to conform, in all instances, to such rules and regulations, as are, or shall be, established for the government of the said Army.

That oath would again change just a year later when the Congress would pass the Articles of War on September 20, 1776. Section 3, Article 1, would offer this oath to the officers and enlisted:

I (name) swear to be trued to the United States of America, and to serve them honestly and faithfully against all their enemies opposers whatsoever; and to observe and obey the orders of the Continental

Congress, and the orders of the Generals and officers set over me by them. [5]

This would change once again in 1779 to a two-part oath that would stay in effect until 1962 as the modern oath seen above. It would be taken by officers and the enlisted men at all levels for all branches. Regulations on who could administer this oath is prescribed by the Secretary of Defense. As can be seen by the evolution of the military oath, change often doesn't happen. The passing down of traditions and responsibilities is basically steadfast and unmoving. While the oath has changed very slightly over time, the tenets of being in the armed forces has withstood the test of time.

For Ray, taking the oath is a simple thing in terms of the process of it. It requires nothing more than standing there at attention and raising his right hand. He is in a room with several young men his age and younger. He would discover that there are actually fellow recruits that are only sixteen years of age when takes the oath. Fortunately, or unfortunately, depending on how one may look at it, these young men joined the military for several reasons. In 1949, some of these fellows are joining to escape poverty, troubled family lives, broken hearts, or just to keep getting a paycheck.

While the process of taking the oath is a simple thing, living up to that oath will take the full measure of a man to uphold. The estimated number of our current military strength is represented as just 1 percent of the entire population. True one-percenters. There is no limit to the amount of thanks and gratitude that should be offered to these men and women, especially the ones who gave their last full measure of commitment to that oath. In an all-volunteer army, even more should be recognized.

NR: DA TT 3426   PAGE 2

All restrictions which have previously prevented the
full utilization of the U.S. Far East Air Forces to support
and assist the defense of the South Korean territory are
lifted for operations below the 38th Parallel. All North
Korean tanks, guns, military columns and other military targets south of the 38th Parallel are cleared for attack by
U.S. Air Forces. The purpose is to clear South Korea of
North Korean military forces. Similarly Naval Forces may be
used without restriction in coastal waters and sea approaches
of Korea south of 38th Parallel against forces engaged in
aggression against South Korean. (End DA-1)

Washington: DA-2.

Imperative that you use every method available to you
to advise Amb Muccio, Korean military leaders and Korean
civilian officials of these decisions as they relate to
Korea. (End DA-2)

Washington: DA-3.

What is your latest information summary of military
situation in Korea? (End DA-3)

Tokyo: FEC item 1.

Summary situation since 270145I last report CX 36812
Chief KMAG quotation N-Koreans have capability to take Seoul
within 24 hr i.e Tuesday/Wednesday. S-K C/S takes attitude
that the fall of Seoul is fall of South Korea. Latest info
to 10 A.M. Tokyo time: Piecemeal entry into action North of
Seoul by South Korean Third and Fifth Divisions has not succeeded in stopping the penetration recognized as the enemy
main effort for the past 2 days with intent to seize the
capital city of Seoul. Tanks entering suburbs of Seoul.
Government transferred to south and communication with part
of KMAG opened at Taegu.

South Korean units unable to resist determined northern
offensive. South Korean casualties as an index to fighting
have not shown adequate resistance capabilities or the will
to fight and our estimate is that a complete collapse is
possible. (End item 1)

Washington: DA-4.

What means of communications do you have now with
Korea? (End DA-4)

DA TT 3426   (JUN 50)

TOP SECRET   COPY NO.

From the Truman Library [1]

As Ray determines how long of a ride it will be from Richmond, Virginia, to Kentucky, the North Koreans and the Chinese are determining how long it will take to get control of the Pusan peninsula. On June 25, 1950, the North Koreans, supported by the Chinese "People's Liberation Army" and the Russians, invade south of the 38th parallel. The 38th is the geographical marker for the world that basically cuts the country of Korea in half. The dispute started in 1945 when Russia declared war upon Japan. Russia influenced the lands north of the 38th, and the United States influenced the land to the south. Both sides of the line set up governments. Both governments declare their legitimacy over the entire country. No specific borders are ever determined in the dispute. By June 25, this dispute would expand into all-out war. Russian support of the Chinese People's Liberation Army had come into play for the North Korean Army's assault into the south of the country. The North Koreans had pushed their way across the 38th and were making their way south to take it all over.

June 27

Two days later, June 27, S/Res/83 (Security/Resolution/83) would be adopted by the United Nations Security Council. It is a complaint of aggression upon the Republic of Korea. Eighty-eight percent of the U.N.'s military force is U.S. personnel. Over twenty countries are in support of sending forces to support the struggling army of the South. Following is a short summary of communications and actions going on behind the scenes.

From the Truman Library

The [United Nations Security Council resolution] . . . did not pass unanimously. That was drafted in my office. . . . I remember that at one stage . . . [Deputy U.N. Representative] Gross and Senator Austin [the U.N. Representative] were on the telephone and said, "We've gone as far as we can. If we could postpone this another 24 hours, we <u>might</u> get the Indian vote, but we're not at all sure, What do we do?"

I've forgotten what the lineup was, but the Indian vote would have been important. . . . I said, "I'll check this with the Secretary, and call you back, but I don't think we can wait. You've given all the arguments and they know this thing. There's a UN Commission in Korean. There was; and they reported there had been aggression and the North Koreans did it." I said, "What more can you say than that?"

Acheson confirmed what I said and I reported back to Senator Austin at the UN, India and one or two other states abstained but the resolution passed.

Assistant Secretary of State for U.N. Affairs John Hickerson
Oral history interview, June 5, 1973 [1]

June 28, 1950

Muccio (John Muccio United States Ambassador to Korea) sent a message to [the Department of] State marked 28 June 10 A.M. (presumably Korean time) with the following statements: "Situation had deteriorated so rapidly had not President's decision plus arrival General [John] Church party become known here, doubtful any organized Korean resistance would have continued through the night. Combat aid decision plus Church's orders [from General MacArthur establishing him to head the U.S. Advance Command and Liaison Group in Korea] have had a great morale effect. . . ."

Administrative Assistant to the President George M. Elsey
Memorandum for the record based on White House Files, n.d.
George M. Elsey Papers [1]

June 29, 1950

Around 7 o'clock in the morning of June 29, a teleconference was held between representatives of G2 [Intelligence] in Tokyo and G2 in Washington, at which State Department representatives were present . . . . At this conference it was reported that the South Korean forces had suffered 50 percent casualties and were attempting to form a line at the Han River, but would fall back to a line above Taegue, if necessary. Reports for holding the Suwon airstrip were favorable.

Administrative Assistant to the President George M. Elsey
Memorandum for the record based on Secretary of State's
Briefing Book "borrowed . . . from Averell Harriman," n.d.
George M. Elsey Papers [1]

The president had appointments up to lunchtime. Shortly after 3:00 P.M. we went into the cabinet room where we held our usual prepress and radio conference session. At the beginning the president read a report on the situation in Korea, which was not too cheerful. The weather has hindered aerial operations, and the situation with the Korean defending forces has deteriorated. The report said they had about forty percent casualties and of those remaining about eighty percent were armed.

We submitted numerous questions that we thought might be asked by the correspondents, especially concerning the situation in Korea and some of the many reports and stories that have been printed. Several columnists and writers have charged that the United States has reversed policy toward Korea and Formosa, and others have said [Secretary of State Dean] Acheson would be forced out of the cabinet or would resign. There was some mention of differences between Acheson and Secretary of Defense [Louis] Johnson, and stories have charged that Acheson opposed action. The president said the fact was they had trouble getting the defense establishment to move. Johnson has talked to much - this is my own opinion, shared by numerous others - and undoubtedly has tried to take as much credit as possible.

"If this keeps up," the president commented, we're going to have a new secretary of defense."

Assistant Press Secretary Eben Ayers
Diary entry, June 29, 1950
Eben A. Ayers Papers [1]

The press conference was interesting, naturally, because there were many Korean questions. One question which had later significance ran as follows: "Mr. President, would it be correct, against your explanation, to call this a police action under the United Nations?"

The President replied: "Yes. That is exactly what it amounts to."

The President also said "We are not at war."

The President had called the North Koreans "a bunch of bandits."

Administrative Assistant to the President George M. Elsey
Memorandum for the record based on the
White House Files, n.d.
George M. Elsey Papers [1]

June 30, 1950

[W]e had no sooner gotten [to Suwon] . . . and the chauffeur of Ben Lim, who was the Korean Minister of Foreign Affairs, came up and said that General MacArthur was on the phone and that he wanted to talk to me. And if it had been anyone else I would have considered him a phony of some kind, because I didn't know of any possible telephone connection from Suwon to Tokyo. I turned to General [John] Church and I said, "If it is General MacArthur he'll probably want to talk to you. How about going along?

So, the two of us drove up to the Post Office in the center of Suwon. The power was off and the only lights in there were a couple of candles. It was a very eerie feeling to go there and see an old French style telephone . . . . And it wasn't General MacArthur, it was General [Edward M.] Almond, the Chief of Staff, MacArthur had already left the headquarters. And that's when I heard that General MacArthur wanted to come over in person and "get a feel of the situation," on Thursday and he wanted suggestions as to where to come to. . . . Well we were there at Suwon where there was a plausible airstrip. But [Korean President Syngman] Rhee and his Cabinet were already down at Taejon. And I flew down to Taejon the next afternoon, Wednesday afternoon, and came back to Suwon, Rhee in one L-5 and I in another L-5, early Thursday morning where we met MacArthur. That was on the 29th of June. . . .

General MacArthur spent the day talking in succession with President Rhee, myself, the American and Korean military and going up for a fleeting view of the Han River. Before leaving he told me he had decided to report to Washington that what was needed were some regular U.S. armed units to firm up the Koreans--"Say, some two divisions." He actually sent his report and request for two divisions while in flight back to Tokyo from Suwon.

Ambassador to Korea John Muccio
Oral History Interview, February 10, 1971 [1]

June 30, 1950, a phone call is made to the White House to President Truman. Details of that conversation are uncovered in this memo from the president.

July 1, 1950

Aboard U.S.S. *Williamsburg*

I was up and about shortly after 8 o'clock, the hour at which the ship was scheduled to leave the navy yard. . . . A little later I had a chat with him [President Truman], alone, standing at the "fantail." I commented that it was just a week since we took off on the trip to Independence, Mo., and that it had been a crowded week. I said I felt that the chronology of events during the week should be recorded if only for historical reasons, and he agreed. He said he had George Elsey at work on it and had had him sitting in on some of the conferences . . . .

On the way through the canal [Charles] Ross and I were with the president on the sun deck outside of his cabin. He talked with us at length about the

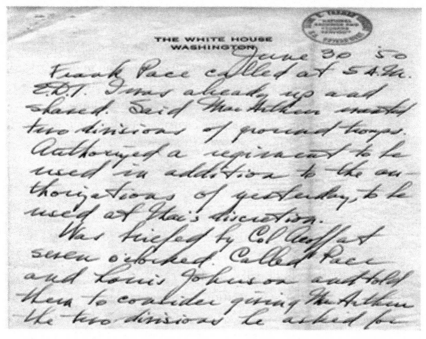

White House Communications to Joint Chiefs of the Military. Doc. 1. Doc. 1 from the White House in Truman's hand reads as follows: June 30th 1950

Frank Pace called at 5 AM. E.D.T. I was already up and shaved. Said Mac Author wanted two divisions of ground troops. Authorizing a regiment to be used in addition to the authorizations of yesterday to be used at Mac's discretion. Was briefed of Col. Acoff at seven o'clock. Called Pace and Louis Johnson and told them to consider giving MacArthur the divisions that he asked for. . . [1]

Korean situation and about General MacArthur, for whom the president has little regard or respect. He feels, as do most others, that MacArthur is a supreme egotist who regards himself as something of a god. The president commented on MacArthur's departure from Manila and Corregidor when the Japanese besieged the Philippines early in the war, and his escape to Australia, leaving General Wainwright to be captured. Wainwright has never recovered from the experience while MacArthur has become a hero and dictator in Japan.

The president said we should have heard John Foster Dulles and what he had to say to the president about MacArthur when he came in to see him this week after returning from Tokyo where, as a state department adviser, he had visited MacArthur. Dulles told him that when word came to Tokyo of the outbreak in Korea, MacArthur knew nothing of it, and [Dulles] was unable to get any of the general's staff to call MacArthur. All of them were afraid to. So Dulles did it himself. Dulles, the president indicated, would like to have MacArthur hauled back to the United States, but the president pointed out to him that the general is involved politically in this country - where he has from time to time been mentioned as a possible Republican presidential candidate - and that he could not recall MacArthur without causing a tremendous reaction in this country where he has been built up to a heroic stature. Dulles agreed, he said. . . .

Assistant Press Secretary Eben Ayers
Diary entry, July 1, 1950
Eben A. Ayers Papers [1]

July 13: First trip to Fort Knox

On July 13, 1950, Ray is arriving by bus to Fort Knox, Kentucky. This is his basic training base for the next leg of his career. More yelling, another haircut, and a new set of clothes that do not fit so well. He is attached to Company C Thirty-Third MTB (Machine/Mobile Tank Battalion). [2]

The morning routine during basic training is the same across the nation. Basic training is managed by SOPs (standard operational procedures). As one base goes, so do all bases. Up at the ass crack of dawn to whistles blowing and a very unhappy platoon sergeant banging on a trash can to get everyone out of bed. Uniforms donned, boots checked for scuffs, buckles polished until a tape measure becomes visible in it, and standing in front of the bunk that was so meticulously made that a recruit's mother would have baked him his favorite cake to see that just once before entering the military. Basic training has the unique ability to get these young men in lock step for the orders that are going to be followed without question. Ego is broken down. Any deviation from orders issued are quickly addressed with push-ups and a harsh chastisement from a voice that could make anyone's spine rattle while standing in place. Every issue is resolved immediately; every question is either answered or removed from the recruit's mind. One wrong step could cost not only the recruit but the entire platoon. Each person learning to think and act as one team. One purpose, one mission, is the expected result. This is not the time to clown around or create waves. Get in line or get pulled out of it. Getting pulled out was always a bad thing.

It is now August. The days are hot. The weather is never good. Even if it was good, it would not matter because the recruit is marching here, cleaning this, working on that. Orders, orders, orders consume the young recruit. If it rained, the recruit feels cooler, but the humidity and the weight of the uniform is a constant bother. As basic training comes to an end, Ray has made a new acquaintance. Lewis Taylor, a fellow Virginian from his childhood is with him at Fort Knox. Lewis has a car back home in Richmond, and the two guys decide to take advantage of some home time and a chance to acquire a ride for their next leg of training. Personal vehicles are not allowed to recruits during basic training. But a personal ride will come in handy for time off in the future.

Lewis Taylor and he leave Fort Knox. The young men start a 600-mile hike by thumb to their hometown of Richmond. They are wanting to get a little home time before shuffling off to advanced individual training (AIT). They have the opportunity to get Lewis's car and bring it back to Fort Knox as their ride back to base.

While in Richmond, they have a little money in their pocket and a little time to kill. Ray is afforded some time to see his sweetheart Lovey on his trip home, and is eager to be there among family and friends. Of course, there is a little garnered respect now that he has a military uniform. He has now started to fill out. There is still a little time for adventure. As the saying goes, "boys will be boys."

The week would end too soon though. Most of their money has been spent, save for a full tank of gas in his buddy's car. With not much time left to report back to Knox, they begin their journey back. Along Highway 44, just outside of Shelbyville, Kentucky, the two soldiers make a discovery: one tank of gas is not enough to drive from Richmond to Fort Knox. Both guys thought that the other had some money left on them from basic, but neither did. Nor did they count on being hungry and thirsty. After all, it was just a half a day's ride back to base.

Pulling up to a gas station, just outside of town on the main road, Ray gets out to speak to the owner. She is an older woman. She's not much to look at and has a bit of an edge about her. She is rough around the edges. Ray, being the wise guy of the two, convinces his buddy that he can work a deal of some sort to get a tank of gas. He walks into the shop and begins to barter with the woman. He offers her the spare tire on his buddy's vehicle in pawn for a tank of gas. He tells her that they will come back in a couple of weeks, after AIT, to repay her and collect the spare tire.

It turned out that this lady would not barter for objects, but she will barter. She argues with Ray and tells him she doesn't take pawns. She doesn't want used tires, rumble seats, or knick-knacks as a trade. She replies, "*I only want cash.*" [2] Basically there is not much that Ray could barter with her to get a tank of gas. Ray asks if there is anything that the two soldiers could do to help her out—move some boxes, do some type of work that would pay for the gas. Things look a little hopeless here.

But as it turns out, there is another opportunity that would help get the guys back. She stops and thinks for a second. She looks Ray over from stem to stern. A twinkle can be seen in her eyes. This is caught by Ray. She tells him that there is something that he can do after all.

This will get them a tank of gas. Ray picks up on her forwardness and responds quickly. *"I really appreciate the compliments lady, but let me suggest this instead. If you take a look outside by the gas pump, you will find a better-looking guy than me. He is taller and better built. I think you would like him better."* [2] She walks up to the window and pulls the curtain back a bit to get a look at Lewis. Turns to Ray and tells him, *"He will do just fine."* Now that half the battle has been won, he has to argue for a better deal.

No good wise guy is worth his salt unless he can get more bang for his buck than what the other party ends up with in the deal. He continues to negotiate just a little further. He recalls, *"I tell the lady that we have been on the road since Richmond, and I ask her if it would be possible to get a couple of colas and something to snack on for the rest of journey"*. [2] With a little excitement in her voice now, she agrees to two bottles of Pepsi and two MoonPies. Ray argues that he should get the gas pumped first to ensure no reneging on the deal. She happily agrees. All he has to do now is convince his buddy to complete the other half of the bargain.

He returns to the car leaving the lady inside and unexposed for Lewis to see. He speaks with his buddy and tells him the deal. All he has to do is satisfy the woman as need be, and then they can be on their way. He says she agrees to a drink and a snack as well. Lewis is taken back a bit by the arrangement and asks Ray for a description of the female. He tells him that she is older but is a handsome lady. Ray is trying to hold back the snickering. He ensures him that it will be okay. Lewis reluctantly goes inside. A few seconds later, the woman peeks out and tells Ray to watch for anyone coming onto the property. It will be his job to stand guard. Ray knows how to do that. The door shuts and locks, and he takes up his post by sitting on the steps in front of the door to enjoy his Pepsi and MoonPie.

Ray pumps the gas and the car is ready to go. It takes about twenty minutes for the business transaction to come to an end. He is seated in the driver's seat as the door opens and a disheveled private first class runs to the car. He is tucking his shirt and trying to put himself back together as he dashes to the vehicle. He jumps into the passenger seat. The only audible word that Ray could make out was "DRIVE." Unable to keep himself from snickering, Ray puts the pedal to the metal and kicks up dust and gravel as he shoots the car out on to the main road. The young man was unable to complete a sentence for next five minutes. Ray says, "*I couldn't help myself from asking. I waited till we got a couple of miles down the road and said to him, 'Did you get your Pepsi and MoonPie?' He yells at me, 'Don't ever talk to me again!'*" [2] They did, however, make it back to the fort on time.

While Ray is being run through the rigors yet again, the war in Korea is heating up fast.

North Koreans have pushed the South Koreans to the deep south of the country.

The young soldier enters his AIT. Before he completes this education, the North Korean Army has pushed their way south to the Pusan Perimeter. The South Korean Army is all but defeated at this point. Support has started to arrive to boost the efforts to keep the North Koreans and the Chinese "People's Liberation Army" (PLA/CCF-Communist Chinese Forces) out of Pusan. Supported by air strikes and the beefing up of personnel, the South Koreans are fighting back with all they have. The U.N. forces are being led by Gen. Douglas MacArthur of WWII fame.

Other generals back in Washington are warning against an aggressive counterattack as given the rough terrain and many unknowns. MacArthur is planning something much larger and faster. While battle plans are being created for an assault, General MacArthur puts in motion what will create a massive retaliation against the North Koreans.

It is now September. AIT has ended. Ray has now been trained in armor. The only thing that he hasn't been trained in at this point is infantry. Having received artillery training in the reserves, he has a leg up on most of his counterparts when it comes to induction and education. He jumps in the car with Lewis and makes his way back to Richmond again for another quick visit home.

It allows Ray the time to reconnect with Lovey. Dating Tootie is not without complications. Her mother is very strict. She is not allowed to leave the yard. She is not allowed to hold hands or go for a ride in the car with him. On occasion, her mother could be seen standing at the door shaking her fist at him as if to say, "I will knock you out if you make the wrong move."

This level of oversight is not uncommon for the time. In a mother's mind, a young teenage girl hanging out with a military man could only lend itself to bad things. Ray tolerates this because his love and concern for Tootie make it worth it. When they part, Ray understands that there will be someone at home who will wait for him. There is some comfort in that thought.

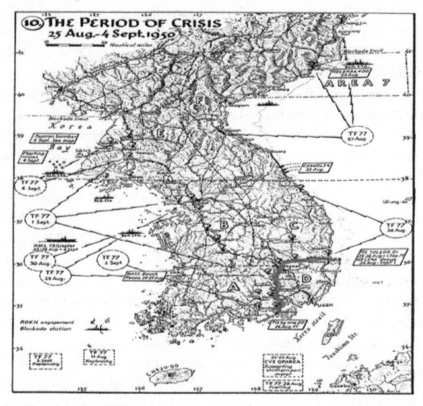

U.S. Navy map. Bold line at South east corner of map represents the Pusan Perimeter. ROK and U.N. forces are southeast of the line. [3]

His next trip takes him to San Francisco. He travels over 2,000 miles just to go another 4,000 miles. His orders have been cut, and he was lucky enough to be out of AIT in time to be sent to Korea for the U.N. forces and MacArthur's plan to push the North Koreans back and beyond Seoul, South Korea, and the 38th parallel. The trip to California is eventful.

The Train to San Francisco

With a little time to be home, farewells having been completed, the two men, Lewis Taylor and Ray, board the train to California. They are to report to the harbor to board a transport ship to Korea. Spending all their money while in Richmond, they hold the belief that they will be there in a day or so. Their thinking could not be further from the truth. With no one to guide or prepare them, and very little understanding of what it takes to travel across the country, their journey begins. Trains are slow and they often make several stops along the way. This trip will take three days. Financial planning is not part of the military training that they have received. Ray knows how to make a buck on the ground, but that is not possible for him on the tracks.

However, luck is on their side in this journey. While sitting in their assigned seats, they think that they can make the whole journey fairly comfortably. *"There was a lady that was sitting across from us in the other aisle. We only took water from the porters because that was free. After the first twenty-four hours, this lady approaches us and says, 'I have noticed that you two men have not eaten since we boarded. Could I buy you two a sandwich?' It was an unexpected surprise, and boy were we hungry. She buys us lunch that afternoon. When dinner time rolls around, she invites us to the dinner train and feeds us again. She tells us that is the least she can do for what we are doing for the country. We couldn't refuse. I was truly appreciative.*

"The following morning, on the last leg of the trip, she takes us back to the dinner car for breakfast. We explained what our future held as we understood it in the small talk that took place. I never got the lady's name, but it was an act of kindness that I will never forget." [2]

The men arrive in the Port of San Francisco. *"After reporting to the post, the receiving soldier tells us that if we have any more leave time left, we should take advantage of it because we will be gone for a long time."* [2] Of course, since they have no money, and little opportunities because of it, the two wait on-site to board. More time is spent waiting for the ships to prepare to leave. The ships must be loaded with gear, ammo, and soldiers. It is managed by the navy. The food is good, but sleeping quarters are compact and must be shared. The weather is getting cooler as the ships depart the bay. They enjoy seeing the Bay Bridge as they pass underneath. It will be some time before they see home again. The next stop is Japan. Other parts of the country are sending troops as well, including Seattle, and Washington.

Lewis, who has been a friend to Ray since the heroic incident at the water spigots, was lucky enough to enter Fort Knox at the same time that Ray had entered. When he receives his orders, it is the same as Ray's. They are to report to San Francisco for departure to Japan for reassignment. They travel to Japan together, neither of them really knowing what they got themselves into. Ray has explained to Lewis by now his experiences in the National Guard. Not that Lewis needed to have his emotions brought into check, but it was convenient to have someone he knew going into the great wide open with instead of alone. Both boys are fit and ready. The likelihood of either one actually showing some raw emotion here is far from realized. It is just not their way.

The U.N. forces, under the command of General MacArthur, are planning a major assault. Ray's role in this invasion will take place at a place called Inchon. The soldiers are being sequestered in Japan before final plans are put into action. They are not allowed much free time while in Japan. Ray is only there for a couple of days. While there, all must remain on base before the assault is to be launched. The two men are separated when they land in Japan, but it will not be the last time that they meet. Life in Japan is pretty straightforward and quick. Report in the morning for orders. Instant assignment to a platoon. Ray is assigned to the Second Battalion Company E of the Thirty-First Infantry Division (2Bn. Co. E 31st Inf.). Lewis, on the other hand, gets assigned to the Third Battalion. It would be some time before the two will meet again.

The Thirty-First Infantry is known as the Polar Bears. Ray is assigned to the 3rd platoon as part of the beefing-up process of regiments that are lacking manpower. The wrinkle in the process for him is that he is now part of an infantry division. Ray has no training as an infantry soldier. This particular group has been especially trained in cold weather conditions. They are based out of Camp Crawford, Japan.

ROBERT BROOKS

The **Thirty-First Infantry Regiment** ("**Polar Bears**") of the
U.S. Army on August 13, 1916, was part of United States Army
Forces in the Far East. (USAFFE). It was in the Philippine
Division during World War II. The unit is rare in that it was
formed and has spent most of its life on foreign soil.

[4]

As part of the Thirty-First Infantry, the Polar Bears, Ray should have
received cold-weather gear: coats (parkas), boots, gloves, and sleeping
bags, but because he arrived in Japan when he did, he was attached to
the Thirty-First and had not received the extensive cold-weather-climate
training that others in the regiment had. A lot of this training would
have taken place in the northern part of Japan in Hokkaido. His stay in
Japan is too short to complete these exercises, let alone lacking the gear
that should have been issued to him for the actions that lay ahead. Ray
is one of many filling in the gaps to get the regiments up to strength.
Orders have been cut for his regiment, and boarding processes for the
trip to Inchon are underway. It will be a few days before he will see land
again. His trip takes him across the Sea of Japan, around the southern
tip of Korea, and up the Yellow Sea.

Hokkaido is a training site for the army. Winter training for this
regiment is located here. It is in Japan where Ray gets assigned to

the Second Battalion Company E Thirty-First Infantry. This will be shortened to 2 Bn. Co. E 31st Inf. or parts thereof. Example, (1) Co. E 31st, (2) Co. E, 31inf) E Co., (4) E 31st, and (5) elements of the 31st. This is not to be confused with a Regimental Combat Team (RCT).

At this stage of the journey, the average company is made up of 200+ men. Each platoon is usually grouped with 4–5 other platoons of 42 men. Those joined platoons make a company. Within a battalion, there could be three rifle platoons, a mortar platoon, a heavy-gun platoon, or any combination thereof. From these groups, parts of them can and will be used to make a combat team, otherwise known as a Regimental Combat Team (RCT). RCTs can vary in size and scope according to the orders and task at hand. For example, a captain can take two platoons and issue this RCT to take a hill. Along with this logic, a colonel can take parts of separate battalions and the companies that make them up to create an RCT to take control and create a perimeter.

Finance Building, Camp Crawford, Japan, Winter 1949. This would have been his training camp had he entered the Polar Bears (Thirty-First) earlier. Ray informs us that he is has no winter gear for his first year in Korea. Winter gear is not given to him until late fall of 1951. Too late for when he needed it most. [5]

A general can create an RCT consisting of even larger groups crossed over with elements from various military groups like army and marine battalions to follow through with even larger objectives. This is the case in Korea 1950. General Almond is over X Corps (Tenth Corp) consisting of army and marine regiments. These regiments or RCTs are managed by generals and colonels. Colonel MacLean and Colonel Faith are such individuals.

It is important to remember that the Korean conflict, as it starts to unfold in August and September of 1950, has many groups that are not up to full strength. Because of this, much confusion can be realized by the individual soldier within his commands as to locations and orders of these groups. Platoons could travel for days, stopping here and there with no idea as to their actual locations. Knowing where they are is left up to the higher elements of the group. After spending some time in the military, a lower ranking soldier such as a specialist or platoon leader will pick up on things and start to make sense of issues like time and location. A private first class (PFC) might know that he is at a river basin or valley but not really have any idea where that location is on a map.

The Korean War is remembered as a "war on a budget." Many groups are short of men, and oftentimes throughout the conflict, they have to be replenished. These shortages are usually resolved with new arrivals and recalls from the National Guard. The ones who are in guard are also referred to as reserves/reservists. These people are the ones who are getting activated.

Top Center, Ray Hooker Cottrell, age seventeen. Suwon airport Korea. Bottom right picture shows Ray in the right-hand lower corner. Picture taken after the Inchon landing, after the taking of the Suwon airstrip heading south to the Pusan Perimeter. Names of his buddies unknown—friends he made once he made it to Korea. [6]

Ammunition and supplies can run short during their engagements as well. Airdrops can deliver these materials, but on occasion they will not drop enough, the munitions will be wrong, or perhaps something completely wrong altogether.

Ray is shipped out from Japan with his attachment to 2nd Bn. Co. E 31st Inf. to be part of what is now called the "Inchon Landing." Military plans identify this as "Operation Chromite." An amphibious landing is devised by General MacArthur against the opinions of those in the War Department and at the U.N. in Washington. MacArthur explained his ideas for the operation and convinced them that this was the way to go. Ray's transport ship is one of some 260+ ships assigned to this task.

Author's note: To produce a better understanding of military strengths, this chart of military breakdown and their leaders as they apply to the U.S. Army when at full capacity will be beneficial. These numbers are general in their addresses and make a basic outline of U.S. military structure as it is realized internationally. These numbers can and do vary from the services over time and countries as they apply respectfully.

General MacArthur is the only five-star general in the Korean War. He is the supreme commander of the engagement, answering only to the president. On his staff, playing a dual role, is General Almond. Almond is commanding X Corps, which is a conglomeration of army and marine divisions, and is MacArthur's Chief of Staff. The marines are under the command of Gen. O. P. Smith. Notable commanders in this engagement for the purpose of this book also include Colonel MacLean, Col. Don Faith, and General Walker of the Eighth Army. The U.N. forces employ a new group known as an RCT (Regimental Combat Team); these forces are a mixture of elements of companies or battalions to make them up on the fly. They can also have as few as one to two hundred men. A commanding officer, for example, could make an RCT of just one company of men to take a hill. We will focus mainly on a group named RCT31. It is commanded by Colonel Maclean. Ray Cottrell is added to Company E of the Second Division of the Thirty-First Infantry Regiment. Artillery regiments, tank regiments, and infantry regiments are deployed together in a hodgepodge of groupings under the makeup of the RCT31.

Fire Team:	4 riflemen/infantrymen
Squad:	10 soldiers
Platoon:	40 soldiers and a platoon sergeant and a lieutenant
Company:	4 platoons of 40+ men with platoon sergeants and a lieutenant or captain/commanding officer in the lead
Battalion:	4 to 5 companies of 800+ men led by a lieutenant colonel or colonel
Brigade:	2–5 battalions 3,000–5,000 men led by a colonel
Division:	3–4 brigades with 10,000 to 15,000 men led by a brigadier general (one star) or major general (two stars)
Corps:	2–5 divisions of 20,000 to 45,000 men led by a lieutenant general (three stars)
Field Army:	2+ corps o f80,000 to 200,000 soldiers under the command of a major general (four stars)
Army Group:	4–5 field armies 400,000 to 1 million soldiers under the command of a general (four stars)
Army Region:	3+ field armies of 1–3 million soldiers under the command of a general (four- or five-star general)

Inchon

Several groups of ships make up "Operation Chromite." When putting together 260+ ships with the intention of having them hit beachheads at the same time, timing is crucial and adjustments must be made. Precision plays a great role in such a program as this. Ray has moved so fast to Japan and from there to his transport ship that he has no recall of his actual location in Japan. It is believed that he boarded his transport ship in Sasebo, Japan. This thought is due in part to the amount of time or rather the lack of time he spent in Japan. These troop movements/ship movements have staging areas to bring all the elements together. Task forces of the navy ships leave harbors in Yokohama, Kobe, and Sasebo. They will rendezvous at a sea location known as Point Iowa. As these three naval fleets join, their next way point will be Point Arkansas. Elements of marines and General Walker's Eighth Army will depart from within the Pusan Perimeter and join the naval groups at this location. The South Koreans and elements of the U.S. Army and others will remain behind at the Pusan area to maintain the lines and hold the area as this group moves out.

Once Point Arkansas is realized, and all groups have joined up, they move up to Point California. The U.S. Air Force, along with navy ships, secure borders and begin circling the Korean Peninsula.

September 4

On September 4, two Russian-based aircraft moved into the Yellow Sea near the joint operations. Radar detects contact at 1:29 p.m. heading south by southwest. This blip on the radar is assumed to have been launched at Port Arthur Naval Base. The base is controlled by the Chinese but leased to the Russians. At 1:31 p.m., the radar contact splits into two distinct contacts. The second contact turns back at a northwesstern direction from whence it came. The original contact turns slightly to a more southern direction.

Map labels:

11

PORT ARTHUR NAVAL BASE AREA U.S.S.R.

HAIYANG TAO

Radar contact 1329

1335

1331

Shot down 1343

Contact splits 1333

THOMAS DD.
Bomber opens fire

1335

Estim. speed 180 kts
• alt. 12000 feet

1337

1338 Merged plot

1337 Twin-engine bomber sighted

1335

CAP-4F4U
10,000 feet

K O R E

KOREA

Sok-to

Chinnampo

Cho-do

TF 77

1330

CAP-4F4U
12,000 feet

Sir James Hall Is.

SHANTUNG PEN.
(China)

Reiss.

THE RUSSIAN BOMBER INCIDENT 4. Sep. 1950

0   30   Naut. miles

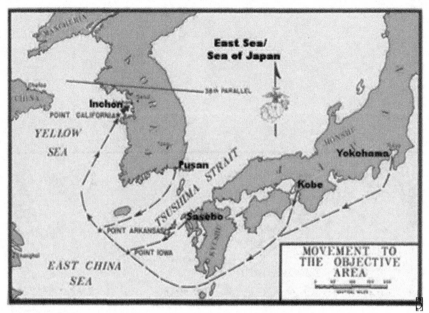

From Wikipedia 08/21/15 *Herbert J. Thomas* had just returned from the Mediterranean and was in Cartagena, Columbia when hostilities broke out in Korea in June 1950. She immediately proceeded to Pearl Harbor and joined the Pacific Fleet. In July she joined Task Force 77 (7th Fleet Striking Force) operating off the coast of Korea in the Yellow Sea effectively checking the enemy. A month later *Herbert J. Thomas* was assigned to the blockading force on Korea's east coast, and rendered highly effective gunfire support missions for our forces at Pohang inflicting much damage on the enemy. While operating with the blockading forces, she furnished interdiction fire all along the eastern coast and fired a diversionary mission for British commandos who were landed from Submarine Perch (SS-176) to destroy a vital railroad tunnel.

At 1329 on the afternoon of 4 September, *Herbert J. Thomas* was on picket duty about 60 miles north of Admiral Ewen's main force when she made radar contact on unidentified aircraft and reported this to aircraft from Valley Forge (CV-45) passing overhead. A division of F4U Corsairs which was orbiting northeast of the force was vectored out. The raid was now estimated on course 160°, speed 180 knots. As the fighters turned to meet it, it separated into two parts, one retiring in the direction whence it came. Sighting the fighters, the bogey nosed down, increased speed and began evasive action, but turned toward

ROBERT BROOKS

Korea rather than westward toward China. The division leader flew over him in an attempt to identify and reported a twin-engine bomber with red star markings. The intruder opened fire and was subsequently shot down. *Herbert J. Thomas* proceeded to the spot where the aircraft crashed and, according to a crew member on the *Herbert J. Thomas* at the time, recovered the dead body of an oriental aviator, and was immediately transferred to the USS Valley Forge.

For the next three months she was assigned patrol duty and operations with Task Force 77. [7]

At 1:35 p.m., a Russian bomber flies near USS *Herbert J. Thomas* (DD-833) (*Gearing*-class destroyer) to its east. It is heading near Task Force 77 operating at the 38th parallel. The plane continues its southern route. At the same time, a group of Corsairs is flying right at it. These aircrafts, a squadron of F4U Corsairs (Cap-4F4U) sites the Russian bomber at 1:37 p.m. The Russian bird makes an immediate turn due north in the direction of the Thomas. Cap-4F4U is now on its tail. On or about 1:41 p.m., the Russian bomber fires its guns. At 1:43 p.m., the intercepting birds from Cap-4F4U shoot down the bomber.

This event verifies the Russian involvement in the Korean conflict acting on behalf of the Chinese in support of the North Korean communists. More verification of Russian involvement comes later when a U.S. Army officer captured by the North Koreans was interrogated not only by the Chinese but by a Russian officer as well. This officer managed to escape after his interrogation and reported these facts upon returning to friendly lines.

The Joint Task Force 7 consisting of U.S. Air Force and Navy and United Kingdom naval forces working in conjunction with the Republic of Korea Navy (ROKN-South Korean Navy) have started to take islands near Inchon. These operations are just south of the 38th parallel. These islands are taken from August to September 20. The bombardments are intermittent along with the taking of the islands by the ROKN. This served two purposes: to soften up the landing that is about to take place and to help secure the area at sea outside Inchon. Additionally, they did not forecast the imminent invasion to the enemy.

Traveling to Inchon

Life aboard the ship en route to Korea is cramped for our soldier's first actions against the enemy. The quarters are tight and compact. Soldiers are expected to sleep in eight-hour rotations. One has to give up the bunk for the next guy in this revolving-door-sleep section of the ship. Rumblings of the ship's motors and the rolling of the waves make a good rest hard to get. The navy eats well though, and the food is hot and good. Ray settles in by meeting and speaking with others in his platoon. Recalling these names and faces will prove hard moving forward. Colonels, captains, lieutenants, and sergeants meet with other officers to discuss plans as they know them and prep their soldiers as best they can for what lies ahead. A good leader will lay at ease any of the questions and fears that their subordinates may have in the free time that they have to speak with them on the journey. Ray pays close attention and tries to absorb whatever he can during this time to help him in his performance when he hits the beach. He will venture on deck very little to view what is outside.

The seas are rather rough. Timing is an issue for this armada as the weather has turned rugged. Typhoon season is on them. Typhoon Jane had formed on August 29 and hit the cities of Osaka, Kobe, and Kyoto. It crosses over the center of Japan and heads back to sea only to hook back over the country once again as it lowers to a tropical storm. Jane dies at sea on September 4. Meanwhile, on the same day, another Typhoon, Kezia, forms and has a trajectory with the main fleet forming up from Kobe and Yokohama, Japan. It is closely following the same path as its little sister. Winds are logged at 115 mph. Carrier vessel *Boxer* was traveling to Japan to offload fourteen spare aircraft. Typhoon Kezia and *Boxer* both arrive off Japan on September 12. *Boxer* is forced to take a 400-mile southern

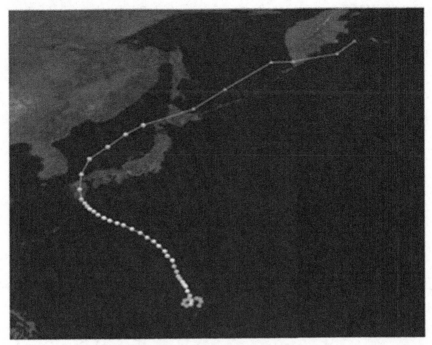

Typhoon Kezia's sustained winds of 115 mph on
September 4–15, 1950. Started the same day Typhoon
Jane that hit the island of Shikoku ended. [8]

route to Okinawa to offload these aircrafts. CV *Boxer* is damaged as it turns to launch these aircraft and is forced to handle its time in Korea with only three engines. The storm would cross over the center of the country, travel into the Eastern Sea of Japan, and cross back over Japan before coming to an end on September 15.

Ray is unaware that the main fleet had basically slipped between these two typhoons to get into position below the 38th parallel in the Yellow Sea on the west side of Korea.

September 5

Carrier strikes were scheduled for Kunsan and other coastal areas as part of an invasion deception. The fleet carriers *VALLEY FORGE* and *PHILIPPINE SEA*, and the escort carriers *BADOENG STRAIT* and *SICILY* were offshore during this period. These ships and others from countries such as the UK have taken control of the seas and skies south of the 38th. On September 8, ROKN troops take the island of Yonpyong-do in preparation for the Inchon landing just a week away. Actions are predominately on the east side of Korea and to the south just above the Pusan perimeter on the south of the Korean peninsula. Support air strikes on enemy forces and supply drops to working regiments are the call of the day as the armada is moving into position.

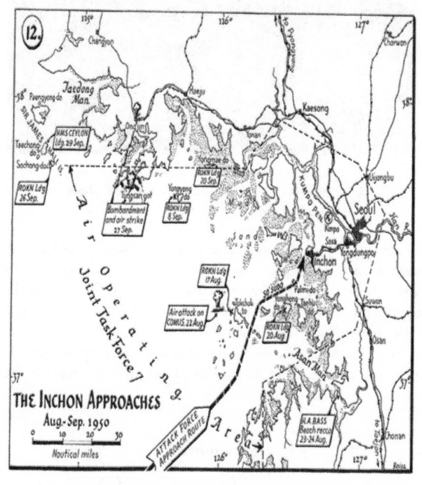

Map shows attacking force approach route. [3]

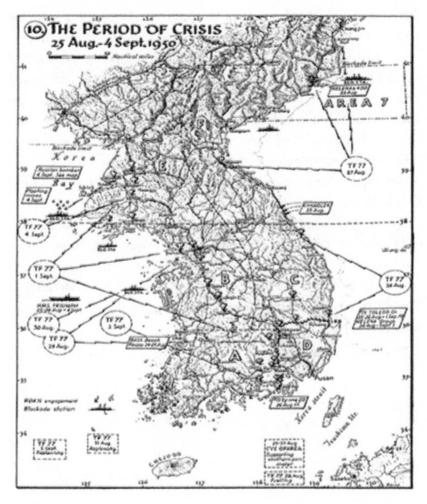

[3]

General MacArthur was meeting with his commanders back in Japan as the operations were getting underway. His chief of staff, General M. Almond, it was determined in this time frame to play a dual role: as MacArthur's chief of staff and as a commander on the ground in Korea over X Corps. This dual position would be played to his favor as much as could be taken advantage of during the hostilities as he saw fit. Others believe that Almond should not be wearing two hats during the engagement. It is believed that MacArthur, who was setting up a pincher move on the North Koreans, would make this engagement short and brief. This lends itself to the belief that General Almond would have no problem in this dual role in the mind of MacArthur.

The basic idea was to cut off the North Koreans south of the 38th parallel by coming in north of the 38th from the west. This would disrupt supply lines of the enemy south of the line. The Eighth Army under General Walker, along with the ROKN, would clear areas, take airstrips, free Seoul, and move south as they captured enemy troops between the forces moving out beyond the Pusan perimeter. This action would trap the NKs between U.N. forces moving south, and ROKs and U.S. forces coming up from Pusan.

Lewis Taylor and Ray are about to make a landing in Inchon. This will be the last time that they see each other for quite some time. When they were in Japan, Ray would go left and Lewis would go right. In their separation there, Lewis was assigned to the Third Battalion of the Thirty-First. Like Ray, he is used to bringing the battalions up to strength.

CHAPTER 3

Operation Chromite

**Photo of Corsair flying over the USS *Missouri* (Old Mo).
The USS *Missouri* was used for the surrender signing
by the Japanese at the end of World War II. [1]**

FROM JUNE 25, 1950, until August, the North Korean People's Army (NKPA) had many successful battles against the south. They would harness a four-pronged attack: a straightforward frontal attack with two flanking attacks and long-range firing positions aiming deep into the southern battlements. Their superior numbers alone would often be enough to keep the South Koreans on the run, oftentimes leaving their equipment behind. The South Koreans' logistical ability to wage war was left in shambles below the 38th. This approach would leave their personnel scrambling in retreat. It would later be discovered that the NKPA was capable of strong first strike abilities, but that would not show itself to be sustaining.

While the NKPA would make good gains, their inability to sustain attacks by its forces would later prove to be part of their undoing. MacArthur planned to assault with an amphibious landing to the middle of the country. This, in turn, would create the opportunity to cut off the North Koreans' logistical abilities throughout the south and effectively allow the U.N. forces to gain some much-needed territory as well, significantly weakening the overall ability of the NKPA as a whole and reestablish the original boundaries of South Korea.

To think that MacArthur would choose an amphibious landing here is no real surprise. Since Bataan, this was typical of Gen. Mac. Deploying around enemy-held islands and establishing footholds gave the navy better control of the seas. Knowing that the air superiority was already held, it only made sense to create a cutoff of the supply lines moving south by the enemy. "An army travels on its stomach" (Alexander the Great/Napoleon). Blind men tend to move blindly. MacArthur was not against such a grandiose address of issues in wartime decisions, but this tactic, while it offered greater rewards, would also require quick decision-making as well. Sweeping the enemy from the flank (rear) and cutting off communications and supplies proved successful many times in the past.

This operation is 261 naval ships strong and is effectively putting 75,000 troops into action. The landing would take place in rough seas at the port of Inchon. Copyright Britancia.com. [2]

September 3: Navy

The navy issued JTF7 Operational Plan 9-50 on September 3, 1950, by Admiral Struble (JTF-Joint Task Force). Under this order and his command, a successful Inchon landing would need the following objectives met. A strong naval blockade would have to be realized on the west coast. D-Day would need a successful launch and landing by forces to the beaches. These landings would need to acquire and defend said landing areas (weather would play a factor in this). If directed, send in reserve troops, supplies, and any following requirements at said objectives. Provide cover support during the entire operation. CV Boxer, a U.S. carrier with marine aircraft, and a small British carrier would provide air support during the operations.

Several smaller task forces were formed under "Operation Chromite" to put MacArthur's vision into the history books. Task Force 91 under the command of Royal Navy Rear Adm. W. G. Andrews held the blockade and offered cover support. TF 79 under Capt. B. L. Austin, USN, provided logistics support. TF 70.1, the flagship group, was directed under Capt. E. L. Woodyard, USN. The Fast Carrier Force was directed by USN Rear Adm. E. C. Ewen. Under USN Rear Adm. G. R. Henderson, TF 99 would hold the job of reconnaissance and patrols. Task Force 90 was an attacking force under Rear Adm. James H. Doyle. Also making the landing would be TF 92. This is the landing of X Corps under the command of U.S. Army Maj. Gen. Edward M. (Ned) Almond. Almond would be chief of staff to General MacArthur in absentia and maintain command of the Tenth Corps for the foreseeable future in Korea.

The value of the Inchon landing lies in the fact that it is the port for the city of Seoul just eighteen miles off to the east. Two airports, Kimpo Airfield to the northeast and Suwon Air Strip to the southeast, would be valuable assets for incoming military actions and would also be dual-purposed in removing avenues of support for the enemy.

Complications in landing at Inchon were weather and tide related. Inchon has tides that ebb and rise to 30+ feet. The summer months are lower while in October through the winter, tides would be higher.

Water depth and timing is critical for the landing. There is a causeway from Wolmi-do and Sowolmi-do Islands. This creates an inner and outer harbor. Deep drafting vessels at high tide could realize 40 feet of water on the outer breakwaters but only feet of water during the low tides. Two channels of approximately 35–60 feet lead into this location between the two islands. The inner harbor, beyond Wolmi-do and Sowolmi-do, has two dredged channels averaging about 13 feet at low tide leaving them surrounded by mudflats.

Ray has boarded his boat and is now prepared for the next leg of his career. In the plan, the island of Wolmi-do will be taken at the first high tide at a location marked Green Beach. Other landings would be realized as well. On ship, bad weather on the seas keeps him inside for the predominant part of the journey. Receiving three hot meals a day, saltwater showers, and an uncomfortable sleeping arrangement makes for a tolerable transport. Luck would be on his side again during this trip as well. Lewis is on board with him. Having a traveling companion came in handy with so many unknowns laying ahead. A chance to play cards, share a meal, or just talk about things back home made things more comfortable and offered a sense of normality to his days. This will not last long. Once the landing starts, they will be separated when the bay doors are opened. Both boys realize this. Nothing is remembered of these last moments when their feet hit the ground.

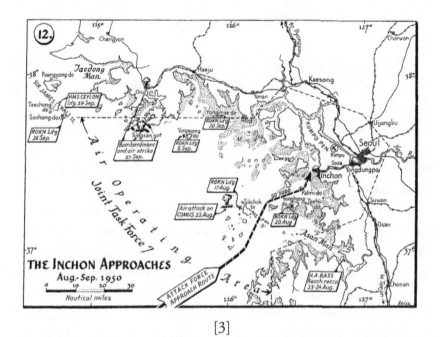

(12.)

The Inchon Approaches
Aug.-Sep. 1950
0   10   20   30
Nautical miles

[3]

The bombardment begins with a series of attacks with the intent of isolating the invasion area. A continuation of these attacks would continue till the 10th. Sixty-five sorties would be flown by the marines on Wolmi-do on the 10th. Two days would pass and attacks would proceed in earnest on the 13th. At 1010, six U.S. destroyers, two British light cruisers, along with two U.S. heavy cruisers under the command of Rear Admiral Higgins, move into the approaches of Inchon. Meanwhile, in the channel, while Fast Attack TF 77 provides cover, enemy mine fields are found. Most of them are taken out by automatic fire. There are now four cruisers taking up positions close to ten miles out as five destroyers slip in closer to Wolmi-do. At 1230, destroyers Collett, Swenson, DeHaven, Gurke, and the Mansfield take up their closer positions to the island and take out five enemy 75 mm guns. Enemy fire kills two (one U.S.). As these destroyers back out at 1347, the cruisers offshore, beginning at 1352, start a ninety-minute shelling campaign. This is followed by an air bombardment from Task Force 77. When TF 77 strikers move out at 1610, the cruisers restart the shelling of Wolmi-do for another thirty minutes.

September 14

D-day-1, on or about 1045, TF 77 restarts a second aerial bombardment. By 1116, the cruisers on position again start shelling the island. This time, they will shoot at targets beyond the island and land them into the forward positions of the city of Inchon. Within seventy-five minutes of action, five destroyers will land over 1,700 shells on Wolmi-do and Inchon. All are silent on the island as they back out of the channel.

Ray's transport ship is close enough now to at least hear the bombing campaigns from a safe distance. Some are topside to take it all in. Rumblings of thunder roll through the air like a Fourth of July celebration that goes on for hours. The sound carries over the waves to far-reaching distances. The more experienced soldiers understand that the more the shelling continues, a better likelihood of success can be realized once on shore. Confidence increases as the time ticks on for these men. To the newly enlisted, imaginations run rampant and, in some cases, out of control. Commanders move among the men and reassure them. They are quick to restate expectations during this time. The repeat of orders to the enlisted ensues so that all questions that can be answered are answered. The men who are not on watch are heading to their bunks, while the others calm themselves and try to get a good night's sleep. Most men are too anxious to accomplish this, but the effort is put in nonetheless. Heads rest on duffle bags or whatever can be managed into a pillow as they try to find a place to stretch out comfortably.

An added value to initiating the attack on the 15th, MacArthur would later come to know, is that the NKs were just weeks away from fortifying Inchon Harbor for just such an event. Had this been realized, Operation Chromite would have received more casualties and the overall event could have ended before it got rolling. On board USS *Mt. McKinley*, MacArthur is getting little sleep as well. He is awake in the predawn hours as the armada moves into position. He takes up a position on the bridge. He notes that there are no out-of-the-ordinary actions seen on shore. Beams from the lighthouses marking the harbors move in their normal patterns, he recalls. It appears to him that they have caught the enemy off guard to some acceptable degree. No extra artillery or troop movements adding to the equation seem present. This could have been disastrous. Generals know how to put boots on the ground, but they are not keen to leave those boots behind (mission 1 and mission 1a).

[1]

SECRET   PARAPHRASE NOT REQUIRED
FLASH

FROM: CINCUNC TOKYO JAPAN SGD MACARTHUR

TO : CINCFE TOKYO JAPAN

INFO: JCS WASH DC

NR : C 63153   15 SEP 50

        Late in the afternoon troops of the First Marine Div,
which this morning captured Wolmi-Do, the island dominating
the harbor of Inchon, after heavy Naval and air preparation,
successfully landed on the beach of Inchon itself and the
beach to the south. They rapidly overcame light resistance
and are consolidating the beachhead.

        Our losses were light. The clockwork coordination
and cooperation between the services was again noteworthy.

        In this instance the natural obstacles, combined with
the extraordinary tidal conditions, demanded a complete mastery
of the technique of amphibian warfare. The command distinguished itself. The whole opn is proceeding on schedule.

ACTION: JCS

INFO : CSA, CNO, CSAF, G2

CM IN 11787   (15 Sep 50)   DTG 151220Z   fcl/D

JCS FORM 270   ~~SECRET~~   COPY NO. 1001
REPLACES CM JCS FORM 22-2, 15 JAN 49, WHICH MAY BE USED.

[4]

D-Day. Recons and air strikes move inland. The way must be made clear. The United States Marine Corps would be the first to hit the ground running. They have three objectives: land, take control of Wolmi-Do and the causeway to the south to Sowolmi-do, and secure the causeway to the east to Inchon. These islands make a breakwater for the inner harbor. Green Beach is located northwest of Wolmi-do and will be taken by 3rd Battalion 5th marines. Because of the tidal movements, they land early in the morning at high tide. Water depth and timing is an issue because of this.

Company A 3rd Bt. 5th marines with a tank battalion will move onto the island with nine Pershing tanks. The battalion landing group readies to move ashore as well. A special radar task force prepares to go in with them. Several attack ships of the gunfire support group move into positions. Fast-moving landing craft along with LSRMs (rocket ships) and one LSD (a landing ship dock) help fill out the forces heading to the island.

At 0500, Corsairs fly overhead just before the launch. At 0530, troops start debarkation and launch to Wolmi-do. The island has a peak that juts up to over 300 feet above sea level. Many niches, caves, and trenches are rumored to be in the hill. Rocket ships issue a barrage on the island just before landing. Three LSVs holding the tanks, and seventeen LCVPs carry the force about a mile to the landing beach on Wolmi-do. The first transports land completely unopposed.

Wolmi-do is captured quickly. Three hundred enemies are captured, and the marines suffer no losses in the engagement. Wolmi-do is laid to waste. Few obstacles and structures are left behind. Marines handle the island so quickly that they are free to watch the campaign of air strikes occurring on the main land by the Corsairs and bomber strike forces. [5]

By 0750, Wolmi-do is secured. A task force is sent across the causeway to Sowolmi-do to capture or kill a small enemy force there. Some of the combatants lurch into the sea to make a swim for it like rats from a sinking ship. The taking of the outer islands breed hope in the commanders hitting the main land that evening.

Because of the ebb and flow of the waterways, the landing is broken up into two events. The unforeseen value of this issue lends itself to more bombing from the air superiority of the strike forces. At 1730, First and Second Battalions wait until high tide and land on Red Beach. At the same time, the First Marine Regiment lands on Blue Beach.

That evening, Red and Blue Beach will be taken as well. Red Beach has walled ruins and create a bit of an obstacle for marines coming ashore. Cover is afforded these forces because there are some structures, but they will still have to overcome the seawall. The landing falls between the northern hill of Cemetery Hill and the southern, marked Observatory Hill. Marines will make this amphibious landing upon which they will scale the walls and move through ruins while facing enemy opposition. As the saying goes, *"That ain't no hill for a stepper."*

Blue Beach is no walk in the park either. It is far from ideal conditions for a landing. It is a swath of mudflats making it tough to get men and equipment ashore. There is no cover for these men at this location. When the doors open on the LSTs, they imagine it to be balls to the wall from then on. Once on the beach, if it can honestly be called that, the men must deal with a sixteen-foot-high seawall that was built for when the tide was in. Debarkation when the water is high is no problem here. Ladders are employed as the men were to cross these mudflats if the tide was low and then scale these walls to start their movement forward. Timing again plays a factor here because of landing craft being stuck in the mud as the retreating waters would hold them in place till the high tide returns. Being a stick in the mud and laying there like a duck are no laughing matter in wartime. The bigger the target, the easier to hit it.

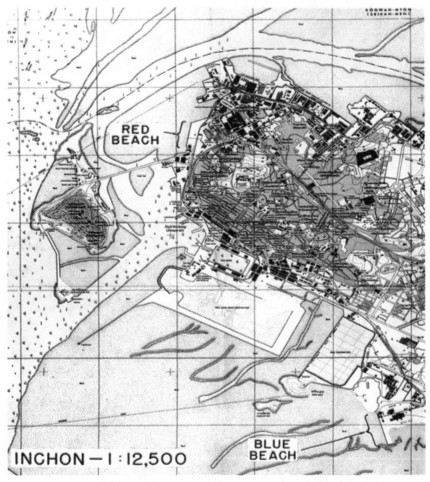

The Inchon Landing, September 15–18, 1950. [7]

With air support from USS *Boxer* and other forces in the harbor area, the landing is plausible and working. Amazing to the casual observer, all the things that could go wrong, didn't. The plan unfolds in less-than-ideal weather, at poor locations, with bad geography, and during record tides of thirty feet. The marines do what they are called to do—take beaches, kick ass, and plant flags. Inchon is no longer enemy territory.

~~SECRET~~

DEPARTMENT OF THE ARMY
STAFF COMMUNICATIONS OFFICE

SECRET   PARAPHRASE NOT REQUIRED
FLASH

FROM: CINCUNC SCD MACARTHUR

TO : CINCFE TOKYO JAPAN, DEPT OF ARMY FOR JCS (CINCFE PASSES)

NR : C 63154   152345Z   15 SEP 50

During the night of 15-16 Sept the First Marine Div
further consolidated its positions in Inchon and to the south
thereof, meeting only sporadic resistance. Coordinated
attacks this morning all link up the two wings of the Div.
ROK Marines, attached to the First Marine Div, are clearing
up the northern half of the city of Inchon.

Preparation for the landing of heavy equipment and
supplies progressed throughout the night. The high tide
this morning will provide the first use of the inner harbor
of Inchon for this purpose. Operations continues exactly
on planned schedule.

ACTION: JCS

INFO : CSA, CNO, OSAF

CM IN 12050   (16 Sep 50)   DTG 152302Z   mld/A

DCS FORM
1 JAN 50 290

~~SECRET~~   COPY NO. 1001

[4]

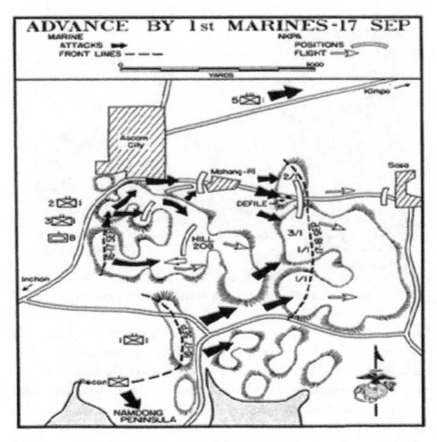

ADVANCE BY 1st MARINES - 17 SEP

On September 18, transport ships unload to smaller landing craft as air support and fire power has been directed at all points outward from the beaches. Soldiers are brought down to the landing craft via nets. These troop transports are known as LSTs.

Inchon Landing with LSTs North Korea, 1950. [6]

"Landing ship tanks" (LSTs) were heavily used during WWII, Korea, and many other actions from several countries. They are built like most ships but have what could be considered a door and ramp on the front of the ship allowing it to close in to shore without beaching. These ships and smaller boats are an important tool for getting men and machine on to land at unimproved landing sites for debarkation. They allow for quick loading and unloading which is a highly prized attribute for wartime efforts. The first LST was first tested in 1945. Four LSTs unload on the beach at Inchon as marines gather equipment to move rapidly inland on September 15, 1950. Landing ships were stuck in the deep mudflats between one high tide and the next.

As for the young warrior Ray Cottrell, he will be required to traverse down a rope net from his transport ship to a small LST for departure to the landing zone. He is the company's radioman. His job is to stay close to the captain and follow orders. Captain Cook is in the lead position of four platoons making their way to shore. The young radioman, heavily weighted with gear, is about to disembark. He is carrying an SCR-300 series radio pack and an additional walkie-talkie system with attached battery pack.

His first duties before offloading is to contact all five companies by the captain's order and have the men strap their helmets to their chins before they climb over. The captain, who is leading from the front, has made his way down the rope netting and made it on to the LST. Ray follows shortly thereafter. Captain Cook, onboard the landing craft, has removed his helmet in preparation for the launch. While working with the cumbersome weight of the two radio sets, Ray makes it over the edge and is working his way down. He is right above the captain when his foot becomes entangled in the netting below. While trying to disengage his foot from the tangle, he leans over to get a look at what the problem is and why he can't get clear. When he leans over a bit too far and looks down, his doughboy metal helmet comes off. He has forgotten to attach his chin strap.

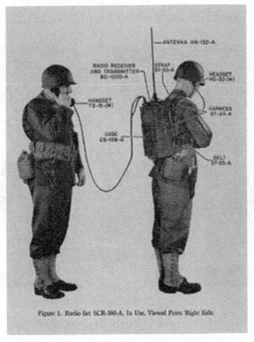

Figure 1. Radio Set SCR-300-A. In Use, Viewed From Right Side.

[8]

His helmet falls and lands squarely upon the captain's head, whose skull is now exposed. It lands edge side down on Cook's head. The captain is knocked stupid from the hit. Blood is leaking from his skin. He is temporarily knocked out. Ray is still stuck in the net when the captain regains his faculties. Cook yells at Ray, *"Cottrell, get your ass down here right now or I will shoot you off there myself."* [9] Not a great first moment for the young PFC. These metal helmets are sometimes used as cooking pots, but Ray has only succeeded in cooking his own goose with it.

The battle at Inchon is a four-day event. The North Koreans, unable to maintain their lines, were overrun by superior forces of army, marines, and ROK marines. It appears that the U.N. assault would be effective at this point. But it would not be without losses. The North Koreans are battle-hardened, but they don't have the manpower in this area to prevent the onslaught. They are stretched too thin. They have another weakness: energy. They are not well-fed. Because they are now fighting on multiple fronts, they have trouble getting resupplied with both men and material. The NKs start to retreat to Seoul. By September 19, Inchon is cleared and the path to Seoul lies ahead.

At some point between coming down the nets and the 20th, Ray is approached again by Captain Cook. Ray tells a buddy, *"He comes up*

to me and tells me that I fell asleep. I tell him that I didn't. Cook restates, 'You fell asleep, I am going to give the radio job to someone else. You will be carrying a bazooka from now on.' [9] Not wishing to be confrontational with a captain at any time for any reason, he dutifully picks up a bazooka. He has had training with this weapon before. While it is heavy as hell, it is not awkward in his hands. It is far from his expectations, but a soldier follows orders. Orders do not get questioned.

Author's note: Ray chose not to attach his chinstrap because the two radios could not be managed for him to hear from with the helmet in the proper place. He is trying to shrug his shoulders to keep them in place at the same time. He tells me, "These damn things didn't have a hook to hang them on." Perhaps if he had a little more time with the contraptions, he could have figured that problem out. Alas, that was not the case.

CHAPTER 4

No Time to Think

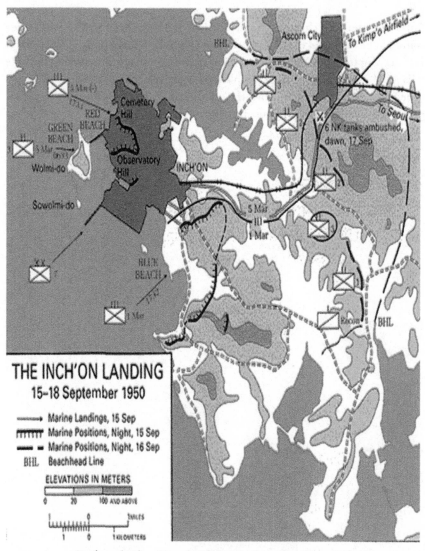

THE INCH'ON LANDING
15–18 September 1950

- Marine Landings, 15 Sep
- Marine Positions, Night, 15 Sep
- Marine Positions, Night, 16 Sep
- BHL. Beachhead Line

ELEVATIONS IN METERS

0   20   100 AND ABOVE

Red and Blue Beach of the Inchon landing. [1]

N O TIME TO think. War is upon him. The 2bn 31st Inf. Co. E has been offloaded by the LSTs and make their way through the mud, up and over the seawall, as they make their way to a gathering position for the march southeast. Movement is fast and with purpose. The platoon is organized and formed up. Everything is checked out—ammo, guns, three days' supply of rations, laced boots. Orders are being barked out to the men by their associated leaders. As they move out, the sound of shells landing off to the east resonates in his ears.

This is real. Ray has always been a fighter, a street scrapper with a keen mind to adjust to changing environments and issues. Fear is something, for him, that is handled after the event. His sharp sense of self-preservation, coupled with an ability to understand things as they develop as a free-wielding youth, would play a critical role going forward. He can handle a gun from all his experiences hunting with his grandfather and friends. This too will be helpful. He is no stranger to the outdoors. All this will come in to play from here on.

Just south of Ascom City, the First Marines had approached Hill 208. The encounter had turned brutal. For the last two days, the area has been cleared by the X Corps. NKs were caught with no way to reinforce or support their positions. The marines move forward to the east creating perimeters as they traveled. A day before, an encounter with six enemy tanks had been overran and taken.

September 18

While the Eighth Army is moving north out of the Pusan perimeter, 2Bn 31st, along with a tank company and mortar teams, is moving their way south to the Suwon Air Strip, the same air strip that had been used by a U.S. ambassador and others just months before. Larger aircraft are able to land at this location allowing for evacuations and deliveries. It had to be regained. Holding this airfield also set up a perimeter preventing enemy forces moving up from the south an opportunity to strengthen the forces at Seoul. Along the traverse to the town around

Suwon, enemy forces, snipers, and mortar squads were encountered. Ray's first personal encounter in combat action is realized.

"For what is the measure of an Army infantry man? No matter the length of his training, the event that he may be killed in action even before he reaches the beachhead, his intensive training—or lack thereof—is then of little value. Likewise, if he is fortunate enough to hit the beach alive, only then can his individual mettle be tested on the battlefield. However, adding to enemy fire, a sudden friendly fired bullet, or an unintended napalm—friendly fire—canister, dropped short, may also snuff out his life in a second." —Douglas MacArthur

General MacArthur looks on at the most northern marine position east of Inchon, September 17. Photo provided by the U.S. Army. The marine center right is holding a Russian-made automatic machine gun, called a burp gun. It is very unreliable in cold weather. The two dead soldiers are North Korean. [2]

Meanwhile, as Ray's company is heading southeast toward the Suwon Airfield, what is about to happen is rarely recorded. This one event, similar to so many other combatants throughout history, is generally never shared especially with those not in the military. These stories generally lay in the sacred grounds of conversations of one combatant to another, or perhaps with psychologists in the privacy of their offices. Rarely with someone from the outside. The simple unspoken acknowledgment is all one generally shares with the others. It is as if they can see it in their eyes when they meet. When two or more of them are together, they will speak of their engagements, their locations, things they have done on leave, but they will tend to avoid the first event: the first killed in action event (KIA). Many events are etched forever in a combat soldier's mind, not unlike memories that are etched within us all. More frequently in the life of the combatant, though, the memory is indelible. It is not looked back upon in a peaceful, meaningful way. It often carries confusion, pain, and uncontrollable emotions. These emotions can be hard to squelch. These thoughts can and will extend many years into their lives. Their repercussions affect not only the individual but also the people that surround them. The strongest of men can be brought to their knees in recall of such events. It invades their sleep and dreams. Rare is the time that a war combatant will put this memory to paper. Each one tends to carry this first event within the confines of their own minds. Some may never share it. It is considered rude and in extremely poor taste to even bring it up, especially if one is not a combatant.

The first time a person takes a life, something changes deep inside. This is a critical moment for the young man. Quick choices will have to be resolved in his mind. The best option now is to block it out and continue with the issues at hand while maintaining a sense of self-control and self-discipline. Preventing it from pervading into his thoughts as he tries to move forward will be the best choice. Another option is to let it consume him and influence him for the rest of his life. Either way, along with other possibilities, the soldier must find some way to come to terms with it, or be ravaged by it forever. Events such as this have been explained as "being HIT." Once he is "HIT," he either gets back up or he never recovers. Ray has the luck of other soldiers around him who have been there before. He can realize support from his brothers-in-arms as time moves forward. He is also lucky in that there is not much time for reflection. There are those who would have him dead if he doesn't stay focused.

Ray's company is spread out as the forces move southward to the town. Korea is a country that relies heavily on water supplies. Reservoirs, creeks, bridges, and dams dot the landscape in no small degree with tough terrain in all areas of the country. In the summer months, steep hills and heat exhaustion are just as dangerous as exposure to cold in the winter. Coupling this with the reality that enemy forces are trying to kill him makes travel in this country not at all easy. When his company approaches an area that has low-lying ground full of hiding places, Ray encounters an opening to a tunnel. As he approaches the tunnel, a fourteen-year-old NK soldier exits as Ray realizes his presence. It is an encounter that is just short of becoming a Mexican standoff. As the two see each other, the NK raises his rifle to shoot. It is either shoot or be shot. Ray fires his rifle. He is a split second faster. His assailant drops out. Our soldier freezes for a moment and makes a mental note of what just happened. He is forced to move forward with his platoon. There is more to do.

Under resistance, Suwon and the airstrip are captured. As the X Corps' tank battalion moves through the town, they get themselves lost and have to radio ahead to reset their destination. They get into position south of the city before the North Koreans advance on their location. Word has come to the commanders that a group of enemy tanks and infantry are making their way northward. This force had been turned around and are retreating to Seoul. They are driving into a trap being set by the U.N. forces at Suwon. Mortar and rifle companies have taken up positions on the high ground south of the airstrip and along the road heading south. They are setting up a crossfire squeeze as their perimeter.

As incoming North Koreans approach from the south, Ray is sent out to confront the enemy with his platoon. He carries his bazooka and takes up his position as assigned with the others. When the surprise attack on the NKs start, he discovers quickly that the bazooka he is carrying is not effective against the armor of the tanks. A direct fire to the vehicle only bounces off. When he reloads and fires again, this time at the tracks of the tank, it reveals its only effectiveness. The blast disables the track. The behemoth is obliged to rotate in the direction of the busted side.

Destroying an enemy tank is no easy task. Disabling the ability to move forward does not remove the danger of the metal beast. It has in its armament a mounted machine gun that can easily take down an opposing force. There are still enemies within that can fire from a relatively safe environment from rifle fire. These men will also have to be taken out before a successful takedown can be achieved.

The battle is long and not without incident. Several enemy combatants are killed or taken at this event. A total of twelve tanks are taken out in this engagement. The U.N. forces are not without losses as well. Parts of the RCTs are moved off to secure and hold the road leading south from the city as well. Their engagement with the enemy puts the U.N. forces in control of the area, and a blocking perimeter is maintained. Superior forces, along with good communication and control of the environment, yield a positive result. Prisoners of war (POWs) are moved south along with the injured. The 2Bn holds here for a very short time. While they are here, camp is set up, and material is flown in. A short respite can be enjoyed now. The journey inward so far has been aggressive and orderly. Reinforcements are brought into this area and command posts are set up. Flights in and out of Suwon under friendly control can now take place. Expansion of controlling and blocking forces can be better served with the airstrip in operation. His short-term rest is broken up by new orders. His battalion is informed that they must pack it up and begin their move south to Pusan.

Ray digging a foxhole. Ray is always digging a foxhole. [3]

Ray is top left with the coffee cup. From his personal library. [3]

**Photos after the taking of Suwon Airfield. At right,
Ray peeking out of bunker with a hat on. [3]**

To the north, Col. Don Faith and the 32nd Inf. are fighting along with marine battalions to encircle and control the city of Seoul. Upon harsh fighting, and many losses, Seoul is recaptured. Some North Koreans manage to leave the city before it can be totally encircled, escaping to the northeast. General MacArthur is quick to reestablish governmental control of the city back to Syngman Rhee, the leader of South Korea. The ceremony was so quick on the heels of the recapture of Seoul that several marines and troops have to be placed in guarding positions around the city during the event. Sniper fire and some mortar shots can be heard during the speeches and the raising of the flag. MacArthur is excited to be able to commit to such a thing so soon. It serves to show what great progress has been achieved back in the United States.

The six-hundred-mile trip from Suwon to Pusan is complicated. Several methods of transportation are put into effect. The Eighth Army is moving northward as the Seventh moves south. Marching, trucks, and trains are employed in this traverse. Upon their arrival in Pusan, Ray's 3rd platoon has 7 survivors. Along with Ray Cottrell, Corporal Carter is one of them. The company is replenished with men and supplies. It will be several days before Ray can put his feet up and write home. The crisscross of forces show a comfortable sign of control over the territories south of the 38th. By October 17, Ray and his company have been moved onto ships in preparation for the move northward.

Left, Ray at Fort Knox, 1950. Right, Ray at Kobe, Japan, 1951. Center, Ray and his friend Sonny Stevens, 1955. [3]

Home by Christmas

The Marine Corps troops under X Corps board the ships to go to Wonsan. South Korean troops who entered Wonsan by land had reclaimed the town. Floating just outside the harbor, Japanese and U.N. minesweepers are clearing the harbor for the marines to land. Bob Hope and his traveling USO show had already arrived at Wonsan, as they wait to get on land. General Almond is a man on the move. His perception of Korea is based on, largely and in part, his connection to General MacArthur. As Mac's right-hand man, his expectations of himself and his underlings are always high. MacArthur had just returned by air from Wake Island just a day before. Many think that this was a publicity photo opportunity for the election cycle that was now in gear. The five-star general has plans to get the X Corps, comprising of marines, Koreans, and the Seventh Infantry up to the Yalu to bring this police action to a quick and resounding end. Concerns over the Chinese and Russian involvement have been addressed. The reality of using a nuclear option is off the table.

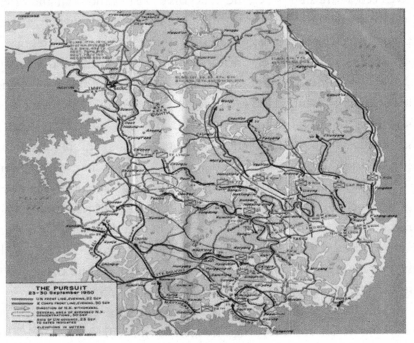

[4]

October 26

The U.S. Marine Corps, under the lead of Gen. O. P. Smith, and answering to General Almond under X Corps begin unloading at Wonsan Harbor at 0730. The following day, at 1000, the command center of the First Marine closes on USS *Mount McKinley* and reopens in Wonsan. By the end of the next day, all troops and supplies have been offloaded to shore. Because of the great success of the taking of this port by land, plans are changed. Taking advantage of the fast-gained ground, Almond decides that his Seventh Infantry will now take the sea town of Iwon as their landing point. The intent is to send both the Marines and the Seventh northward from their respective azimuths to move northward to the Yalu River.

Ray and his Seventh has spent the last ten days in the Pusan Harbor. Almond has been routing materials and supplies from Japan and U.N. supply stores to fill his regiments up to par. The Marine Corps had been receiving most of their supplies via the navy. Almonds S2 and others have been addressing issues and concerns as fast as they can and often find themselves under stress to fulfill the requirements as they arrive. Almond's penchant to oversee everything to the nth degree creates many opportunities for mistakes, but the men under his command keep up and are sometimes ahead of the general's orders before they even come down. General Almond likes to have his I's dotted and T's crossed, but sometimes, he could be thought to be overdoing it. On the 27th, Almond issues orders to have the Seventh move out of Pusan and onto Iwon as their azimuth to get them to the Yalu. MacArthur believes that he can get all forces north to Yalu, the Chinese will not intervene, and some of his troops could be routed back home by Christmas. MacArthur had no intent of crossing the 38th into north Korea but south Korean Chairman Rhee has forced his hand. The joint Chiefs in Washington agree with the UN that the NK must be pushed all the way back and the country unified after the ROK continued to push over the 38th parallel.

Gen. O. P. Smith, who is in command of the First Marines, is following orders and preparing his men for movement up to the east and west side of the Changjin Reservoir, also known as the Chosin.

The overall plan is to get the X Corps to the Yalu. ROKs will take all areas east of Hyesanjin. It is decided that no American troops will be within sixty miles of the Russian border. The First Marines will take the Chosin Reservoir and move north to the Yalu from there. The purpose of keeping the American troops away from Russia is seen as an attempt to keep the Russians out of the entanglement that is Korea. It is not well-known to most of the U.N. and U.S. forces on the ground, but the Russians have already flown missions against the Western forces.

Status Quo

CIA intelligence has identified Chinese forces building up on the northwest edges of Korea just north of the Yalu. It is anticipated that the Chinese have no more than sixty thousand troops in this area at the time. It is considered a manageable number. The Eighth Army has been pushing northward to this location but has yet to reach the Yalu. The ROKs are to take the eastern border. U.S./U.N. forces of the 17th Inf., 31st Inf., and 32nd Inf. will take the northcentral border at the Hyesanjin area. The First Marines will move northward from the Chosin Reservoir area and move northward to the Yalu as well. This movement by the marines will close up the central area of the country north to the Yalu. If the Eighth Army can take their area of operation all the way north, then complete control of the country can be realized. MacArthur will be quick to hand the entire country over to Chairman Rhee, and this conflict will, for all intents and purposes, will be completed. MacArthur will have succeeded in pushing back the communist expansion and finish out his career on a high note.

Best-Laid Plans

Under the current conditions, the following issues are playing out behind the scenes. General MacArthur and President Truman are not the biggest fans of each other. Truman is concerned with his reelection and is concerned that MacArthur, like General Eisenhower, will take advantage of his support in the United States and make a run for office. MacArthur is concerned and upset with the president over fears of not getting the support that he needs to complete the job that he was assigned to do. Meanwhile in Korea, General Almond is not happy about, well, most everything, but especially with Gen. O. P. Smith. General Smith is not satisfied with the planning and delivery of actions as ordered by General Almond. Nor is he happy about being under operational orders of a U.S. Army General. He believes that the army is underserved with so many raw recruits and a general lack of training and supplies. He doesn't trust the abilities of the raw ROK soldiers brought into the control of the U.N. as well. General Walker, in the meantime, has his hands full leading ROK soldiers along with the Eighth Army north. All of them are settled in the uncomfortable belief that their mission is close to completion.

Time stands still for no one. The Chinese have entered the war en masse. The PLA/CCF (People's Liberation Army of China–Communist Chinese Forces) has been sending troops across the northern borders to the west side of northern territories by bridges that can only be monitored by day. The nights are long. This permits the Chinese to move across under concealment of the darkness. They are well-versed in using camouflage and have been quite successful in hiding in the mountain passes and terrain as recon missions from the U.N. forces try to discover locations and strength levels as they fly overhead.

MacArthur has been informed that his request to bomb the Korean side of the Yalu bridges has been denied by the administration. The general is more than upset by this. He offers, *"How can we successfully finish what we started if we can't stop the influx?"* The administration is concerned that the bombing of these bridges on the Korean side will have collateral damage and motivate the Chinese and the Russians to get involved. Hydropower in the Eastern borders supply Russia with electricity. Chang Hi Shek would later post in Chinese newspapers that if he knew that these bridges would be blown, he would not have sent his men across to be captured. But the news report would show that in some way, Shek was informed that they would not be blown and thus he could get his armies involved.

The sixty thousand Chinese that the higher-ups at the Joint Chiefs of Staff and the U.N. had believed were in force for the Chinese were in fact south of the Yalu River already. On October 26, the G2 of the Far East Command sent a letter to Washington believing that the Chinese would only slow down the U.N. forces even though they had basically wiped out the ROK II marines the night before. General Walker sends troops in support to prevent further collapse in the ROK's area of operations.

October 29

O. P. Smith has started moving his men out to the west to take up their positions in Hagaru, Hudong-ni, and Yudong-ni around the Chosin Reservoir. Movement is not fast but with purpose. Resistance on the east coast is broken with intermittent engagements. Smith proceeds with caution. He moves too cautiously, and at times, his forces only move 1 mile a day. Marines take land and set up flags. They are designed to clear paths and let the holding of those territories be left to the army. They would rather be coastal than in country. The ROKs continue their movement up the east coast of Korea to take the northeast territories. They will come up short of the Russian border of the Yalu with the First Marine Division ashore at Wonsan and South Korean troops rapidly moving along North Korea's east coast. Most of the Navy's amphibious shipping are still occupied with Wonsan-related chores, so the soldiers were mainly brought north from Pusan in merchant-type ships, then transferred to LSTs and smaller beaching craft while anchored offshore.

The operation went slowly but smoothly, assisted by a total absence of enemy resistance. Following the now-mandatory mine clearance operation, the army forces are beginning to reach the shore. The entire embarked force was ashore by November 8. From Iwon, much of the Seventh Division moved inland against slight opposition.

October 31

It has only been forty-three days since Ray landed at Inchon. He is still seventeen years old. Captain Smith sends for Private Cottrell to report to his quarters. The innocence that was in his eyes as a sixteen-year-old standing in front of the principal back in Virginia has been altered. Captain Smith has an order for Ray. He informs him, "You are now the platoon sergeant of Company E." Ray is taken aback by the statement. He fails to prevent the next two words that fall out of his mouth faster than a bullet leaves a barrel, and says, "*Why me?*" [3] Smith, with a smirk on his face, tells him, "*Because you are lucky, son.*" Privates are not prone to questioning a captain in this manner, but Ray continues on in a disoriented and confused voice. "Why am I lucky?" Cook retorts, "Because we gave you the bazooka son, and we didn't think you would survive. That makes you lucky! Anything else?" [7] Ray has talked backed before and was fined for not following orders. He does not want to repeat that now. He replies, "No, sir." [7]. Ray has talked backed before and was fined for not following orders. He does not want to repeat that now. He replies, "*No, sir.*" [3] The captain eases his mind on what his responsibilities will be. Cook recounts to him that he was really only joking about falling asleep with the radio position but was surprised when he took up the bazooka so readily. Ray salutes him before exiting and heads back to his quarters a little more at ease.

Field promotions are not unheard of, especially in warzones. As one man is taken out of commission, another steps up in his place. For example, if a captain is removed from action or killed in action, the next in command is immediately transferred control and responsibility of the ones below him. Ray has much to think about now. He knows that, as the platoon sergeant, he lacks a lot of skills that generally go along with it. Reading a map is just one of the things that he will have to learn. It is not that he does not understand the requirements of the position; it is his lack of experience that has him unsettled. Because of his time in the National Guard, he comes to peace with the new assignment and immediately starts to work on improving his shortcomings as time will allow.

November 19

With the Seventh Division headquarters set up and a perimeter created around Iwon, reconnoitering begins. Almond is holding troops in the back of these forces as reserves. Ray will move with his group northward in the operational area east of the Fusion Reservoir. The Fusion lays just twenty miles east of the Chosin. Small groups of enemy combatants are taken as they move through the mountains to Hyesanjin. The winter weather of the north is setting in. Up until now, Ray's summer gear has yet to be augmented. With the weather turning sharply cold, travel becomes very difficult. High mountain paths are starting to be covered with snow. A support group of ROKs are attached to his group. Their job is to capture or kill any enemy forces in the area. Most of these enemy combatants are offering little fight or surrendering en masse. They are cold and hungry. On November 19, travel has become severe. Some of the men of this Polar Bear group have not been through the rigorous training that would have occurred in Hokkaido had they been assigned earlier to the company.

Ray is one of these men. They have been traveling in a foot of snow up and over a mountain. The area of operation for the Thirty-First is wild and virgin. It overlays the southern hunting grounds of the Siberian tiger. This land has high passes and poor roads that are inaccessible by track or vehicle. Oxcarts and manpower are used to move equipment and machines around. Cold temperatures of -40 degrees Fahrenheit are not uncommon in these parts. As the evening sets into darkness, the group has managed to make it to a perimeter of the 7th Div. Company B 31st Field Artillery.

[5]

The following is an excerpt from the magazine 'American Heritage', Winter on the Yalu by James Dill. He speaks of a splintered E Co. coming into camp. This is from pages 38–39 of a very old copy of Dill's article. Lt. James Dill was a member of Battery B, Thirty-First Field Artillery Battalion (155 mm towed), Seventh Infantry Division, which operated from Iwon to Kapsan, then back to the Hungnam perimeter. Those of us who knew that the Second Battalion, Thirty-First Infantry, had arrived at Koto-ri less E Company, and that B Company (organic to First Battalion) arrived earlier to take part in Task Force Drysdale where they suffered serious losses; it was unclear where E Company was and what they were doing. Part of the answer lies in James Dill's article. The severity of the cold is well described in the excerpt.

ROBERT BROOKS

My notes for the 18th of November begin: "Snow, almost a foot has fallen. The snow, however, seems to have warmed up the country somewhat." Warmth is, of course, relative. In this case it meant the temperature was only about twenty degrees below zero. This day we sent a wire crew on foot into the mountains in an attempt to lay a phone line to the front lines to supplement our erratic radios. They were not able to push through and ran into an enemy patrol. Only a few shots were fired, and the North Koreans surrendered. The wiremen brought in a total of six POWs. The patrol might be better described as stragglers, as they were so cold they gave up to keep from freezing to death. . . .

Early the next morning we received notice that tour mission with the 31st Infantry was to end, and we were to move even farther north and support the 32d Infantry Regiment in protecting our ever-lengthening MSR (main supply route) as the division neared the Yalu. . . .

Company E of the 31st Infantry (Rays Company) came down into our battery position about dark after a hard march over the mountains. The company commander told us he had had no way of carrying anyone who fell out, and since anyone who did would either die in the snow or be killed by the enemy, he took a drastic step. The first sergeant marched at the rear, and he was ordered to use his rifle sling as a whip. Any man who fell was lashed until he got up and kept going. The captain said he had more difficulty keeping his ROK's going than his Americans. We had always regarded them as tough., wiry men who cold keep going longer than anyone else, but we concluded that, at a certain point, physical condition gives way to basic stamina. The Americans were going on a lifetime of beef and potatoes, while the Koreans were going on a lifetime of fish and rice. One man suggested that this proved bourbon was a better conditioner than sake.

We parceled infantrymen out among the gun sections to get warm at our fires and sent off a hurry-up call to the nearest quartermaster for more rations. Our cooks prepared a meal for them. It was hashed corn beef and bread, but the hot food did wonders for them. Trucks arrived sometime after midnight to take the company away, and they left expressing deep thanks for our hospitality.

On the twenty-first we learned that the 17th Infantry had reached the Yalu River at Hyesanjin. We did no firing from this position, but the journal notes show we moved the guns which had pointed west to point north. On the twenty-second we received some much needed winter clothing. It was not enough-we still did not have any overcoats-but we did get the "arctic shoe pac" to replace our combat boots. This item was rubberized and watertight. Body moisture was absorbed by a removable felt inner sole. The soles along with the socks worn each day were place next to the skin at night to dry out from body heat, adding a piquant aroma to bodies long unwashed.

Adequate clothing was not issued until after we returned to South Korea. My clothing was fairly typical of what everyone wore. Under my helmet I wore the hood for the field jacket buttoned down to the jacket shoulder loops. Most of the men had these hoods, those who did not wrapped towels around their ears. We had not yet been issued the fur cap that made everyone look like an illegitimate son of Mao Tse-tung. I had a scarlet artilleryman's silk scarf, which I wound around my neck to prevent chaffing. . . . From inside out I wore a T-shirt and drawers, more for cleanliness than warmth, since they could be easily washed; a set of wool longjohns that had been issued at Pusan; a standard wool uniform shirt and trousers-the famous "shade 33s"; two fatigue jackets and two fatigue trousers; and lastly I wore my field jacket, not lined but a good windbreaker. I also wore two pairs of sock at all times. Except for some spare socks and underwear and two handkerchiefs, this completed my wardrobe.

Our worst shortage was gloves. Nobody had anything but leather work gloves which gave almost no protection from the cold. It was impossible to touch metal at any time, be it howitzer, ammunition, or truck, with the bare hand without having the skin stick. I had a pair of leather dress glosses I had brought from Fort Sill. . . . The worst problem was where the fingernails joined the skin. Here the flesh split into deep furrows that bled almost constantly. I managed to keep my sores fairly clean, but many men developed bad infections. In the cold our lips cracked and bled. I had had the foresight to put chapstick in my pocket when I left the States and so got some protection. The battery aidman finally managed to get some kind of salve, which the men smeared around their mouths. It was a white paste that made everyone look like a character in a minstrel show. A few of the men had sweaters of some kind, but I did not. Fortunately we did have winter sleeping bags, without them we would not have made it.

On the twenty-third we moved up to the ancient walled town of Kapsan, passing evidence of hard fighting along the way. The town itself was almost entirely destroyed as a result of the recent fighting with only a few pathetic residents left, and they were freezing in makeshift shelters. Large sections of the walls had crumbled away, but there were sections still standing up to seven or eight feet high. I think the walls were about ten feet thick at the bottom. James Dill. [6]

Author's notes: 2Bn Co. E, along with ROKs, had been traveling for over twenty four hours when they reached the B Battery FA location along the supply route. The company was completing a sweep for enemy forces in their Area of Operations. It is believed that they are then moved to the fighting northward in the area of Kapsan from Pungsan. [8] His platoon would be moved further north to the operational area near the Yalu. Those that sustained frost bite and other enjuries were sent back to Pusan for treatment. This time gap before and after the B Co. FA location on Nov 19 and their next stop near the Yalu River has yet to be confirmed by military documentation. Freedom of Information Act requests are being sought to find the movements of the company from their landing at Inchon to November 23. The following information is provided by the best recollections and oral history of Ray Cottrell and laid out in order as they are overlaid with current available information. For a large number of men involved in the Korean War, their actual locations, waterways, orders, and positions were not known. The movements are fast creating difficulties for the enlisted to keep up with the dramatic changes as they occurred. It is not until the 1980s that some of the information of the army's realities were now starting to come out. This knowledge, or rather the lack of it, has garnered this conflict the title "The Forgotten War." As an example, some top-secret operational orders were not released until late 1979. [9] Some other documents have not been secured to the public until the 2000s, some fifty years later. This book wants the reader to keep this in mind. As time unfolds, more information will trickle out and either confirm or correct the information that is in this document. As of this writing, a confirmation that E. Co. 31st Inf. can be realized as being separated from the bulk of the 2Bn which can be located near Pukchong and or Hamhung operational areas per the statements of James Dill above. The author believes that E. Co, along with a group of ROKs, has been sent out to recon, capture, or kill enemy forces as part of a reconnoitering order before they encounter the B BAT. 31st.

November 22/23

After several fights with the enemy, Ray is as far north as any American soldier can be. He has made a walk out on the ice of the Yalu River. Looking across, he can see the Chinese communist world of Manchuria. He is located near Hyesanjin. He could not have imagined from the beginning of 1950 that this is where he would be now.

With Thanksgiving being celebrated in the States, the U.S. Army is sparing neither expense nor effort to get the men a Thanksgiving meal. Morale for the troops will be best met by the high command's opinion by getting them a hot meal. For him, this will take place near a school house near Untaek. A mess tent has been set up. On November 22, he is finally issued some winter gear. He is given a set of arctic shoe pacs that will help in keeping at least his feet warmer. A mess tent has been set up, and a warm meal can now be enjoyed. It would be the first warm meal that he has been able to enjoy since early September.

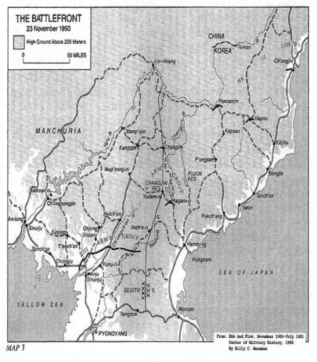

MAP 3

[8]

Dinner will have to wait just a little longer though. The army has a tradition that must be met. When it comes to dinner, the soldiers eat first. Ray is positioned near the tent opening as his men move through to get their meal. Their meals, once outside, will freeze fast. They had to eat quickly or the mashed potatoes would turn to ice. As he stands by, and as the men are eating, a group of men enter the tent. Ray notices them as they enter. There are about eight of them. One of them comes to him directly. Ray sees the five stars attached to his shoulders. The others standing behind him have stars as well. They range from 2–3 stars per person. He knows that this guy is important. The general asks him, "*What are you doing here, son?*" He replies, "*I am waiting for my men to eat, sir.*" As the platoon sergeant, this is a requirement. The general questions on. "*How old are you, son?*" Ray decides for the first time in his formal military career that it is time for him tell the truth on that subject and says, "*I am seventeen, sir.*" The commander tells him, "*Why, you are not even supposed to be here. You have to be eighteen to be in the army. It will be okay, son. You will be home by Christmas.*" [7] The general and his entourage head back outside as if they are in the wrong place.

A few seconds later, Captain Cook runs up to him and says, "*Why didn't you call me over?*" Ray tells the captain, "*He didn't stay long enough.*" Captain Cook questions him further, "*Do you know who that was?*" Ray reports, "*I only know that he had five stars.*" In disbelief, Captain Cook informs him, "*That was General MacArthur!*" [7] Ray stands there a bit surprised but not as moved by the event as his captain. After all, ten months earlier, he was hustling newspapers for a few extra pennies. Sixteen-year-old boys don't spend much time reading the newspapers, save a quick review of the Sunday comics. How would he know what General MacArthur looked like? He was doing good just to know his name back then.

General Almond had left the deck of USS *Missouri* to make this encounter to Hyesanjin for the photo op. The plan now is to move elements of this group southward and then back up to the Changjin Reservoir area to replace a marine battalion currently occupying the east side of the Changjin. Those marines, who originally climbed up the high mountain pass of Koto to face a cold arctic wind and enemy resistance, had taken over the area. The temperature had dropped over forty degrees in a day just before they reached the Changjin. With the ROKs making such a rapid advance from Suwon on the 18th to their new area of operation in the northeast, MacArthur had issued orders for the X Corps to make plans to go north from the Changjin.

With regard to engagements with the enemy, a pattern of attack and disappearance has become the standard for operations for the NK/Chinese forces. Except for a few larger encounters where the air force and the marines working together decimated a large regiment of the PLA south and east of Changjin, the U.N. forces are basically moving at their own

Author's note: Regarding the meeting with the generals, it is believed that this is November 23, Thanksgiving Day. It is believed that General MacArthur is under the first leg of his journey to recon the entire northern lines of the U.N. forces. On November 24, MacArthur is on the west side of Korea with General Walker looking over the front lines. For MacArthur to be in this position with Ray, he must have been flown in by helicopter near the area from the decks of ships of the line. USS *Mount McKinley*, USS *Missouri*, or USS *Boxer* are likely launching points. Freedom of Information Act requests are being sought of their flights for those days. James Zobel, the archivist of the MacArthur Memorial Library, believes that the general is spending Thanksgiving with his family on this day at the U.S. Embassy in Japan. It is quite possible that the general made his visit with the troops that morning and still had time to make it home for dinner that evening. No other historian reporting the whereabouts of the general have been noted, filed, or discovered at the time of this writing. Fly time from Pusan to Japan is about thirty-five minutes. Other historians don't believe that this event took place, but as of this writing, no reports contrary to Ray's recollections have been found. [7]

From left to right, these are Generals Kiefer, Hodes, Almond, and Barr. Picture taken November 21, 1950. They are located at Hyesanjin on the Yalu River. The generals believe the war is about over. It is the following day or the next that MacArthur is reported to have met Ray at the mess tent. These men are believed to be part of MacArthur's entourage that day. [2]

pace. Most encounters up to now have been blocking forces to prevent advances, and no direct offensive has been realized. As the 17th and 7th work to clear what is considered stragglers escaping north, and a larger run in with the enemy in Kapsan, an easygoing attitude is starting to be realized. What seems more to be the case is the enemy baiting the U.N. and ROK forces into a position of their choosing. No American force has ever done battle in such a cold environment before.

Ray overhears of an event involving the 17th Inf. battalion. As the men attempt to keep warm by the fires, an accident occurs. Hand grenades that had managed to get too close to the fires had exploded. He does not hear of any injuries. The result of this action will be detrimental to the regiment. Parts of the Seventeenth are loaded onto trains and are required to move out. No big guns were mounted to the top of the train cars for this journey. A short time later, this train moving troops is attacked, and because they don't have the grenades and large guns mounted, many are captured or killed. By November 24 on the west side, the Eighth Army had advanced to within ten kilometers of the Yalu.

On the eastside on the 24th, Ray's company is packing it up from Hyesanjin and heading for the train station. They are attached to a group heading south. The men have been ordered to replace the Marine Corps' location east of the Chosin Reservoir. The trains will move the men over rough terrain on narrow tracks built by the Japanese in WWII. Spare parts can be garnered for these engines and train cars from supplies in Japan. By November 25, they make the turn at ORO and are approaching the Changjin Reservoir from the south. The bulk of the 2bn 31st is working in the area of Pukchong and moving southwest to get to Changjin. The logistical problem of having trucks and machinery to move the men northward is being resolved as best as can be done. A tank battalion and Company C will be a day behind Ray's company, who is traveling with the group from Hyesanjin. The orders are to replace the Fifth Marines that are operating east of the Chosin. Almond has directed this group (RCT31) to that position to move northward to the Yalu again. This will secure the area west of Hyesanjin. The Fifth Marines are to move to the west of Chosin and join the marines there under Gen. O. P. Smith. Smith is to move his marines westward to the Yudam-ni. From there, they will move west and join the Eighth Army under General Walker to move north and close out the end of the campaign.

THE X CORPS ZONE
26 November 1950

Forward Positions, Evening, 26 Nov

⊙ Airfield

0   40 MILES

TO MUSAN

TO HOERYONG

Tumen R.

Ch'ongjin

ROK CAP

CHINA

Yalu R.

Hyesanin

32 Samsu

17

Hapsu

ROK 3

B

Changjin

Kapsan

Kilchu

7 ROK I

P'ungsan

1 MAR

PUJON RES

Songjin

EIGHTH

CHANGJIN RES

Tanch'on

Yudam-ni

5 MAR

7 MAR Hagaru-ri

Kot'o-ri

Pukch'ong

Chinhung-ni

Sinhung

SEA

Sudong

Majondong

OF

Sach'ang-ni

Oro-ri

JAPAN

Hamhung

Chigyong

Hungnam

ELMS 3

Yonp'o

Wonsan

CHINA

Tumen

U.S.S.R.

Hoeryong

Musan

NE KOREA

Ch'ongjin

0   40 MILES

From: Ebb And Flow, November 1950-July 1951
Center of Military History, 1990
By Billy C. Mossman

MAP 5

This C-47 is being unloaded at the tiny Hagaru-ri airstrip at Changjin (Chosin) Reservoir. From here, 4,312 wounded and frostbitten men were evacuated by air in the five days before the retreat to the sea began (U.S. Marine Corps photo). [2]

CHAPTER 5

Changjin - The Chosin

MUCH INK HAS been spread about the actions and issues of the "Frozen Chosin Campaign." This chapter will attempt to relate the actions and participants in a shortened version of these events. It has been the subject of much debate and discussions. What this author wishes to convey is based on the best research that is available at the time of the writing and the subject Ray Cottrell. The bibliography of material used in the research and oral history of Ray Cottrell is brought together for the composing of this chapter. There is still much to be learned about these events. There is still much to be uncovered. We will let that work be carried out for future historians, although Freedom of Information Act requests are being sought for verifications. Further studies of the battle of the Chosin Reservoir should include 'What History Failed to Record' by Ray Vallowe of the 57th FA attached to RCT31. You can also access 'Chosin Reservoir' group page on Facebook.

November 25

The CCF/PLA, or the People's Liberation Army as they call themselves, had been moving across the Yalu River to the northwest of the country. The Twentieth Army of the CCF had crossed over the Yalu on the Tenth on a pontoon bridge just six miles away from Mupyong. A fifty-five-mile march through high passes and cold weather is realized at this point. By November 13–15, they have amassed just west of Yudam and replace the CCF's Forty-Second, who will move west to support the efforts against the U.S. Eighth Army. The CCF's Twenty-Seventh crossed the Yalu later at Lin-chiang one hundred miles due north of the Changjin. The CCF Command Post is set up just ten miles north of the Chosin. For the CCF, three armies consisting of twelve divisions commanding thirty-six regiments are in play during the actions of November 27. An additional army is in reserve north of the Yalu in China above Lin-chiang.

The Eighth Army had moved as far north as the ten kilometers of the Yalu. A rough terrain of hills and forest separate the Eighth Army from the river's edge. Walker's 8th Army supply lines are stretched to the maximum, and orders are issued to recall them back. While the area is under surveillance by air during the day, the Chinese forces have been poring over the Yalu by night. The bridges that MacArthur wanted to blast on the Korean side, but denied by the Truman administration just days earlier, were being used by the enemy to amass their troops on the Korean side. President Truman held that because the electrical power generated by the river and the close relationship that China had with North Korea, he believed that any aggression of this type, or to attack any part of the Chinese infrastructure and installations north of the Yalu, would kick-start WWIII. Word is spread in Russia that a plan was being hatched to resolve the issues in North Korea by the Chinese.

Working on the west of North Korea, the Eighth Army, General Walker, and the high command are not aware that the Chinese had been camouflaged from their enemy's eyes and had unleashed hell on the front lines to the west of the country. Original expectations of the Chinese were sixty thousand troops beyond the north side of the Yalu. However, thousands of troops stood before the Eighth Army on the south of the Yalu River and had them in their sights. By July, the U.N. forces had gained numerical superiority over the North Koreans, but with the CCF getting involved, all that is about to change.

Several American positions under the bugle sounds and whistles of the CCF command are overrun. Armed with grenades, burp guns, and overwhelming forces, a section of the front lines under the control of the ROK was all but destroyed. The U.N. forces are covering a thinned four-hundred-mile expanse as the war front is immediately deteriorated by the CCF. General Walker is gathering reinforcements and moving to get the hole plugged left by the ROK 7th on the right flank. This is the right flank that O.P. Smith and his marines would be scheduled to close in on and offer support as a blocking position for Walker. The Chinese had managed to circumvent detection and were bringing their forces to bear down on the unsuspecting U.N. forces. Unable to communicate via radios, the Chinese use whistles, yells, and bugles to move their regiments en masse. Under these cold conditions, radios oftentimes failed even for the U.N. forces. Batteries would not remain charged.

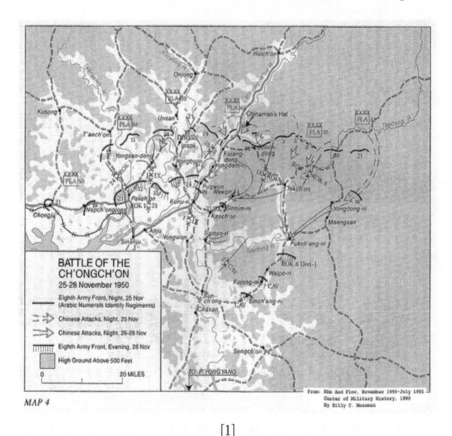

MAP 4

[1]

Meanwhile, in the east, Faith and the men under his direct command had made the turn earlier in that day at Oro-ri and were heading north now to the Chosin. Perimeters are being set in the west of the Chosin by the Marine Corps. Traditionally speaking, the Marine Corps would take a position and the army would hold it. That is not the plan going forward. Each has their own task, and surviving the coldest situations that any U.S. forces have ever dealt with before is just one of them.

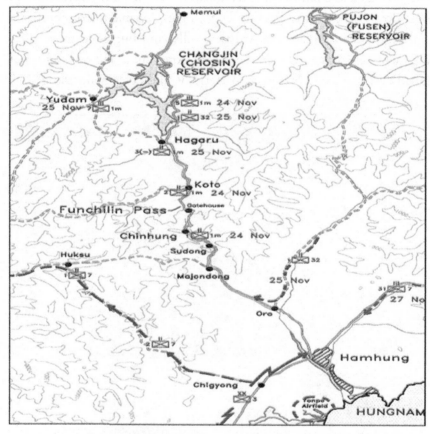

Ray Cottrell is traveling with the 1/32 through
Oro on November 25 from the Yalu. [1]

Faith's 1/32 moving through Oro and taking their position replacing the 1/5 Marines east of Chosin. The 1/5 Marines will move down to Hagaru and then join the 1/7 Marines at Yudam. The marines' orders are to proceed westward to Mupyong fifty-five miles west along the road from Yudam. The bulk of the 7ᵗʰ Div. 2/31ˢᵗ is moving through Hamhung from Puk'chong under orders to join MacLean and Faith on the east of Chosin.

Gen. O. P. Smith had been slow in forward motion. At one point, his group of marines would move no faster forward than a mile a day. This movement, or lack thereof, had gone on for thirteen days. The continual conflicts between Smith and General Almond of X Corps kept creating difficulties that had to be adjusted. A group of twenty thousand should have been moving much faster. Almond had proven that himself with his U.N. Army forces in the north and east traveled farther and faster with much less. Arguments and debates keep the tensions high between the two men. General Smith is purposely delaying his men, and arguing with Almond and the Joint Chiefs in Washington regarding the command structure here.

From the west side of the country, elements of the Eighth Army had moved further north than the marines had at this point. This is upsetting to General Almond. A company of the ROK had been taken out at the extreme southwestern perimeter of the Eighth Army advancement there.

The discovery of the Chinese entering the war at this point creates difficulties for the Far East Command. General MacArthur and his commanders in Japan are adjusting to work with this new revelation. His fears of Chinese interventions had been realized. Intelligence reports still suggest manageable numbers of Chinese forces. With the support of the navy, marines, and air force, they believe that the superiority of the air will keep things well in hand. These Chinese forces, believed to be relatively small in number and poor in supplies and morale, keep things moving forward to the Yalu. While some plans were adjusted, the expectation of pushing these forces back across to the Yalu and northern boundaries is still the main objective.

Maj. Gen. O. P. Smith is getting supplies and air support from the Marine Corps under the U.S. Navy. These men are well supplied with food, munitions, and medical support. Choppers are even used to move the wounded and to transport the commanders from site to site. Meanwhile, General Almond is forced to work with logistical problems. His supply chain is built by any ways and means as could be mustered. In other words, his supply commanders are using every measure possible to ensure that the army and ROK forces are receiving the food, munitions, fuel, and medical supplies from every other point possible. Some of these supplies are being sent in from points as far east as the country of Japan. It is a war on a budget after all.

General Almond is an exacting man. As the right-hand man of General MacArthur, he has extremely high expectations of himself and the men under him. To have Smith, who is supposed to be under his control, ignore, refuse, or fail to follow through on orders by Almond is completely unacceptable to this chief of staff. Major General Smith continues to offer that his actual line of command falls under the Department of the Navy, but General MacArthur's orders clearly state otherwise. The conflict between the two men would set into motion more strings of events that would help in creating confusion and conflicts later. Under Smith's command, perimeters are set up at Hagaru-ri. There are two companies of men in place along Toktong to keep the main supply route open. General Almond wants movement.

MG Smith is cautious and appears to drag his feet in Almond's mind.

Gen. O. P. Smith (left) and Gen. Ned Almond (right) confer.

November 26

On the east side of the mountains at the Chosin, General Smith was gathering his Fifth Marines back from the east side of the reservoir, passing through Ray's position and that of RCT31. This creates a delay for RCT31 to get into position, while at the same time the 5th Marines are late getting to Yudam. They stayed on the east of Chosin one day beyond orders. Ray's unit and others of RCT31 give way as the marines pass through. He notices the warmer parkas that the marines are wearing and wishes that he had one. Soldiers in his regiment are using towels, scarves, and whatever they can find to protect their faces from the cold. Socks over gloves help insulate the hands but had no effective value for shooting their weapons. For those with no lip balm, a salve had been given out to the men to help fight the bitter cold. His fingers are cracking to the point of bleeding at the fingernail. No information of the marines' destination is given to him, and he holds no speculations of it. They are better dressed for the equations of this wasteland. Ray had passed through Hudong-ni, a small milling town that had capitalized on lumber production. It is desolate now.

November 27

A forward command post that had been set up by the Marine Corps is now being utilized by the army in this location. Col. Allan D. "Mac" MacLean is the commander of this task force regiment (31RCT), which had been formed in mid-November at the Yalu. The remaining elements of Ray's 2Bn Co. E 31st Inf. has been attached to this command because of his proximity to Hyesanjin. Col. Don Faith had taken his 1/32nd Infantry consisting of Companies A, B, and C to the position just north of the inlet bridge previously held by the Fifth Marines. These forces had been there alone with no artillery support for a full day.

Nightmare at the Chosin

Task Force MacLean consisted of the following units: the 2nd and 3rd Battalions, 31st Infantry (2/31 and 3/31); the 31st Tank Company; the 1st Battalion, 32nd Infantry (1/32), under the command of LTC Don C. Faith; the 57th Field Artillery Battalion, equipped with 105mm howitzers; and a platoon of eight antiaircraft vehicles (M19s with dual 40mm cannon and M16 quad-.50 halftracks) from D Battery, 15th Antiaircraft Artillery (Automatic Weapons) Battalion. In all, Task Force MacLean numbered about 3,200 men, including 700 ROK soldiers. [3]

Author's note: General Almond is planning to move this group north to the Yalu again from the Chosin Reservoir. Replacing the marines and their orders and giving those task to the 7th Infantry U.S. army personnel.

On 25 and 26 November, the lead elements of Task Force MacLean, Faith's 1/32 Infantry, relieved the 5th Marines, which redeployed to join the rest of the 1st Marine Division along the west side of Chosin. However, because of delays with the rest of the task force's redeployment, the 1/32, which occupied the Fifth Marines forwardmost positions, stood alone without artillery support for a full day.

Don Faith, commander of the 1/32 Infantry, was considered one of the most promising officers in the army. The son of a retired brigadier general, he had been handpicked from the Officer Candidate School at Fort Benning by then-MG Matthew B. Ridgway to serve as his aide-de-camp. He served with Ridgway throughout Europe and jumped with the Eighty-Second Airborne Division on D-Day. In battle, Faith was considered a virtual clone of Ridgway: intense, fearless, aggressive, and unforgiving of error or caution.

Most of the remaining units that comprised Task Force MacLean arrived on the east side of Chosin on November 27. MacLean was among the first to arrive and immediately jeeped forward to confer with Faith. He confirmed with Faith that the task force would attack north the following day with whatever forces were on hand and that the 1/32 would spearhead the attack. [3]

ROBERT BROOKS

Of the forces under MacLean, it is estimated that about two thousand U.S. soldiers are north from Hudong-ni, the timbering town on the west side of the reservoir to Faith's most northern perimeter on the east side of Chosin.

Up until now, General Almond and others believed that a quick and speedy end to the engagement is close at hand. A communication from the Far East Command in Japan had been sent to Washington from the observations of the G2 officer there. He offered that things were well in hand and a progression to the north again to the Yalu could proceed. Gen. O. P. Smith's marines are to move westward to pinch off the CCF between them and the U.S. Eighth Army. MG Smith has sent out elements of his marines in the western direction to Mupyong from Yudam only to be halted by heavy resistance of enemy CCF forces. It was believed that they would cut off the CCF supply lines and encircle them with support from the Eighth Army and marine aircraft. Smith is cautious with his actions and his men. He is prepared for a major conflict.

Ray's 2nd Bn. E/31st is in a position just south of the 57th Field Artillery position creating a blocking position on their southern flank. While at this location, Ray befriends Macca Peter Hansen. Hansen is a corporal and a company runner for the 57th Field Artillery group just south of the inlet. His position is also south of the 15AAA, presumably in the foxholes left behind by the marines on the north side of Hill 1221 looking down at the FA and the AAA units to their north. They will await the arrival of the remainder of the 2Bn/31st coming up from Pukchong through Koto.

The cold weather had taken many men out of the equation because of frostbite. Colonel MacLean, who had just arrived, was in a jeep and heading a couple miles north to Faith's location to confer over the current situation. They are under the current order to gather all the 2bn 31st and the ones already in position at Chosin to move northward back to the Yalu River as MG O. P. Smith's marines move off to the west from the reservoir at Yudam-ni to cut off supply routes of the CCF. MG Smith is to pinch the enemy with the forces of the Eighth Army with General Walker.

Because of weather conditions of -35 to -40 degrees Fahrenheit, radios are not working properly. Telephone lines are difficult to lay from the CP that had been set up at Hudong-ni, and will never get up to the forward positions. Radio communications with Faith's 1/32 and the rest of MacLean's 31RCT are broken at best with the command group in Hagaru, and the 7th's command south at the Pukchong operational area. 31RCT is basically alone on the eastern front of the Chosin. MacLean will drive down to Hudong-ni and back to the CP of Faith by nightfall.

MacLean's vehicles must be kept running for fear that they may not start once turned off. These also provide a bit of warmth for the soldiers who are congregating around the exhaust. Those that are not in a perimeter position post have more opportunity to stay warm, but none of these men are comfortable. A reconnoitering group consisting of intel and recon platoon of the 31st (I@R) had been sent out eastward to ascertain troop movements, if any. Lieutenant Coke, originally of Company E 2/31, took the lead position of this platoon. They hoped to capture some of the enemy for interrogations if possible. Twelve hours later, MacLean and Faith realized that none of these men will be returning. All were considered either captured or killed in the cold frozen wasteland of Chosin. There was a small group of survivors from this group as they were manning the security position along the road that the I@R platoon had traveled. Roy Shiraga, a Japanese-American, was one of these men who would not be captured. MacLean and Faith were still holding out hope at this point, but their fate had been set. Korean radio reports from enemy announcements offer a few names of this platoon weeks later, verifying that all were not killed. Colonel McCaffrey hears these on the radio himself. These men were used as propaganda against the U.S./U.N. forces.

The land mass here is granite-based. Rock and very little brush cover make up the bulk of the ground. Covered in snow or ice, metal tracks can slip, especially when making turns. On the perimeter, because the ground is frozen several inches deep, the men have to break through to make their foxholes. They always dig foxholes. It seems to Ray that whenever they stop, it was time to dig a foxhole. The work is tiresome. Extreme cold winds moving across the area are no help. It could take twelve hours to dig a foxhole in this location. Fires have been started to help keep warm the men who are closer in from the perimeter lines. If one of them took a gun into a warming tent, the humidity would put moisture on the weapon only to refreeze it later and yield it inoperable when returning it back outside. Makeshift cookers are being used to warm food only to have it frozen again before it can be eaten when it is exposed to the weather. Men on the perimeter lines, away from the fires, are wrapping themselves up in their sleeping bags to fight off the blistering cold.

MacLean and Faith are in conference at the northern command post as the evening starts to set in. During that meeting, they are discussing the orders at hand and are debating the whereabouts of the I@R platoon that was sent out earlier to the east. Considerable effort was given to try to locate any of these men returning to camp, but none were to be found at that time. They are under orders to group up and move northward. During this meeting, a bugle is sounded, and yelling is being realized on the 1/32nd perimeter. The fight has begun. The CCF was sending their army in.

The Chinese are behind their own schedule. Groups of enemy forces charging with arms locked with each other are attacking forward into the perimeter gaps as probing forces. It is now past 1000. The CCF has little regard for their own men. They do not have enough rifles to supply everyone. The A and C Company of the 1/32nd are hit first, while a group is moving in on B Company to the left flank. Perimeter lines are broken and the enemy has entered deep within it. This first major group is repulsed but not without injury to the 1/31st. With the sounding of the bugles and screaming, most men take up arms to address the attack. Two divisions of the CCF, the 80th and the 81st, have begun attacking all the units east of the Chosin and north of Hudong-ni.

The A Company on the west side of the perimeter was hit hard, and the commander was killed in the first night of battle. Marine captain Edward Stamford, who was handling air support communications, takes charge of A/31 and guides this force to retake the perimeter line. However, orders by Colonel Faith gave command of A/31 to Lieutenant Smith that Stamford should have remained at the command post where he could have directed air support, instead of just directing air support as he saw fit from his self-chosen positioning. The fighting would continue throughout the night at all these positions. Waves of Chinese would advance. When they are cut down, another soldier would come up behind them, grab their rifles, and continue moving forward. With poor communications between these units and their commanders locally or with the ones further south at Hagaru, Hudong-ni, and Pukchong, their leaders must do what they can with what they have. It is a battle of three divisions with upward of 20,000 troops against a group of only 3,200. During these frontal attacks, other enemy forces are setting up roadblocks to prevent the U.N. forces from moving out or getting support sent forward.

Cold-weather conditions, three divisions hitting them in the face, and confusion on the battlefield are not the only issues. Air support is not available because the pilots would not have the ability to separate friends from the enemy at night. The Chinese are aware of this. This knowledge fits well into their plans. The attack is so gruesome that U.N. artillery guns that were to be used for air attacks are leveled directly at the incoming enemy. Ray can see these guns from his higher position at Hill 1221, but he and his men are pushed off that location during the fighting of the first night. They would be forced to move in closer to the artillery guns to their north. His attached ROKs and the depleted E/Co. would be depleted even more. With ammo low, and many dead and injured, the only recourse is to regroup northward.

Unable to communicate in good order as well, the CCF commanders use bugles and whistles to direct their men. These forces incorporate screaming, yelling, and singing, as they move in and over the perimeter lines adding to the confusion and mayhem. Many U.N. forces personnel believed that their enemy was on drugs as they fought. The battle takes place in stages. The first waves of attacks start at 2200. Surrounded from three sides and the ice at their backs, under extreme confusion and cut off from support, these men are now fighting for their lives.

A few miles south of Faith's 1/32 position, the situation for Ray is much the same. The perimeter south of the inlet and across the bridge, the 57th FA, 3/31st, and elements of the 2/31st are getting hammered by another group of the CCF. The Eighty-First Division of the CCF has started their attack south of the inlet on these U.N. forces at the same time. Wave upon wave of enemy forces would battle in sessions throughout the night. A wave would hit, and fighting would ensue, and then the enemy, those that were not cut down, would back away in the darkness to regroup. A medical group in the area is attacked. Some of these men make it back to Hudong, while a few others make it north of Hill 1221. Each attack is led with bugles, yells, and whistles. Blocking forces of the CCF are in positions along the road north from Hudong-ni to the inlet. They have created barrier roadblocks on the bridges to prevent any units from moving south or north along the road from Hill 1221 to the north. The fighting is brutal, intense, and long-lasting. The CCF commanders are working under the orders of total decimation of these forces around Chosin. All the U.N. forces are taking heavy losses. Ray reports to one of his comrades that night, *"They fall like sticks. Just as soon as you wipe out a line of them, another man is coming up from behind picking up their dropped guns and continue charging forward."* Some of the men started whistling and yelling in hopes of confusing their attackers.

Ray's E2/31 Co. had been moved off the north face of Hill 1221. The 15th AAA and the 57th B Co. are to their backs. The 2Bn mortar team that was also attached to 31RCT from the Hyesanjin area of operations are in front of the 57th and tucked behind 3/31 I Co. Ray is facing south and directly in the way of a large group of the CCF's 81st elements who had captured Hill 1221. As with other perimeter lines that are broken, so is his. With it being night, and Stamford being put in charge of the 1/32 A Co. to the north, air support here is never realized. Men in foxholes are using everything that they have to prevent the enemy from moving in, but the numbers are great. Flashes from mortar shells landing create silhouettes that can be aimed at and shot for. Men are running low or out of ammo. The Chinese are taking guns off their fallen comrades as they fall and continue to press forward. These men too are cut down. U.N. forces in the mess tents have also been overran. Even the cooks have taken up rifles and put themselves in positions to fight back. All of this is happening under a full moon lit night.

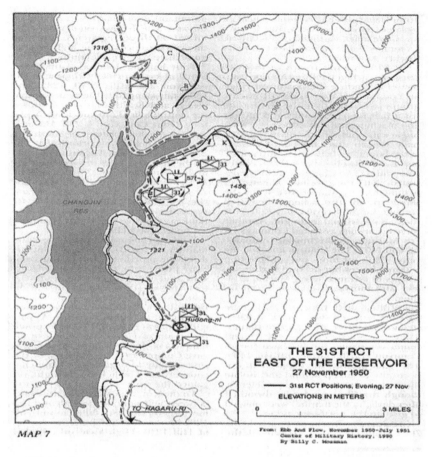

MAP 7

From: Ebb And Flow, November 1950–July 1951
Center of Military History. 1990
By Billy C. Mossman

This map has been altered to show the approximate location of elements of 2E/31st Inf., Ray's platoon. It is believed that they are around the north face of Hill 1221 and the south/southeast face of Hill 1250 just south of the 57th FA battalion. [1]

It was heard above the den that any man who runs away will be shot. The last wave of these forces make their final assault before sunrise. The yells of the ROK and Chinese forces make it even more difficult to ascertain who is in trouble and who is fighting whom. When the CP of the 57FA is blown up by a grenade landing near two gas cans, enemy soldiers are seen warming themselves by the fire as they came into the perimeter. Confusion and misidentification are hindering all forces from distinguishing each other. After considerable losses, all these waves

ROBERT BROOKS

have been repulsed. There will be many survivors. There will be many boots left there. Dead and wounded account for sixty people north of the inlet with MacLean.

September 28

By sunrise, the devastation is evident. In the cold and ice, dead soldiers from both sides are frozen in the positions that they died in. Anyone who had fallen during the night and didn't get help would die from the cold. Some are on their knees with their hands frozen to the rocks that they were trying to prop themselves upon. Limbs and torsos are scattered about as if some macabre horror flick was about to be filmed. Coated in dusty windblown snow, everything looks like a black-and-white motion picture from the past. The men are hungry, distracted, and confused. Senior officers are in high gear in an attempt to reorganize the men. Small-arms fire is present the entire day.

South of Hagaru-ri, it is reported that a few of the Chinese had buried themselves on the icy ground under the cover of the snow during the attacks that night. They would hide in their positions for a couple of hours after the attack. When they thought that they had the advantage of surprise, they would jump up and come forward firing, hoping to catch friendly forces off guard and get a couple of kills before they are cut down. It is not known how many of these sleepers actually died of the cold as they laid in wait to attack. One U.N. soldier worn out from the nights fighting found a rock near a fallen CCF soldier. He used the rock as a chair and the folded position of the enemy who had died frozen into spot as his table. [4]

The situation on the west side for the marines is a little better but not by much. The CCF's is attacking the forces at Yudam from the north. The CCF's 89th division is attacking the northwestern and western points of the perimeter of the 7th, 5th, and 11th marines entrenched there. The marines of Charlie Company at Toktong Pass (C/7th) and Fox Company (F/7th) at Fox Hill near Sinhung-ni are battling by the CCF's 59th Division. The marines' advantage over the army positions lays in the numbers. There are approximately twenty-thousand marines in these locations. While they are fighting off three divisions of the CCF, the army has about two thousand men fighting three divisions of the CCF. The marines are equipped for the cold, and they can be better supplied by airdrops accounting for a wider area to put the materials on the ground. Because the Marine Corps have a wider perimeter, airdrops land in the area and are readily gathered by these forces. Troops on the northeast side of Chosin are not that lucky. Airdrops had to be fought for to prevent the enemy from receiving them. One drop south and east of MacLean's position north of the inlet falls completely into the hands of the Chinese.

MacLean and Faith are holding their positions to the north. The troops south of the inlet are regrouping and fortifying. Most of the day is spent preparing for the night. During that afternoon, a helicopter is spotted overhead. It is headed to the perimeter to the north to see Maclean. It is General Almond. During the afternoon of November 28, a helicopter landed in a rice paddy near the battalion's command post buildings. General Almond, on one of his frequent inspections of his front lines, stepped out of the craft. He discussed the situation with Colonel Faith. Before leaving, General Almond explained that he had three Silver Star Medals in his pocket, one of which was for Colonel Faith. Faith is asked to pick two men to receive these medals. Faith picks the first two people he sees. The first was Lt. Everett F. Smalley, Jr., a platoon leader who had been wounded the night before. He was awaiting extraction. The second was Sgt. George A. Stanley, a mess sergeant who happened to be passing by. They were both asked to stand at attention to receive them. Almond expects the group to continue to move northward to the Yalu as previously planned. After pinning the medals to their parkas and shaking hands with the three men, General Almond spoke briefly to the assembled group, saying, in effect, *"The enemy who is delaying you for the moment is nothing more than remnants of Chinese divisions fleeing north. We're still attacking and we're going all the way to the Yalu. Don't let a bunch of Chinese laundrymen stop you."* At this point, Almond believes that all is still going forward and this was just a temporary setback. His comment is intended to bolster morale but fails to do so.

General Almond, using the top of a jeep, spread a map out and was pointing north. After a brief conversation with Colonel Faith, he boards the helicopter to depart. Colonel Faith, pissed about the issuing of the Silver Star, stripped it from his parka and throws it to the ground. Maj. Wesley J. Curtis walks back to the CP command post with him. He questions Faith, *"What did the general say?"* Faith replies, *"You heard him, remnants fleeing north!"* Lieutenant Smalley went back to his water can. *"I got me a Silver Star but I don't know what the hell for!"*

Colonel MacLean went to see Faith's battalion. As nighttime approaches, he attempts to go south of the inlet to his 1/31st but is stopped by a CCF roadblock there. Realizing that the 32nd is surrounded, he is forced to stay on the north side of the inlet.

Air attacks commenced between 1700 and 1730. Planes struck what appeared to be a battalion-sized enemy group that was marching toward the battalion perimeter from the north, still two or three miles away. The tactical situation, even during the daytime, had been so serious that many of the units did not take time to carry rations to the front line. When food did reach the soldiers after dark, it was frozen and the men had no way to thaw it except by holding it against their bodies. By this time, most of the men realized the enemy was mounting more than light skirmishes as they had the previous evening. [5]

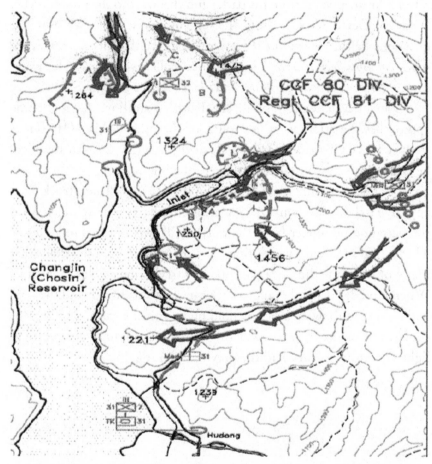

The above map is an illustration of the Communist China Forces (CCF/PLA) as it represents the attacks on the night of November 27.

Operational Orders and the Confusion

OPO 25 Rays orders revealed.

82 Mossman, Ebb & Flow, CMH: GPO. p.129
As defined above by X Corps: —c ‖ .
The huge huge error via a sin of omission.
Below is not the 7th Inf. Div: Mission!
Rather one assigned exclusively to the 31st-RCT, by Division-Commanded by Colonel Allan Duart MacLean!
MacLean's timeline is W/O Delay-and is not the set timeline: **270800I Nov**!
-RECALL-
7th Infantry Division: Zone of operation.
—c. **7th Inf Div:** (1) Attacks N at **270800I Nov** from CHOSIN Reservoir, advance to the YALU River, and destroy En in zone. (2)Secures PUNGSAN area, after coordinating with I ROK Corps. ‖
Ironic as it turns, the only one of the three division regiments assigned to the Changjin Reservoir and within their *legal zone of operation* would be the RCT-31 of the 7th Division! Lacking one battalion 2/31-delayed at Koto-ri-it would never be a full RCT-31 as envisioned by the planners. [The 7th Infantry Division now has the 1st Marine Division's Yalu River zone reassigned to this Army Division of Singalpajin. Task Force Kingston of the 32nd Regiment will seize this objective on 28 November miles north of the Yudam-ni area!]
****
RCT 31- [Declassified 1979-by someone unknown to me: My copy of that copy; obtained 7/13/91.]
27 Nov 50
Opn O 25 Map: KOREA 1:50,000, Sheets 6625; I, II, III, IV.
[Section 1-G-2-Division-Input to order]
1. a. Intel summaries
[G-3, Division-Input to order] 86

b. 7th Inf Div atks 270800 Nov, seizes MUPYONG-NI, adv to YALU RIVER, destroys en in Z. Secured PUGSAN area. [Typo (Pugsan) corrected in Captain Rasula's unclassified S-3 copy as PUNGSAN) ABOVE: What the DIVISION is required to DO. / BELOW: What 31st RCT is required to DO.

[Regimental S-3 Input to order]

2. a. RCT 31 atks w/o delay N from CHOSIN Reservoir, sz Objs A, B, C, D, E, prepares to continue atk to sz CHANGJIN and atk to YALU River.

b. Annex 1, Opn Overlay,

3. a. 1st Bn, 32d Inf:

(1) Sz and secure Obj B w/o delay.

(2) Be prepared to sz Objs C, D, E on O.

(3) Outpost w/o delay Obj C.

b. 3d Bn, 31st Inf:

(1) Sz and secure Obj A w/o delay.

(2) Be prepared to sz Objs D and E on O.

(3) Protect RCT E (right) flank.

c. 2d Bn, 31st Inf:

(1) Close vic Obj A w/o delay.

(2) Prepare to atk to N on O.

d. 1st Bn, 31st Inf: Atched: C Btry, 57th FA Bn. Continue present mission. Review original Archive Document for all remaining orders:

OFFICIAL: MACLEAN

s/LTC Berry K. Anderson Col S-3 5 [11]

Author's note: OpO 25 above, courtesy of Ray Vallowe, in his book *What History Forgot to Record*: *Chosin Reservoir: A Phantom Force - Lost to History*, ISBN 978-1-63068-144-9, gives a great recollection of his actions with the Fifty-Seventh FA as it is realized at the Chosin Reservoir. A fuller and more accurate breakdown of orders and how they pertain to the actions of the U.S. Army under the commands of Marine Corps MG Smith and the U.S. Army's General Almond can be better understood by this book. I highly recommend it. Errors recorded under Appleman's and Mossman's books can be adjusted by Vallowe's accounts and understanding. Vallowe had spent twenty-seven years massing the data to produce this piece. Certain aspects of Vallowe's account have been incorporated in this publication as a result of his findings.

On the previous page and above, one of the accounts realized by Vallowe is shown. In his breakdown of Operational Order 25 (OpO 25), we see who was to do what and when, and who wasn't. Appleman's *East of Chosin* and Mossman's *Ebb and Flow* will give a good layout of most of the events that occurred In Chosin as a whole, but the fuller, more complete actions and how things should have been and actually were under the army's rules and regulations can only be understood by reading Vallowe's *What History Forgot to Record*. What is missing from Vallowe's account and the others is the placement and attachment of Ray Cottrell's E Co. 2Bn 31st Inf. It is believed that elements of Co. E were attached to perhaps I@R platoon as they are sent from Hyesanjin down to Chosin. Note E Co. is not with the I@R platoon as they were sent out on November 27. Rather, they are located on the south of the 57th FA units south of the inlet. Lieutenant Coke is in charge of the I@R platoon. He was formerly the first lieutenant of E Co. 2Bn 31st prior to

ROBERT BROOKS

his assignment to the I@R platoon. It is from this location, south of the 57FA, and north of Hill 1221, that all of Ray Cottrell's recall of the events of the Chosin come into play. It is here that all those recollections could have possibly occurred at the Chosin. Corporal Richard Eugene Hutton and Cpl Carter are with Ray Cottrell as part of 2E/31 east of Chosin.

For the purpose of understanding, the following abbreviations should be understood as listed below: Z - zone, Sz - seize, Objs - Objectives, atk - attack, Opn - Operational, Btry - Battery, destroy en - destroys enemy.

Three factors prevented the situation from being hopeless. First, airdrops were delivered on the afternoon of October 29. The first drop landed on high ground to the east, and friendly forces had to fight to get it. They recovered most of the bundles and captured several Chinese who had also been after the supplies. A second drop went entirely to the Chinese, landing outside the perimeter to the southwest. A third drop was successful. One airdrop consisted of rations, the other of ammunition. The second factor was the marine tactical air support, which constantly harassed the enemy with napalm, rockets, and machine-gun fire. Throughout November 29 and 30, the black Corsairs hit the enemy even during the night between the two days, when they operated by bright moonlight. Pilots later reported that so many enemy personnel were in the area, they could effectively drop their loads anywhere around the perimeter.

The third factor was the hope that friendly forces would break through the Chinese from the south and effect a rescue. There was talk that the assistant commander of the Seventh Division (General Hodes) had even then formed a task force and was attempting to join them. This was true. Colonel MacLean had asked for help the day before (November 28) when he realized he was surrounded. In a message to X Corps, he had asked that his Second Battalion, then at Hamhung awaiting orders from corps, be dispatched to him at once, even if it had to fight its way north. [6]

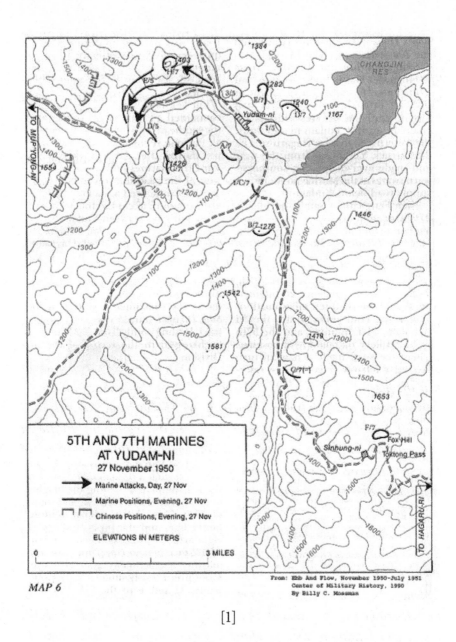

**5TH AND 7TH MARINES
AT YUDAM-NI**
27 November 1950

→ Marine Attacks, Day, 27 Nov

▬ Marine Positions, Evening, 27 Nov

⊓ ⊓ Chinese Positions, Evening, 27 Nov

ELEVATIONS IN METERS

0   3 MILES

MAP 6

From: Ebb And Flow, November 1950-July 1951
Center of Military History, 1990
By Billy C. Mossman

[1]

    The 2d Battalion 31ˢᵗ Infantry's main force, meanwhile, waited for orders. Late on the afternoon of the 28ᵗʰ, X Corps ordered it to set up a blocking position at Majon-dong, a third of the distance from Hamhung to Hagaru-ri. It was to move by rail, with its trucks following by road. A little later, X Corps changed the orders. The Second Battalion was to move by rail to Majon-dong, the next morning. From there, X Corps would furnish trucks to haul the battalion north to help Colonel MacLean. The battalion arrived at Majon-dong and spent the entire day waiting for X Corps trucks. None came. When the battalion's own trucks arrived, as part of the initial plan for establishing a roadblock in the village, X Corps ordered them off the road. Because of the confusion at X Corps headquarters, the battalion's own trucks were not released to it even though the promised X Corps trucks did arrive. Thus, two entire days passed without progress in providing relief for Colonel MacLean's surrounded battalions. It was while his Second Battalion waited at Majon-dong that Colonel MacLean disappeared at the enemy roadblock.

Finally, on the morning of November 30, the relief battalion got underway. Before it had gone halfway to Hagaru-ri, it came under enemy attack itself and did not reach Koto-ri until the following morning. By then, the road between Hagaru-ri and Hamhung was threatened by the enemy, and it became necessary to divert the Second Battalion to help protect the entire corps withdrawal route, and it was therefore held in Koto-ri.

Ten miles above Hagaru-ri, Colonel Faith's task force beat off enemy probing attacks that harassed his forces in full scale during the night of November 29–30. The Chinese concentrated on the two points where the road entered the perimeter, and on the south they succeeded in overrunning a 75 mm recoilless rifle position and capturing some of the crew; however, the perimeter was still intact when dawn came. It was another cold morning. The sky was clear enough to permit air support. Inside the perimeter, soldiers built fires to warm themselves and the fires drew no enemy fire. Hopefully, the men decided they had withstood the worst part of the enemy attack. Surely, they thought, a relief column would reach the area that day.

November 30

A letter-bearing helicopter made two trips to the area on November 30, carrying out four seriously wounded men. Fighter planes made a strike on high ground around Task Force Faith, and cargo planes dropped more supplies, some of which again fell to the enemy. As the afternoon wore on, it became apparent that no relief column was coming that day. Colonel Faith and Major Curtis organized a group of men to serve as a counterattack force to repel any Chinese penetration that might occur during the coming night. As darkness settled for another sixteen-hour-long night, commanders tried to encourage their troops: "Hold out one more night and we've got it made."

On November 30, again beginning about 2200, the Chinese made another of their dishearteningly regular attacks. From the beginning, it showed more determination than those the two previous nights although it did not appear to be well coordinated or concentrated in any one area. Capt. Erwin B. Bigger (CO, Company D), in an attempt to confuse the Chinese, hit upon the idea of firing a different-colored flare every time the enemy fired one and blowing a whistle whenever the enemy blew one.

Soon after midnight, when the enemy attack was most intense, a small group of Chinese broke into the perimeter at one end. Faith sent his counterattack force to patch up the line. From then until morning, there were five different penetrations and as many counterattacks. One of the penetrations, just before first light on December 1, resulted in enemy seizure of a small hill within the perimeter, thus endangering the defenses. Battalion headquarters called Company D to ask if someone there could get enough men together to counterattack and dislodge the Chinese.

Lt. Robert D. Wilson, a platoon leader, volunteered for the job. "Come on, all you fighting men!" he called out. "We've got a counterattack to make." During the night, Lieutenant Wilson had  directed mortar fire, but the ammunition was gone by this time. Assembling a force of 20 or 25 men, he waited a few minutes until there was enough light. His force was short of ammunition—completely out of rifle grenades and having only small-arms ammunition and three-hand grenades. Lieutenant Wilson carried a recaptured tommy gun. When daylight came, the men moved out, Lieutenant Wilson out in front, leading. Near the objective, an enemy bullet struck his arm, knocking him to the ground. He got up and went on. Another bullet struck him in the arm or chest.

"That one bit," he said, continuing. A second or two later, another bullet struck him in the forehead and killed him.

SFC Fred Sugua took charge and was in turn killed within a few minutes. Eventually, the remaining men succeeded in driving the Chinese out of the perimeter.

Even after daylight, which usually ended the enemy attacks, the Chinese made one more attempt to knock out a 75 mm recoilless rifle that guarded the road. In about two-platoon strength, they came up a deep ditch along the road to the south. Lieutenant Campbell rushed Corporal Armentrout forward to plug the gap with his machine gun. Hit by a mortar round the night before, the water jacket on the machine gun was punctured and, after several minutes, the gun jammed. Armentrout sent his assistant back for the other heavy machine gun, the last good one in the section. With it, and by himself, Corporal Armentrout killed at least twenty enemy soldiers and stopped the attack.

At 0700, December 1, as Lieutenant Campbell was telling the battalion S4 (Capt. Raymond Vaudrevil) that everything was under control, a mortar shell landed ten feet away and knocked him down. Fragments sprayed his left side and wounded two other men. Someone pulled Campbell under a nearby truck and then helped him to the aid station. The aid-station squad tent was full; about fifty patients were inside. Another thirty-five wounded were lying outside in the narrow-gauge railroad cut where the aid station was located. Dazed with shock, Lieutenant Campbell lay outside about half an hour. Colonel Faith appeared at the aid station and asked all men who could possibly do so to come back on line. "If we can hold out forty minutes more," the colonel pleaded, "we'll get air support." There was not much response. Most of the men were seriously wounded. "Come on, you lazy bastards," Faith said, "and give us a hand."

That roused several men, including Campbell. Because he could not walk, he crawled twenty yards along the railroad track and found a carbine with one round in it. Dragging the carbine, Campbell continued to crawl to the west. He collapsed into a foxhole before he reached the lines and waited until someone helped him back to the aid station. This time, he got inside for treatment. The medical personnel had no more bandages. There was no more morphine. They cleansed his wounds with disinfectant, and he dozed there for several hours.

As it was everywhere else in the perimeter, the situation at the aid station was most difficult. Near the medical tent, a tarpaulin had been stretched over the railroad cut to shelter additional patients, and other wounded were crowded into two small Korean huts. Company aid men, when they could, assisted the medical officer (Capt. Vincent J. Navarre) and three enlisted men who worked continuously at the aid station. [5]

November 29-30

31RCT/Task Force MacLean is renamed Task Force Faith, from the remnants of 31RCT/Ebb and Flow

At around midnight on 29 November, the CCF 80th Division attacked Task Force MacLean once again. The fighting was savage, often hand to hand. At around 0200, MacLean, still in the 1/32 perimeter, ordered the battalion to withdraw south in the darkness to the 3/31's perimeter, taking all weapons and wounded with them. The move was to be a temporary one to consolidate forces before attacking, as ordered by Almond, the following day.

After disabling and abandoning several vehicles and loading the wounded into trucks, MacLean, Faith, and the 1/32 began moving south at 0500. Darkness and falling snow made the maneuver difficult, but fortunately, the CCF did not attack. Along the way, the task force gathered up the 31st Heavy Mortar Company, which was located halfway between the 1/32 and 3/31 and had supported the two battalions during the CCF attacks.

By dawn, the battalion reached the 3/31 perimeter, only to find it under heavy enemy attack. Without communications, attempting to enter the perimeter would be an extremely hazardous operation. Furthermore, the Chinese had created a roadblock at a bridge on the road leading into the perimeter. Faith led a party of men that successfully drove the CCF off the bridge and cleared the block. MacLean then came forward in his jeep. He spotted a column of troops whom he believed were his overdue 2/31. The troops within the 3/31 perimeter, however, began firing on the column, much to the dismay of MacLean. The troops were actually Chinese. MacLean, still believing they were American, ran towards them, shouting, "Those are my boys." He dashed out onto the frozen reservoir towards the perimeter, attempting to stop what he believed was friendly fire. Suddenly, CCF troops concealed near the bridge fired on MacLean, hitting him several times. MacLean's men watched in horror as an enemy soldier grabbed him and dragged him into the brush.

Unfortunately, there was no time to attempt a rescue of MacLean. Faith had to focus on getting his men into the 3/31 perimeter. With the men crossing the frozen stream on foot and the vehicles with the wounded dashing across the bridge, most of the column made it into the perimeter.

Once in, Faith surveyed the carnage. Hundreds of American and CCF dead littered the ground. The 3/31 had suffered over 300 casualties and its L company had ceased to exist. With MacLean gone, Faith assumed command and did his best to strengthen the perimeter. Marine air controller CPT Stamford also called in for Marine close air support and an airdrop for desperately needed supplies, especially 40mm and .50 caliber ammunition. Faith then sent out search parties to look for MacLean, with no luck. MacLean was declared missing, but later, an American POW stated that MacLean died of wounds on his fourth day of captivity and was buried by fellow POWs. He was the second and final American regimental commander to die in Korea.

On the morning of the 29th, Drake's 31st Tank Company made another attempt to reach the 3/31 perimeter, only to be driven back to Hudong by CCF troops dug in on Hill 1221. For the remainder of the day the newly designated Task Force Faith remained in position. With nearly 500 wounded, the force was in no position to carry out the attack ordered by Almond. Yet, Faith had no authority to order a withdrawal. The situation was helped somewhat by Marine close air support and an airdrop of supplies, although the drop lacked 40mm and .50 caliber ammunition. A Marine helicopter also flew out some of the most serious wounded. Task Force Faith's situation, however, remained desperate, particularly since it had still had not established communications with the Marines or the 7th ID HQ.

MG Dave Barr, commander of the 7th ID, flew in by helicopter to bring Faith more bad news. All the units of X Corps, including Task Force Faith, now under operational command of the Marines, were to withdraw. The Marines would provide Faith with air support, but other than that, the men would be on their own. To make matters worse, the task force was burdened with wounded, which would make their withdrawal even more difficult. Furthermore, the 31st's CP, the 31st Tank Company, and the HQ Battery, 57th FAB, had evacuated Hudong for Hagaru-ri, further isolating Task Force Faith.

At about 2000, the CCF launched another attack. While killing large numbers of Chinese, Task Force Faith suffered another 100 casualties. Faith soon concluded his force could not survive another major attack. He summoned his remaining officers and told them to prepare to move out at 1200. The task force, after destroying its artillery, mortars and other equipment, began to move south, carrying 600 wounded in thirty trucks.

With a twin 40mm gun vehicle leading the way, the column began to move at around 1300 hours. It immediately came under fire. Stamford called in Marine air support, but the lead plane's napalm canisters hit the front of the column, engulfing several soldiers and creating panic throughout the task force.

The situation quickly grew worse. Heavy fire from the flanks killed many of the wounded in the trucks. The fire grew more intense as the column reached Hill 1221, which dominated the surrounding area. At the north base of the hill, the CCF had blown a bridge, forcing a two-hour delay as the lead A/A vehicle had to winch the thirty trucks across a stream. A roadblock then held up the task force, while the CCF troops on the hill kept up their heavy fire. There was only one way to break through: take Hill 1221. Several hundred men charged up the hill, including many of the wounded, some of whom said they preferred to die on the attack than while waiting in the trucks. Despite heavy casualties, the men drove the CCF off most of the hill. Many, however, simply kept going over the hill and down the other side, venturing out onto the frozen reservoir and walking towards Hagaru-ri.

The task force then ran into another block at a hairpin turn. Faith led an assault that cleared the enemy from it. However, he was struck by enemy grenade fragments and mortally wounded. Once Faith was lost the command structure of Task Force Faith collapsed. As the 1/32's S-1, Robert Jones, described it, "When Faith was hit, the task force ceased to exist." Faith would later be posthumously awarded the Medal of Honor.

While some such as Jones and Stamford tried to provide leadership, Task Force Faith quickly fell apart. Another roadblock, this one comprised of disabled tanks from the 31st Tank Company and other vehicles, furthered delayed the column. At Twiggae, the CCF had blown another bridge, forcing the column to attempt a risky crossing of a railroad trestle. All the while, the vehicles were under fire. Many men left the trucks to hide or tried to escape over the reservoir. Many died from wounds and exposure, or were captured.

Just north of Hudong-ni, the task force ran into yet another roadblock. This spelled the end for Task Force Faith. The CCF brought heavy fire to bear on the column. CCF troops lobbed grenades and fired rifles into the trucks, killing masses of wounded. Those who could escape ventured out onto the reservoir and began the arduous march to the Marine lines at Hagaru-ri.

During the night of 1-2 December, survivors straggled into the Marine lines. Many came through a sector held by the Marine 1st Motor Transport Battalion. LTC Olin L. Beall, commander of the battalion, led a rescue mission across the ice by jeep, picking up over 300 survivors, many suffering from wounds, frostbite, and shock. In all just over 1,000 survivors reached the Marine lines, and of those, only 385 could be considered able-bodied. The survivors, along with other 7th ID soldiers, were organized into a provisional battalion and attached to the 7th Marines. Known as the 31/7, the battalion participated in the 1st Marine Division's breakout from Hagaru-ri to the coast beginning on 6 December.

For years afterward, the saga of Task Force MacLean/Faith had been largely ignored. Many believed that the collapse and panic that engulfed the task force had brought great shame to the Army. Upon closer examination, the task force's role in the Chosin battle proved to be much more noteworthy. Many historians now agree that Task Force MacLean blocked the Chinese drive along the eastern side of Chosin for five days and allowed the Marines along the west side to withdraw into Hagaru-ri. Furthermore, the task force destroyed the CCF 80th Division. In recognition of their bravery, Task Force MacLean/Faith was awarded a Presidential Unit Citation in September 1999.

For additional information on Task Force MacLean/Faith, please read: Roy E. Appelman, *East of Chosin: Entrapment and Breakout in Korea*; Clay Blair, *The Forgotten War: America in Korea, 1950-1953*; and Anthony Garrett, "Task Force Faith at the Chosin Reservoir," in Infantry, (September-December 1999).

31st infantry regiment, 7th infantry division, 8th us army, battle of the Chosin reservoir, task force faith, task force Maclean [1]

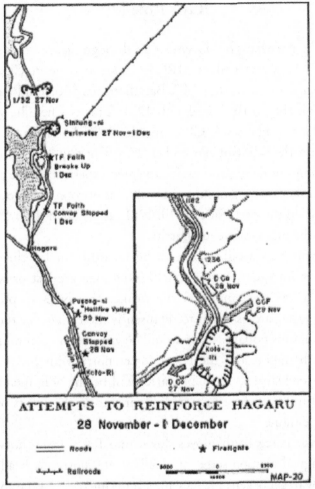

This Marine Corp map was created in 1957. It omits the 2Bn Tank Company under Drake at Hudong. Hudong is located on the map where TF Faith convoy gets destroyed. At 00:01 on the 29th Gen. O.P. Smith is given control of all actions at the reservoir. Col. Drake had sent out 4 tanks north to support Col. Faith but they were destroyed on the 28th. At 1730 on the 29th the 2Bn tank co. pulls into Hagaru by orders of O.P. Smith or General Hodes to reinforce Hagaru. This will in effect lead to the destruction of TF Faith. Faith was not given orders by Smith to return to Hagaru on the 29th like the tanks were. Why? Thirty hours after the tanks arrive at Hagaru, TF Faith arrives at Hudong to find no one there on December 1st. This omission of events will be hidden or waxed over for the next 50 years.

Ray's Role [7]

During the events of November 27 through December 5, elements of 2E/31st were attached to 31RCT. Upon arriving at Chosin, Ray is established south of the 57FA Battalion, north of Hudong-ni. His group is on the north side of Hill 1221. This is where he will meet Macca Hansen. Hansen is CP runner for 57th FA. As the CCF moves in on them the night of November 27, this group will realize many losses. Many confusing and undocumented experiences take place that night. On the morning of November 28, his platoon will move further northward off the north side of Hill 1221 just south of the 57th FA. The events of the night before are horrific.

November 28 would prove to be no different for this band of brothers. With each passing attack, more men are lost or wounded. With each loss of manpower, the weaker the forces to protect the perimeters they are assigned to. Hansen is the runner for the 57th FA CP. Without his updates, there would be virtually no communications with this battalion and the larger forces north with the 3/31st. Cpl Macca Peter Hansen, and Cpl Carter will be the only men that Ray can recall from all the events he is a party to in the events of Chosin Battle time frame.

As Task Force Faith moves down into Ray's area, and with Ray being assigned platoon sergeant of 2E/31 at Chosin, he heads toward the convoy to get orders. He sees an outranking officer as he approaches and asks him, *"Who is in charge?"* The man replies, *"Colonel Faith, he is in that 3/4 ton over there."* Pointing to the road just north and east, he sees the vehicle. Worn down, hungry, tired, and still only seventeen years old, the young sergeant makes his way to Faith's vehicle.

Ray notices that Faith has been injured in the shoulder/chest area of the parka he was donning. Firm and confident, after identifying himself as the sergeant of his company, he asks the colonel, *"What are our orders, sir? What is the plan?"* Faith replies, *"We are moving out back to Hagaru. I want you to take your company and fall in line in the back of the convoy. Your task will be to cover our flank as we move south."* Ray retorts, *"Sir, there are only seven of us left, myself included."* It is unclear the reason behind the decision that comes from Faith at this point, but an idea can be formed from his last orders. Faith says, *"I want you to take your men and infiltrate your way south to Hagaru. Someone is going to have to tell what happened here."* Ray salutes the colonel and moves off to confer with the remainder of his men. [7]

He gathers his men and explains what has just happened and what is expected. In an attempt to ensure that at least some of them make it through the CCF soldiers that are pocking the landscape, Ray decides to spread his team out into two groups. He will keep two men with him. The other group of four will head out first. Colonel Faith and his task force will continue to move on past Hill 1221. Faith will move forward no more than one mile before he is killed attempting to get past yet another roadblock put into place by the enemy. Ray has no map to work with, but he does know what direction south is if he follows the ice of the reservoir. He enters the ice somewhere between Hill 1221 and Hill 1250. He was close to the Fifty-Seventh, but that group, or rather who was left of it, had joined the convoy and would continue the fight south.

Author's note: As the fighting continued southward around Hill 1221, more and more men were forced out on the ice. A jeep would set out from Hagaru on the ice as soldiers started to walk into the perimeter. Many of these men dropped their rifles. There was no point carrying a weapon that weighed 10lbs that had no ammo to fire. Many would be rescued via that one jeep, but that was not the case for Ray Cottrell.

There is no guarantee that the U.S. forces will be there when they arrive. It is a risky trek with a very low chance of success.

The three men are moving slowly over the ice. In an attempt to stay out of sight of enemy forces, they walk at night in some of the worst weather ever dealt with by a U.S. soldier. Fear of walking on thin ice is a concern but not relevant to the situation. The cold weather would have seen to that by now. Not knowing the conditions of ice thickness, though, keeps the men fairly close to shore at night. The first two nights are wrought with the echoes and flashes of light from the fighting coming from the east. It is the sounds of Task Force Faith fighting CCF on their way back to Hudong-ni, they will be broken up and destroyed before they reach Hagaru-ri. Fuel dumps and supplies that were at Hudong-ni, which would have been helpful to the TF, are no longer there. Neither is the tank group that had been there only 30 hours before. That group had been recalled by MG O. P. Smith back to Hagaru-ri to help reinforce the RCT there. TF Faith would have to fight all the way back to Hagaru-ri. They will not make it.

As the morning approaches, the men take shelter in the darkness under overhangs of the water. This will stand to cover the group from any enemy forces lurking about on the shoreline. A warming fire is not an option. On the third night, December 3, the small band takes shelter under a large outcropping over the ice. As they crawl under and in, they discover an army captain propped up against the back of the sheltered area. He is extremely wounded. Coagulated blood can be seen outside of his clothing. His legs are frozen to the ice just above the knees by the blood loss. The man sits there with his wallet opened to a picture of his newborn daughter. He explains to the guys that he has never seen her before. She was born while he was at war in Korea. The conversation doesn't go far beyond this. Ray explains what has happened further north and what had happened in their location thus far.

Ray realizes that the captain held on to a glimmer of hope that they would take him out. The men had been on the ice for three days and two nights at this point. Traveling was slow and dangerous. Ray knows that they are in no condition to carry the man out and that the man is in no position to travel. He is frozen to the ice itself. The captain is aware of the situation as well.

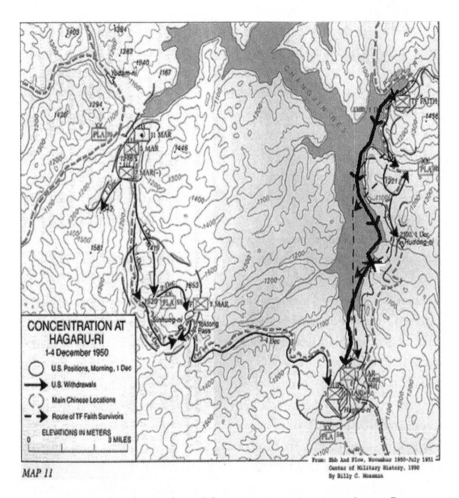

From: Ebb And Flow, November 1950-July 1951
Center of Military History, 1990
By Billy C. Mossman

MAP 11

This map has been altered from Mossman's original to reflect
when and where Ray Cottrell enters the ice from the location
of TF Faith near the inlet. He is told to take his six soldiers to
Hagaru as Faith's convoy moves southward along the shoreline
next to the train track. He enters the ice north of Hill 1221.
The black line represents the suspected traveling route of Ray
Cottrell and the remaining members in his platoon of 2/31 E Co.
The black X along this route represents the suspected location
of the injured captain on the ice along the shoreline. [1]

December 3

As the sun starts to set, the men start their preparations. What little food the men had has already been given to the captain. It serves no real purpose, but they have so little to offer the guy. His fate had been set when he made his way down to this spot. No words are spoken as Ray removes the dog tags from the captain's neck. He puts one in his own pocket. He then reaches down to grab the boot of this fallen man. He turns his foot upright to put the other tag on to his boot. The captain's foot breaks away from his body. Ray tucks the tag in. He feels no pain in this. They both know what will happen next. Ray will hold this memory for all the years to come. The men make it to their feet and move off into the darkness. They were forced to leave the man behind. The tag will be turned in at the CP for recordkeeping.

That evening, they approach the end of the reservoir. It is a dangerous thing for anyone outside of a perimeter to attempt to move into it. Often-used code words are changed daily. Ray has no idea what that might be this night. Attempting to just get the attention of the soldiers holding the line could result in immediate death by friendly fire. It is a game of trust as they approach, during which they have become very vulnerable. Each man has his rifle held clearly with both hands over their heads. The fear of being shot by their own men is also complicated by the fact that they have to be exposed this way allowing any nearby enemy a free shot at an unprepared soldier.

In loud voices, as clearly as they can, they identify themselves. Questions are asked from the soldiers inside the line to verify who it is outside. Clothing does not secure the men. Enemy forces had been known to wear uniforms of their adversaries as a means of attacking a perimeter. After a few short desperate moments, the men are allowed to approach and enter into the relative safety of the perimeter at Hagaru-ri. They will not be the only ones. Stragglers from other forces from the east and west of the reservoir had been trickling in over the past couple of days. For the night, the men are safe.

It is now early morning on December 4. In the darkness, the men are directed to a warming tent. They have been offered some food as well. Confusion is still an issue here. Broken groups of battalions are being assigned to new groups as the stragglers come in. Some of these men were able to locate their original commanders and slip off their assigned groups to rejoin the men of their original battalions. This will create a nightmare for the morning reports at the command post. There is not much time for rest for any of these men. This entire group will soon fight to Koto-ri.

Author's Perceptions and Synopsis

On November 17 or 18, 2BN Co. E 31st was sent out from Pukchong as a recon and cleanup taskforce. Attached to them is an ROK unit. They move north. It is believed that Lieutenant Coke is one of the officers in the event. With no radio communication as they set out over the mountains, they come into the area of the field artillery perimeter as reported by Lt. Dill in his story in American Heritage. In the attempt to see that these men are put into a position of moving north to the Yalu, they are trucked out further north and find themselves at the Yalu by November 23.

To ensure that all possible forces go to the Changjin/Chosin reservoir, all available forces are being sent from the Yalu to the reservoir. Injured and frostbitten soldiers of Company E are sent out south to Pusan for medical attention. The remaining elements are sent out to the Chosin Reservoir under the newly formed 31RCT under the command for Colonel MacLean. From these men of the 31RCT, the I@R platoon is formed. Lieutenant Coke, previously of the 2Bn E Co 31st Inf., is put in charge of this platoon by his request. Platoon Sgt. Ray Hooker Cottrell is not part of this I@R platoon but is traveling with the new 31RCT. A small group of men were holding a position on the road east of Chosin as the I@R platoon was moving east. Ray Shiraga was part of this guard duty for the I@R platoon along this road. Lieutenant Coke and others would be killed or captured on this mission.

As these forces are moved into the Chosin Reservoir on the 27th, Ray Cottrell and the remainder of Co. E would take up positions on the north side of Hill 1221 overlooking the 57th FA position directly to their north along the east side of the Chosin ice. Cottrell will make his first run-ins with Cpl. Peter Hansen at this location. These men would offer infantry support for the 57th FA using the foxholes and bunkers built and left behind by the marines a few days earlier. This location, Hill 1221, would have been the location that the bulk of 2Bn 31st Inf. would have taken up had they made it to Chosin. They did not. (This is formalized in the documentary *Task Force Faith*.) The remaining force of the 2Bn 31st under Colonel Reidy would be held at Koto-ri with the marines under command of Col. Chesty Puller.

When the CCF forces take Hill 1221, Sergeant Cottrell, Cpl Carter and Cpl Richard Eugene Hutton and the remaining men would be pushed off the hill and into the area of the 57th FA area. Ray would meet Colonel Faith as the convoy moves on to Hill 1221 and is sent with the remainder of his men on to the ice. Several books have been put out on this subject over the past sixty-five years, with each one bringing new light to the subject.

The documentary *Task Force Faith* [10], produced a few years ago, offers the best photography and cinematography on the events as they unfolded. Enemy footage is brought to bear in the documentary as well and offers a great linear description of the events. Photos of 2/31 Inf. can be seen in Chosin Chronology by George Rasula. [9]

CHAPTER 6

Out of the Pan, Into the Fire

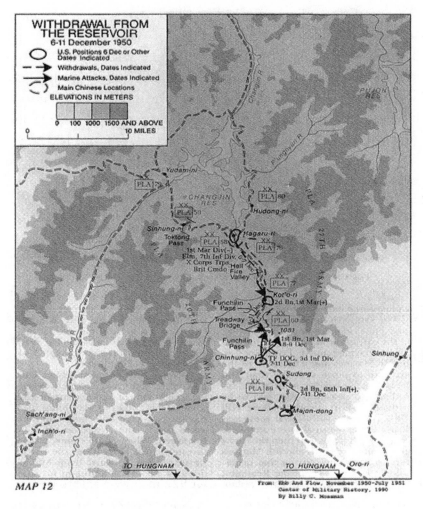

WITHDRAWAL FROM
THE RESERVOIR
6-11 December 1950

○ U.S. Positions 6 Dec or Other
Dates Indicated

Withdrawals, Dates Indicated

Marine Attacks, Dates Indicated

Main Chinese Locations

ELEVATIONS IN METERS

0   100 1000 1500 AND ABOVE

0   10 MILES

MAP 12

From: Ebb And Flow, November 1950–July 1951
Center of Military History, 1990
By Billy C. Mossman

[1]

December 5

WITH GENERAL SMITH'S marines returning from Yudam-ni to get back to Hagaru and what is left of Faith's TF coming into Hagaru from the ice, there is little time to rest. The SNAFU (situation normal, all fucked up) that has been the Chosin campaign is far from over. At best, it is only halfway done. On December 29, General Almond, who has had his fill of dealing with MG Smith, has now turned the defense and movements of what was X Corps' thirty thousand soldiers and returned to Hungnam. General O.P. Smith is now the commander of all actions at Hagaru. Smith had finally gotten his way again. General Walker's Eighth Army is in full retreat now in the west. X Corps is now fighting for their lives to get back to the port of Hungnam. ROK soldiers in the extreme east are moving back down the coast that they so readily had taken just a couple of weeks before to get back to the port. Chinese forces are bent on the destruction of all U.N. and U.S. forces above the 38th.

Task Force Drysdale

Ray and the survivors of the ice walkers have been reorganized. With only seven survivors of his 2bn 31st Infantry at Hagaru-ri, he and his men are scattered into different fighting groups for the move south. Lt. Col. D. B. Drysdale and his 41 Commando group was ordered by Chesty Puller to clear the road to Hagaru from Koto-ri. It would be the Forty-First's first actions in Korea. Even though their orders were to reconnoiter the south of Toktong pass. They would never get into position to fulfill that order. General Smith believes that such a small force was not enough to breakout makes arrangements to increase this TF. By the end of its organization, over 922 men were able to start the move northward to clear the road. On November 29, men, trucks and tanks attached to this group are sent out to clear the path for Smith's group to make it south. Several attacks on this TF in Hell Fire Valley would exert a heavy toll on the soldiers. At one point, the TF is split into three distinct groups. Of the encircled men to the south, only some would make it back to Koto-ri and Chesty Puller's command. As the group on the north of the break head to Hagaru-ri, they are met with a formidable force of CCF that would block their path. Some will make it to Hagaru. Some will not. Of the 922 men of Task Force Drysdale, approximately 300 arrive at Hagaru-ri, 300 are killed or wounded, and about 135 are taken prisoner, with the rest making it back to Koto-ri. Seventy-five of the 141 vehicles were also destroyed. These vehicles will serve as roadblocks later as the Hagaru group moves out southward.

In the breakup of TF Drysdale, on the morning of November 30, Major McLaughlin, who had only joined up on to TF Drysdale as passenger, ends up in command. Out of ammo and surrounded by the CCF, he is forced to accept the conditions of surrender. A captured soldier is sent back to this group to inform them that the CCF stated that they had fifteen minutes to surrender or be destroyed. McLaughlin stalls for as long as he could in the hopes that the tanks to the south would make their way north to help out. That group is turned back by the roadblocks that had just previously been cleared by the frontal section of TF Drysdale. Between 0300 and 0400, he makes his decision. In a few minutes, Chinese soldiers stand up all along the railroad bank, across the narrow road, and ridges on the hills beyond. Once agreed upon, the CCF springs to their feet from positions all around the perimeter. They are virtually unopposed in their wave-after-wave attacks. [2]

Meanwhile, at Hagaru-ri, airdrops and some of the injured are flown out from the airstrip that the engineers had lengthened in the short time that they were there. Only 500 marines are flown in from the 10,000 in reserve at Hungnam. No thought of flying in more troops to this airstrip is realized. With air strikes and early morning fog, the X Corps begin their fight back through to Hungnam. Up first would be Hell Fire Valley, well named for the intense battles that had occurred there along the narrow road from the Funchilin Pass. A high pass to one side, and the drainage of the Chosin Reservoir to the other side. There is little room to operate on most of this road.

December 6

On December 6, remnants of RCT31 are attached to the Seventh Marines. This group would make up a provisional group known as 31/7. Ray would find himself in one of the two groups created under this provisional battalion. One is 3/31, Ray's group, and the other is the 1/32. Commanders would be put over these two smaller battalions. The marines lead out at the start of the move in the early morning before sunrise. Within a mile of the withdrawal, the lead tank is hit by the CCF, and all things are halted for a couple of hours. Marines are sent out to take the east hill that was held by the CCF to give the main group a fuller road to travel.

Marines watch napalm from Corsairs as they move
out Hagaru. U.S. Marine Corps photo. [3]

ROBERT BROOKS

TF Drysdale encountered most of the resistance coming from the east as they moved into Hagaru, and this was figured into the logic of the withdrawal. Infantry battalions of the 3/31 and the 1/32 took their positions on the way out. In the masses of men moving south, elements of the CCF were captured and sent back into the military police for control. Over one hundred are captured. A lot of time had been lost from the onset, but alas the main group was again on the move south. Next up would be Hell Fire Valley. It was named as such by Colonel Drysdale from the battles that had occurred as his TF fought their way to Hagaru earlier.

As the main group enters Hell Fire Valley, the CCF takes advantage to dig in deeper. The 3/31st would be taking the left (east side) of the road back and would take casualties. The commander would be injured earlier before they even get to the valley. Air strikes on the left would result in more Chinese surrenders. This would suggest that the CCF forces are dwindling. This eleven-mile valley will take thirty-eight hours to move the entire group within the perimeter of Koto-ri. The Thirty-First Tank Company which were at Hudong on the 29th was the last to make it in as they were covering the rear of this ten-thousand-plus-man convoy of trucks, jeeps, and tanks. While in Koto-ri, a small rest can be taken, and some hot coffee is available to some of the men here. Soldiers separated from their companies begin to slip out of the provisional battalion to get back with their own men and platoons. "SNAFU." This would create problems as the provisional battalion started to regroup.

Marines take up temporary positions along a ridge
during the breakout from the reservoir. [3]

Army casualties from Hagaru to Koto have never been formalized. Marine casualties in this eleven-mile trek would realize 103 killed, 506 wounded, and 7 MIAs. During the surrender by McLaughlin, one soldier would report seeing a fellow soldier with an open belly wound and his guts hanging out pushed off the side into the raven to die along Hell Fire Valley. This was the environment and the ravages of war.

**Three hundred eighty-five able-bodied survivors of
Task Force Faith move out of Hagaru. Ray would be
part of the 129 U.S. Army from TF Faith. [3]**

A U.S. Marine Corps battalion was also in force at Koto-ri. MG
Smith had Chesty Puller and his marines in Koto-ri over Lieutenant
Colonel Reidy's 2/31st less elements of E Company make up the forces
here. Puller's 1/M were supposed to be at Yudam earlier but were held
back due to Smith's lack of movement forward earlier in the campaign.
Puller would send out a TF along the east side of Hell Fire Valley. They
would slip behind the CCFs attacking westward to the road to Koto-ri.
Ray is part of the Provisionary 31/7 moving south along the east side
of Hell Fire Valley as well. Traveling over snow bitten rough terrain,
they encounter CCF groups on three different occasions before joining
the main group on the road to Koto. Puller's TF and Rasula's 31/7 are
heading toward each other on November 7. As the main group is using
the road from Hagaru to Koto, a CCF roadblock is encountered that

would have to be overcome. The CCF attacking the southbound main force of marines is being hit by three sides here. Forces from the road, the 31/7 heading south and the TF sent out by Puller, are converging on the CCF forces along the east side of the road. The roadblock created by lost vehicles of TF Drysdale two days earlier are in their way and are creating yet another entrapment by enemy forces. Hell Fire Valley is cleared, and all survivors of the Chosin at Hagaru are making their way into the perimeter of Koto-ri. On the evening of December 7, the last of the main force has made it to Koto. The night is basically quiet. Elements of the shrinking CCF forces are moving south along the west of the road and Koto to take up new positions on both sides of Funchilin Pass north of the Gate House. The men get some much-needed rest even if it is short term. A WWII veteran was asked by a younger man, "How do you drink your coffee? Black?" He replies, "You will drink anything hot when you are freezing to death in a foxhole."

Moving out from Hagaru as the road ahead is cleared of CCF forces. U.S. Marine Corps photo, 1950. [3]

Koto-ri would hold a surprise for Ray Cottrell. Lieutenant Colonel Reidy had taken up at Koto-ri on December 1. His 2nd Battalion 31st Infantry was holding the perimeter here along with Chester Puller's marines. Reidy is his commander. He is finally back with familiar faces for the first time since mid-November, or at least with men that bear the same patch. When Reidy arrived here, he sent out men to take Hill 1328 and prevent enemy sniper fire from coming in. This action would also serve to expand the perimeter of the Koto-ri encampment. Back at Hungnam, the divisional command is working feverishly to get plans and things in motion to get these men not only out of Koto-ri but also off the docks at Hungnam should they make it back there.

U.N. dead taken out of Hagaru and brought down to Koto. Chinese stripped the dead of clothing for warmth. [3]

The dead that were brought down to Koto are offloaded from the trucks that bore them. Considering the breadth and scope of the actions passed and yet to come, these men are put into a mass grave here. A ceremony is held for the fallen. It is important to remember that these bodies had at one point been frozen in the conditions that they died. Action had to be taken to straighten the dead to accommodate the space of the trucks themselves. Limbs would sometimes be broken to get the corpses into the trucks. The registration teams work overtime to accommodate for the dead. A bulldozer is employed to create a mass grave for these fallen soldiers. As ghastly a sight as one would ever dare to witness, orders required it to be done. Necessity of this action is the motivation.

U.N. forces moving south are again waiting for the clearing of the road to move forward. DOD photo. [3]

**U.S., British, and ROK being offloaded at
Koto-ri. U.S. Marines photo. [3]**

December 8

Task Force Dog had moved out early in the morning to the east of the road leading to the Gate House of the Funchilin Pass. Their objective was to take Hill 891. They succeeded. Meanwhile, Reidy has sent a group out to take Hill 1328 on the southwest corner of the Koto perimeter. From here, air strikes could be generated against CCF forces trying to move south on the west side of the road of the Funchilin Pass. His 2F/Co would be replaced by 2G/Co there. Marines would be in the lead coming out of Koto. Just over halfway down the pass, the 1/7 marines would take on another CCF force to the west of the road, a few miles north of the Gate House. With most of the road cleared to this point, the rest of the troops in Koto are preparing and moving out of there. Several forces have taken positions on the west and east of the pass out of Koto to ensure that the main group could move forward.

The 31/7 Army and the 1/5 Marines had moved out of the south of Koto tracking the hills in a snowstorm. Their objective on the east side of the road is Hill 1358. CCF forces south of Hill 1358 were set up to attack the road from the east, due west of the CCF just taken on by the 1/7 Marines. A crossfire was to be expected on west and east by the CCF forces. This too was broken up allowing the main forces to get to the Gate House and to install the Treadway Bridge. The high ground was controlled by friendly forces on both sides of the road now. Artillery fire and close air support helped in securing the road as they moved down.

Surveying the damage at the Gate House on the Funchilin Pass above the pipes. The Treadway Bridge comes into play here. [3]

December 9: The Gate House

At the Gate House, a small contingent of CCF forces guarding it were found frozen to death, sitting in the positions that they died in with their hands frozen to their weapons. Sections of the Treadway Bridge had been airlifted and dropped off for assembly in the Funchilin Pass. Two sections would not be used. One was dropped in enemy-occupied territory, and one was found to be unusable. They did, however, manage to get enough there to get the pass open so that the tanks could cross. General Almond had overseen a test of the Treadway Bridge being dropped and secured some days earlier. Engineers worked feverishly to get the pieces put together. For all practical purposes this process went off with just a bit of a hiccup. Work on the bridge was done by 1500, at which point the marines and their army attachments started crossing. By 300, these groups would be in the perimeter of Chinhung-ni to the south of the pass. This is the first time an entire bridge had been air dropped. Vehicles would cross one at a time, and the tank treads would overhang on both sides of the Treadway bridge as they crossed over the gap.

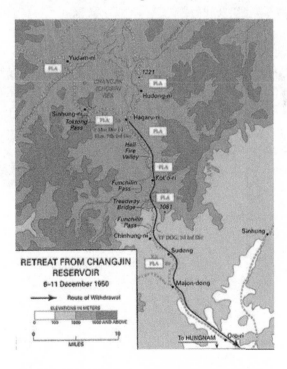

December 10

Around 1500, the First Marines began moving out of Koto. The 185th Engineer Battalion that was attached was in between Ray and his 2/31 and the First Marines as they leave Koto. By 1800, as darkness started to fall, the trains moving out of Koto-ri would run all night. The last out would be the tank company that had a reconnaissance platoon attached to it. Behind them would be refugees, more than could be expected to be handled at Hungnam. One of the issues with refugees coming down with the remnants of X Corps is the infiltration of Chinese regulars mixed in. Task Force Dog is securing Sudong as the troops moved through by 1300. They would remain behind and destroy supply dumps at Sudong. By 1400, they would start clearing the town. They would be attacked south of the city, but Quad-50s and air support would get them out of the jam.

Marines carrying out wounded. [4]

December 11

By 2100 on December 11, all forces were in the Hamhung perimeter with the exception of Dog Company, who entered the 65th Infantry perimeter by 2200 at Majon-dong. TF Dog would continue south to Oro-ri followed by the 65th Inf. The Sixty-Fifth would close into the Hamhung area and be the last of the journey back to the Port of Hamhung. Many refugees would follow this group into Hamhung along with the thousands that were already there. The refugee count was so high that U.S. forces were scrambling to make accommodations for this extremely large, hungry, freezing group of survivors. A semirigorous systematic screening process was put into place to weed out Chinese soldiers that have infiltrated the group. Security of the Hamhung area was supported by air support and artillery fire from the ships in the harbor area. A mad rush to screen refugees and load trucks, tanks, and supplies to the ships was in high gear. It was believed that ships brought into play would only be making one trip south to the Pusan perimeter, but history would show that a routine of loading at Hamhung, unloading at Pusan, and heading back to Hamhung would be needed to get the people and materials out. A few soldiers were upset that their commander's jeep was lost in the battle north of Hell Fire Valley days before and thought that it deserved to be replaced. As a means to rectify the loss of the jeep, they located the gray jeep of a one-star naval officer's jeep parked nearby. They stole the jeep and parked it in an abandoned garage, at which point they began the task of painting it green to match their commander's vehicle. The best-laid plans of men are often wrought with missteps. Once it was realized that the jeep would not pass muster as an army-issued vehicle, they were forced to ditch it to prevent them from getting in trouble. Unfortunately, the taxpayers had paid for a jeep that could not float itself to safety. It was launched off an unused portion of the wharf at Hamhung into the ocean to secure the men's safety.

At the docks, loading of the LSTs continued. General Almond, realizing that there was room to work with here, began loading cleared refugees in any open space that could be secured on the LSTs and ships as they were boarded. Every spare inch was utilized. The sounds of artillery fire whizzing over the town didn't hamper this debarkation.

Snipers had moved into the Hamhung area that was now desolate. Hamhung became emptier by the hour. Ammo for each soldier had been limited. Gasoline and other supplies had been loaded and sent off as the occupying force became fewer and fewer.

Nonessential material was left on the docks to be lost by explosive charges set to be ignited once all were secured offshore. Part of the stores left behind were tons of juice. Apple juice, grape juice, and other juices were sent ashore. Little good it would do for the end user considering it was frozen solid and undrinkable. Kestner, who was one of the engineers assigned to wiring the docks, along with another engineer of Dog Company, was loaded onto fast-moving boats along the docks. They would have to be tethered as they hung over the sides of the boats to ignite the charges along the waterfront. As the fuses are lit, they make a mad dash to their transport ship at the edge of the harbor. They look back as the explosions take place. Once this starts, bombers are employed to create a scorched-earth approach to ensure that the destruction of the docks is complete. Any CCF infiltrating the town of Hamhung by this time has walked into a really bad place.

Loading at Hungnam. There were ninety thousand refugees taken back to Pusan from this location. DOD photo. [3]

ROBERT BROOKS

Ray has seen enough of the cold side of Korea at this point. He had made his way below deck of his transport ship to escape the cold. Once below, he gets instructions to find a duffle bag that he can use to change from. Several hundred duffle bags of unused uniforms are available because of the loss of men from the previous weeks of deployment. Ray and the others will have to forage through these to get something fresh to wear. A fairly cold shower of saltwater to clean off and get back into some fresh clothing is a welcome thing. Donning new clothes, even though they are clean, is not a satisfying experience. He knows he is wearing the left-behinds of a departed compatriot.

U.S. forces making their way down to the LSTs at Hungnam. U.S. Army photo. [3]

Hagaru port being exploded. The two boats in the foreground is probably those of Kestner's Dog Company who helped set the charges. [3]

Some of the men had taken to playing cards on the ship as a means to pass the time on their journey back to Pusan. He would join in, but he hasn't seen pay in weeks. He will have to be satisfied to just watch. He decides this might be a good time to cut a letter to his family back home. He is sure that they are worried.

The journey back to Pusan is not long. He has become somewhat accustomed to travel by sea. Cloistered with others of the 2bn 31st below deck, he finds little comfort. Conversations among the men are slight. Sleep is more needed than hanging out with brothers-in-arms. Most of the time is spent sleeping or resting when he has to give his bed up. He makes a point to get a hot meal when he can. A sense of relief and somberness is beset on the men down below. He is content to hear of the others' stories, those who would talk about them, than adding to the stories with ones of his own. It is not that he feels outcast or unequal to the other men, but he has his own things to be more concerned with. Thoughts of Tootie and Lewis Taylor enter his mind. Memories of the past few days also have to be digested, scrutinized, and organized in his mind.

He pays close attention to the conversations of the older men so that he might better understand what should be taken away from the past events. He is still growing here, and although he has been through some terribly turbulent times, he takes stock of his position and what may lay ahead for him. Ray is a doer, but he is also a thinker. He wouldn't have made it this far by going off half-cocked. But he also knows that because of these experiences, no one would look over at him and consider him a boy. He virtually skipped those awkward teenage years and went straight into manhood. He understands this and takes stock of his new position in life. The age of wisdom has truly begun for him.

Ray has survived the Chinese war of attrition so far. It could be considered a moving version of the Alamo. The Korean conflict up to this point had so many components, all of which played a role in its successes and failures; there are too many to list. All these successes and failures are relative to the perspective of the individual looking at it. War is never a pretty sight. In his travel on the ship to get back to Pusan, Ray ventures topside only once, and only for a few minutes. A break in the action is welcomed, but a vacation would be better.

Upon his return to Hamhung, the men are sent out into the areas of their respective quartering. When he gets to his personal tent, Ray starts seeing some of the men that he had previously fought with back at Inchon and the east of Fusion Reservoir. These men had been recouping from their wounds of the previous entanglements. The war so far has been a SNAFU of "ifs." It was his E/Co that had been attacked back in September along with their attached ROKs. Some of these men were fighting frostbite as they marched over the mountains to reach LT. Dill's artillery battalion. What had started out as a recon assignment had led to his separation from the bulk of the 2Bn 31st in the first place. Had it not been for the army's push to ensure that they all received a Thanksgiving dinner, he may have never ended up in Hyesanjin and later attached to MacLean's 31RCT. If Almond had not been as motivated to move all resources down to Changjin, he still may not have been part of this Alamo. If MG Smith had been more active and reticent to following the orders of X Corp, General Almond may not have been so anxious to move this thrown together battalion to Changjin in the first place. If the intelligence and recon groups were more accurate in their reporting, different plans could have been brought to bear on the enemy forces countrywide. If General MacArthur was not so motivated to get all the forces to the Yalu, many lives could have been spared and the Chinese may not have been involved. If the South Korean government wasn't so motivated to cross the 38th parallel, perhaps none of these actions would have been sent into history. Ray's mind is full of many ifs, but these don't interrupt or hamper his thinking at this point. For now, decent food, rest, and recuperation are closer to the top of his thinking.

General MacArthur and President Truman are planning a way forward from this debacle/conglomeration of unfortunate incidents. While generals, captains, and colonels are dealing with the aftermath of the events so far, some attention had been turned to the men in terms of what can be done to lift them up. The military had taken a stance in seeing that the men should and would receive some much-needed rest and relaxation. In light of the many horrific instances and circumstances the men have endured so far, Ray is issued passes back to Japan for a quick respite from the battle zone. A few of the able-bodied men of E/Co have been loaded onto planes for the trip over.

Upon arrival at the U.S. base, one of his fellow soldiers hatched an idea. He had discovered a hole in the fence behind the barracks that they were sent into for quartering. On the other side of the fence, about one hundred yards away, is a small river tributary. He had discovered a brothel/bar was on the other side. With a little bit of cash, a ferryman would load the men into the boat and take them across. A little more scratch would get the men back. He starts the conversation out as expected, *"Have you ever been to a whorehouse?"* Of course Ray would answer, *"No."* Understanding his youthful demeanor, Ray asked, *"How do you know we can get in?"* The soldier replies, *"You got a uniform on, don't you? They don't care what you look like, as long as you got money! Besides, it ain't like we will be the first to do it. How do you think I found out about it?"*[5] With a little trepidation, but showing no fear of it, he agrees. A little excitement and perhaps a chance to get a drink is part of his motivation. The war had not knocked out his sense of adventure.

As night falls, the men head out. Clearing the fence and walking in eight inches of snow down to the water line, the young soldier saw all things as he predicted. There was a small ferryboat there with a man warmly dressed controlling it. After paying the guy, they both hop in and the boat ventures to the other side. Ray is not too used to things going as planned since he left Virginia back in 1950. It was a bit of a welcome relief. As they reach the front entrance to the small building, he notices a large collection of boots sitting outside. Each one neatly paired up but spread about the porch. The Japanese cultural rule of entering a house without shoes is adhered to here. It would be the first that Ray had heard of such a thing, but he follows suit. "When in Rome" as they say, "do as the Romans do." [5] He notices two things aside from the Asian décor of the room. It is dimly lit, and there is the promised bar.

The young soldiers stay for only about an hour. Ray is not as comfortable in these surroundings as he thought he might have been. It is not like the bars back in the states. It surely is nothing like the bars on base, smothered with uniformed service men getting smashed. When his companion returns, he urges him to leave. The Saki isn't all that good anyway. His buddy gathers himself together. The guys head outside to fetch their boots. "Oh great!" Ray exclaims, *"Where the fuck are my boots?! I put them right here and they are gone! Someone has taken my damn boots! I put them right here on the end so that I could find them easier. I knew this was a bad idea to begin with!"*

He carefully looks through the hodgepodge collection of footwear, and the matter only gets worse. His partner tells him, *"That's fine, just take someone else's shoes."* Thoroughly pissed and anxious, Ray tells him, *"That's GREAT, but nobody here wears anything bigger than a size five. I couldn't fit in the sandals inside. What makes you think I can wear the shoes they left out here? I am screwed!* [5]

He does the math. They don't have to go far to get back to the boat, and the journey back to barracks doesn't seem that far either. It's twenty yards to the boat and another hundred yards to the barracks. What is another eight inches of snow after all the shit he had been walking in so far in Korea? His buddy urges him to make the dash. If they run really fast, it will not be that bad. A small dose of alcohol fuels his adrenaline, smattered with a dose of ego and small helping of testosterone. He removes his socks. Coupled with the need to succeed, the two of them launch from the porch and start their run.

When the two reach the boat, he falls into it as fast as he can. Getting his feet off the ground is first priority once he gets there. He had not accounted for the small case of frostbite that he had developed, and no one would report such a thing on purpose lest they get rolled out of the military for having it. The army would have soldiers change socks every two hours in this kind of weather to keep them from harm. But when in the height of battle, it is not like anyone can tell the enemy, "*Hey, stop shooting. I have to change my socks here.*" [5]

His toes sting like he had been walking on frozen broken glass. Getting his feet dry is the second priority. He rushes to get his socks back on. He buries his feet into the sleeves of his coat. They give the ferryman some coin as if they were two ancient warriors crossing the River Styx. This has become an epic adventure. As they approach the other side, Ray is psyching himself up for part two of his quest to get warm.

The process is in reverse when they land on the other side. He removes his feet from his coat and removes his socks for the run. For just a moment, he has to put his feet back into his coat. He has to keep the maximum amount of warmth on them to the last moment. As the boat approaches shore, he visualizes the number of steps he will take and even where they will land. He calculates just how much time he must endure to get to the safety of a warm place.

His buddy's snickering over Ray's plight isn't helping, but he knows to keep that to a minimum lest Ray kick his ass once they get back. The time to laugh and joke will be when it is all over. The look of determination and solemn silence coming from Ray is warning enough not to push this too far.

The boat lands as Ray takes a deep breath. Surging from the water's edge, he bolts to the fence. His feet are slowly cooling and the stinging is starting to kick in as they pass through it. He rocks his feet from using his heels to the ball as he goes. It is an attempt to minimize the effects of the cold. He discovers that this is harder than he thought. With every step, the cold seeps in. He moves as fast as he can. He thought he could sprint to the building, but the eight inches of snow prevents him. The long and arduous journey back comes to an end when they reach the back door of the barracks. Once inside, he dashes to the showers to get warm water on his feet. He will explain his problem of the missing boots to his commander later. Getting his tootsies warm takes priority here.

A perfectly good night was turned to crap all for the lack of boot security. Freshly recovered from the ordeal, the two have time to reflect. After everything is said and done, it dawns on the two men that a lot of this could have been avoided had his buddy just piggybacked him to and from the boat. Then again, no respected platoon sergeant would be caught in such a predicament.

His leave comes to an end, and he returns to Korea. Back with his company once again in a war-torn country, it is time to get back to business. The gap in time has allowed for the company to be brought back up to strength. Some replacements are new recruits fresh out of the states. Some have been called up from the reserves. A few have been returned to active duty from incarceration from their personal indiscretions. When soldiers go into the stockades, their time as active soldiers is put on the shelf. If a soldier signs up for three years of active duty, and for some reason he is locked up for six months for breaking the rules, then that six months does not get taken out of the three years that he committed to. Instead it is stuck on to the end of their original agreement for the same length that they were incarcerated. A three-year hitch can easily turn into a five-year hitch if that person spends two of those years under lock and key. Getting in trouble in the military isn't like getting locked up in the civilian world. They have their own set of rules and regulations, lawyers, judges, and tribunals. It all depends on the severity of the infraction and the sentence passed out. These were the types of men that Ray was leading, almost of all them older and with more experience.

**Ray Cottrell (center right) with buddies in
South Korea, spring 1951. [6]**

The Summer of '51

General MacArthur has been replaced for political reasons by Truman. It is in the general's speech that we hear, "Old soldiers never die. They just fade away." The general was asked to give a keynote speech at the Republican convention, and suspicions that he would run for office were starting to ease. He would be asked to join the Republican ticket but turned it down. General Dwight D. (Ike) Eisenhower would go on to win the presidency.

General Mathew Ridgway would replace MacArthur as the Supreme Commander of the East. By summer of '51, the routine is back toward the front lines. Upon taking control of the battered Eighth Army, one of Ridgway's first acts was to restore soldiers' confidence in themselves. To accomplish this, he reorganized the command structure. During one of his first briefings in Korea at I Corps, Ridgway sat through an extensive discussion of various defensive plans and contingencies. At the end, he asked the staff about the status of their attack plans; the corps G-3 (operations officer) responded that he had no such plans. Within days, I Corps had a new G-3. He also replaced officers who did not send out patrols to fix enemy locations and removed "enemy positions" from commanders' planning maps if local units had not been in recent contact to verify that the enemy was still there. Ridgway established a plan to rotate out those division commanders who had been in action for six months and replace them with fresh leaders. He sent out guidance to commanders at all levels that they were to spend more time at the front lines and less in their command posts in the rear. These steps had an immediate impact on morale. A request by MG O.P. Smith to be attached to the IX Corps would in effect get him relieved of duty and shipped out of Korea all together. Ridgeway was not up for negotiations with Smith. He had a war to run. Favors played no role in the matter.

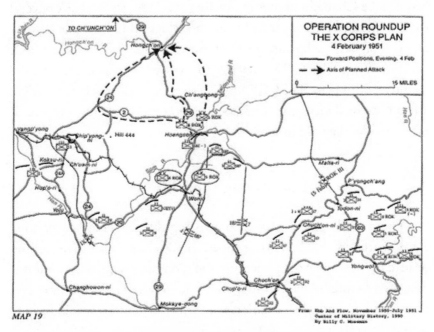

MAP 19

Cottrell is with the 2bn 31ˢᵗ (2/31) holding the '60' road from Yongwol to Todon-ni. See map lower right. This is the refortified troops of the 2/31ˢᵗ during Operation Roundup. They are located just north of 1/31st along the road, and south of 3/31st at P'yongch'ang. [1]

He oversees all actions in Korea. Ridgway had been selected not only for his exemplary actions in WWII but also for his ability to recognize and plan as well. He had helped write the plans of "Operation Overload" and the invasion of Normandy. He helped in the planned invasions of Sicily and others by paratroopers. Ridgway had discovered the weakness in the Chinese attacks and was planning to exploit it. It appeared to him that the attacks were never sustained. Their attacks were hard rushing while exploiting their numbers against the U.N. forces. It was a war of attrition for them. General Ridgway noticed that they would attack, regroup immediately, and then charge ahead with reserves and survivors of the first waves. This concept showed itself in the Chosin Campaign, where the fighting would continue like this all night long for days, and then fall back in the daytime for fear of air superiority.

The Chinese, pushing south, had been successful at recapturing Seoul since Changjin and were pushing the U.N. troops back beyond the 38th parallel once again. This methodology would show itself time and time again. Each time, the U.N. forces would be put on their heels and forced to fall back. Ridgway had to come up with a plan that would counteract this plan. The CCF would also go in under the cover of night and set up roadblocks and hindrances to prevent the enemy forces from escaping like they did in Chosin.

Countering the Chinese

The general's plan was all-encompassing. The Chinese were fighting a war of attrition but had no air superiority, so he decided to use ammo instead of men. He would put more shells on the enemy than what was ever used before. If the pushing back against the U.N. lines was ever to come to an end, then a different order of operations would have to be put into effect.

To fight against this push, he concluded that every time the U.N. forces gained ground beyond the front line, a new line would be set up. The previous line would be reinforced behind the new line. Each of these front lines would be named after states in the United States. This would stop the fast-moving Chinese by giving the front line guys a safety net behind them in which to regroup and hold the previous line. It became a leapfrog effect of moving forward without having to give up all the ground if a line was lost.

The general's expanded use of artillery saved many U.S. and U.N. lives as well as having the repelling effect against the Chinese onslaught. Coupled with air superiority, the Chinese were losing ground once again. As a perimeter front line was established, the soldiers were sent forward to determine enemy locations, size, and capabilities. It would be the same from Ray. In the summer months, with heat being the new weather enemy, his platoon was tasked with this order. They are to move beyond the front lines into enemy territory and from there assess the enemy forces before returning to the lines for reporting. The intelligence gathered from these recon missions would be used for further planning and attacks of the commanders based on real-time spotting or as close to real time as could be done.

Ray finds himself on such a mission in the blistering heat of the summer. They had moved up a ridgeline to the top, giving themselves a solid view of the area. Orders were to not engage the enemy if they sighted them first, but to withdraw upon meeting. It would be the job of the artillery units and the air force to take out those forces. But the Chinese are well-versed in camouflage. In this particular encounter, the platoon, along with some ROKs, stumbled on such an encampment. They are standing sixty men strong. Unfortunately they were noticed first. The fight had been brought to them. The soldiers were quick to take cover, but they were also fast in understanding that they were grossly outnumbered. The order was given to back the men out and off the ridgeline. Ray, along with two other men, would take on the assignment to cover their flank with gunfire.

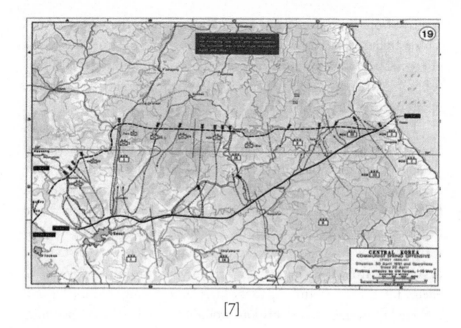

[7]

This tactic had a two-pronged advantage. It would provide cover fire to the men moving out. It would also give the belief to the Chinese to move forward cautiously, allowing more time to get the men out. It is a daunting task to be one of three men against a regiment of enemy soldiers regardless of the intent or outcome of the engagement. Yet the thought of being killed doesn't enter into the men's minds. They would fire repetitively and move back a few yards to the next available cover. Reloading as they went, they would set up and fire repetitively again. The cover would confuse the oncoming forces with regard to the size of the troops that they were attacking. By the end of the engagement, all the troops have made it back to the safety of the front lines. Only three injuries were realized in the fighting.

A few weeks later, Ray finds himself up on the front lines once again. It was his shift. Sitting in a foxhole and guarding against the enemy. On a hot day, he hears his name being called out. *"Cottrell! Cottrell! Ray Cottrell, front and center."* Surprised by this, Ray sticks his head out of his foxhole and looks behind him. It is a colonel making his way to his position. Ray may not know what is going on right here, right now, but he knows to get up and face the man calling his name.

He climbs out of the hole and stands at attention to the fast-approaching colonel. It is Colonel McCaffrey. As Ray stands at attention, the colonel informs him that he has become aware of his actions at the engagement just a few weeks before. *"As a result of your selfless commitment to your men in keeping with the highest traditions of the United States Army, I want to present you with this Silver Star."* Ray is speechless and struggles for the right words to say. Colonel McCaffrey pins the star to his pocket. Ray is still frozen in his boots. He only manages to spill out a few words as he salutes. He musters a "Thank you, sir," the general response to such a situation and the most logical. [5]

McCaffrey sticks out his hand to shake Ray's and continues by saying, "A job well done, son. Keep it up the good work." [5] He asks Ray a few questions about his current assignments and offers a few words of encouragement. Small talk really. Ray becomes more relaxed as the colonel disembarks. He understands that usually when a commander is yelling his name, it generally isn't for anything good. This time, it was.

Ray is not a boastful sort. He had proven to his men that he could lead from the front and could protect their backs, but the opportunity to wear the Silver Star is no small matter for him. Youthful and a bit prideful of the accomplishment, he decides to wear the thing around camp for a little while. There would be no papers for this star. Nothing to register with the recordkeepers back in Washington. This is a field-issued Star. No orders will be cut for this award. Receiving it alone would be its own reward. He had unknowingly gotten himself decorated. This acknowledgement would not just raise his spirits but encourage him to be even better as a soldier. As for Colonel McCaffrey, he would continue on and become General McCaffrey.

The last bit of his hitch for this engagement would be harrowing from time to time, but his sense of what to do and when to do it would garner him the confidence to get it done. There would be more engagements. There would be more close calls to face. But for now, it is time to get back to work. After wearing the star for a couple of weeks, he decides that it would be better served to be stowed away.

Fun and Games

Back at base, things were progressing. More men, and now women, were filling up the ranks. A hospital had been set up for triage. More ammo was being loaded in for the artillery attacks planned by General Ridgway. The general was setting up as part of his offensive northward to bring down a rain of bombardments on the Chinese. But for Ray, again, a little free time and a curious mind could land him in pile of shit real fast. At eighteen, and with a gallon of testosterone running through a curious mind, he again finds himself in an ill-laid plan, as young men tend to do.

As far as the army was concerned, following orders, fighting on the front lines, and reading maps and compasses are starting to become easier for him. But that dangerous drug called curiosity was consuming him once again. Another buddy in his company had suggested that they go out for a little sightseeing adventure. He tells Ray, "It will be worth your time. It isn't dangerous, and you will not even have to leave base. You want to go?" It was nightfall and it wasn't like he had anything better to do. He thinks a little mischief might make him feel normal considering the conditions.

The two men move out to the main thoroughfare of the base. As they make their way toward the end of the road, they approach the area of the women's barracks. Just off to the side of their quarters, a tent had been erected for showering. The plan was easy: stand out of line of sight until a nurse goes in. From there they would move in darkness behind the tents and make their way to the rear area of the showers. Trying to be nonchalant, they stand near a light post keeping a wandering eye on those that go in to the tent. Determining who was going in to get a shower was not complicated.

It doesn't take long before a group of three young women enter the tent. The men make their move to position themselves behind the tent. They travel quietly and quickly behind a row of tents and turn toward the showering tent. Darkness is their friend and also their enemy. Approaching the back of the tent, his buddy trips on a retaining rope, causing the tent to shutter from the action. The two men are trying to be quiet, but the action has created what they perceived as concerns from inside. The sound of footsteps coming out of the front warn the two to flee. The men shoot out into the darkness to get away from being discovered. As they run away, their path is hindered by a pit. The pit was used to secure human waste and shower water. They both had fallen into it hip high. It was an unsecured unpotable water that had no cover. Soaking wet and covered waist high in sludge, the smell is unbearable. Trying not to throw up, they make their way out. No one had noticed that they were back there. They had overreacted to the situation. Seems like the nurses were not the only ones in need of a shower that night. Yet another evening turned to crap.

Wrapping It Up

December slowly approaches and Ray takes the time to ensure that he would not get caught up in such harebrained ideas again. Early in the month, Ray is hanging out in his hooch when his commanding officer comes in. He is holding the paperwork that Ray was awaiting. It is his orders to cycle him home. His days are numbered in Korea. His tour of duty is coming to a close. Thoughts of getting home are taking up more and more time of his thinking. He takes in the time to celebrate with his men. He prays that there is nothing that will get in the way to prevent him from making it out of here in the short time that he has left.

The Korean War would have to go on without him: a situation that he welcomes down to his very bones. General Ridgway would continue to keep the NKs at bay. The fighting would continue at locations like Pork Chop Hill and several points north of the 38th to the east. The U.N. and U.S. forces would force a stalemate with the communists. Negotiations would start and stop again and again before this war would come to an end. The Chinese, at one point, surrounded the neutral land of the peace talks only to acquire more land possession during the process. Many opportunities would come and go before a true resolution would be reached. General Dwight D. Eisenhower would get elected to office of the President of the United States. General Ridgway would elevate to the Joint Chiefs of Staff in Washington. When everything comes to an end, the lines are drawn basically where they were before. Along the 38th parallel, Ridgway's plan was working, but the Chinese support of the North Koreans, along with U.S. sentiment back home to bring the war to a close, brings about the end of the engagement. In the peace talks, the Chinese insist that they sit in an elevated state above the other negotiators as a sign of their dominance over the situation. These were the kinds of things that slowed the entire process. Both sides treated the other as if they had won.

For Ray, all this would happen when he is not there. He was aboard a ship heading back to Osaka in late November of 1951. Upon his arrival in Japan, the process was rather simple. He is to walk off the gang plank and proceed to one of three long tents awaiting him. The first tent required him to strip down to bare ass. All his possessions would be gone through as he disrobed. From here, he would move to the next tent for delousing, being chemically hosed down for lice and other varmints before he moves on to the showers and the doctors for a final examination. The whole process is somewhat humiliating, but he does what he has to do. Getting home is his greatest motivation.

The final tent is for receiving new uniforms. A new set of duds and new footwear will go a long way right now. Everything would be restored right there on the spot. From stem to stern he would be restored, at least on the outside, to what he looked like before he arrived in Japan in 1950. Now a Master Sergeant, his stripes would be added to his uniform as he waits for their completion. Unit badges are sewn to his blouse's shoulders. All will be made new again. It will be a couple of days before he loads the boat to America, but alas he will be going home.

CHAPTER 7

Home for Christmas This Time

ON DECEMBER 27, 1951, Ray arrives home after a long trip from Japan to Washington state. When he boards the train this time, he has a little money in his pocket. Lesson learned. His sister has married Lovey's brother and had taken up residence in her mother's home while he was away at war. A few blocks away, Lovey had found a place of her own to call home. It had been a year and half since the two had seen each other. On the behest of his new brother-in-law, he offers to Ray that he will go and get Lovey and bring her over to the house. Ray was settling in at home when Lovey arrives that same day. After a little hugging and some happy comments of "welcome home," the four of them have a conversation over what it was like to be in Korea. Ray's sister and brother-in-law head off leaving the two alone together for the first time in what seemed like forever. Knowing that Lovey was at home waiting for him made a difference for him while he was away. It took no time at all for the two of them to fall back in love again. They spend no time waiting to start dating again. This time, they were not obliged to sit on her mother's porch. There are no teenagers in the '50s, just children and adults.

On one occasion, the two reunited lovebirds were cruising around town with a friend. In the conversation, the friend announces that there were wedding plans in motion for Lewis Taylor and his beautiful fiancée in the coming weeks. They are both to attend. When their friend is dropped off, the conversation of marriage continues. Without much hesitation, Ray offers his intentions to Lovey and he proposes. The news spreads quickly amongst the two families, and plans are made to get the ceremony done.

Ray is only home for a short time but long enough for the mail that he should have received while in Korea has been bounded together and sent to the house, compliments of the U.S. government. Sitting around the house one day, he decides to go through the letters. While some of the letters are from family and friends, a curious letter from Lovey is found in the stack. As he reads it, he discovers that it was the proverbial "Dear John" letter. Lovey had revealed that she had started to date a marine while he was gone to war. As it turns out it was not that big of a thing, because her actions and commitment to marry him were already settled. Evidently, Ray had cut off a marine without even knowing it. Before all these plans can be realized though, he must reenlist.

The paperwork is being finalized while he waits at home to get his orders. The military is in a growth spurt at this time. Actions in Korea are continuing under General Ridgway, who had just taken control of the U.N. forces there the previous summer. General Ridgway had discovered a weakness in the CCF/PLA forces there and had begun to exploit it. As the U.S. forces move out again from the south of the 38th parallel, he sets up perimeter lines that continue to push forward. With every push forward, the previous perimeter is held in place to ensure that if a strong push southward from the NKs and CCF should move them back, the U.N. forces would only have to fall back to the last perimeter lines that were still intact. But for Ray, after being on these front lines for months, it is now time for him to find his place in the military.

He wants to be able to care for Lovey and support her. The best way he knows how to do that is to stay in the military. It is rare for an individual to find what it is that he is good at and even rarer for him to like it enough to build a career out of it. Ray understands this. He is not only good at soldiering, but he likes it enough to stay committed to it. Lovey is a supportive person. She will follow Ray wherever he goes. She understands the issues of being a military wife and, while uncomfortable, supported to the idea. Being with him is more important than the trials and tribulations of military life. To be in the military means to be able to move at the drop of the hat. It provides difficulties for any relationship and even more so for a married couple. Both are committed to the idea and hold no reservations for what could lay ahead.

Ray's orders arrive and they point to Maryland. Upon arrival there, confusion about where to put him abound. The U.S. military is being built up at this time, and had been for some time. In this growth pattern, many men are being shuffled around to get them to where they are most needed. He is almost immediately sent back to Virginia for fifteen days. But while in Virginia, and in between orders, the two are able to find time to get a wedding pulled off. Family members are brought together and the ceremony is held in Richmond. This did not mean that they got to be together right away though. It is now July of 1952.

Copy of marriage certificate of Cottrell wedding. [1]

The new orders are for Ray to take up a trainer's position in Fort Riley, Kansas. He will be assigned to the Tenth Mountain Division when he gets there. This is not the only issue at hand. Housing will have to be secured for his new wife and new life as a husband. As he acquires an apartment on base, his position as platoon sergeant breaking in new recruits is well underway. Lovey and her mother take a bus ride together to Fort Riley to make this apartment a home. Things are moving at a fast pace, but the young couple start to settle in.

Lovey is getting used to Ray being in the field at all hours of the day and night, while Ray is learning the ins and outs of being a better platoon sergeant and how to get things done. Along with the ever-important lessons of how not to piss off his commanders, his days are full of breaking in the new recruits. He is required to get up well before his soldiers and is commonly still with them when they head to the racks to sleep. Luckily for him, he is ideally qualified for these short sleep cycles. He had been doing it for a couple of years now. Lovey's days are adjusting to his. As his routines get settled into, the better she becomes at it.

Money is tight for the young couple. When his paycheck would come in, it would get them through the first three weeks. The remainder of the month was subsidized by pawning an old shotgun of his that he had sent to him from Virginia. It was not a gun of any particularly great value, just an old hunting gun from his previous years as a teenager hunting in the hills around Richmond. The routine of pawning his gun every month went on for quite some time before they would get their bills under control. Lovey was pregnant now and every penny counted. Pennies are something Ray knows something about.

It was then that they discovered something uncomfortable. Should a soldier be killed in battle or in the field, and they have a spouse back home on base, that spouse would have about thirty days to clear out. Once removed from base, her connection to the military would come to an end. From then on, only a stipend for loss of the loved one would be received and the spouse would be left to her own to reconstruct their life.

Being in the military, a soldier surrenders himself to the U.S. government as his priority. Along with that priority is keeping personal debts under control. If a soldier were to get in debt and start missing payments, the first sergeant or someone of higher rank would get notified by the company holding the debt. These lenders would have to turn to the soldier's commanders to collect. This is not the kind of conversation that a commander wants to spend his time dealing with. Along with being in debt, if a soldier is reported on enough, the ill effect of preventing the young man or woman from moving up in rank

ROBERT BROOKS

could be realized. It would definitely prevent the soldier from getting a secret military clearance. Soldiers in debt become likely candidates to be caught up in compromising situations. This cannot be tolerated by the military. The soldier could be convinced to give away intelligence, government data, or property.

On February 24, Ray receives his second promotion. He is moved from Company D of the Eighty-Fifth Regiment, where he was a platoon sergeant, to Company C Eighty-Fifth Infantry as an instructor. The extra money would come in handy. But like every young couple, money remains tight, albeit more tolerably. As they prepare for the arrival of their first child, the days are filled with heading to the field, managing recruits, and preparing for the following day's requirements. Meanwhile Lovey's days are spent managing the household, dealing with doctor visits and the uncomfortable environment of being a stay-at-home military wife.

On August 6, on a dark and stormy night, Brenda Cottrell is born in a military hospital in Fort Riley, Kansas. Ray was lucky enough to be out of the field when Lovey first broke the news to him that it was time. He was lucky enough to be there for Lovey for the delivery. Nothing will motivate a change in a young father more than to hold his firstborn child for the first time. Few things will break the rough exterior of a streetwise combat warrior than being presented with an innocent daughter. Up until now, Lovey was the only one who had access to his deepest feelings and the keys to his heart. He would now share that space with Brenda. A hard day in the barracks or on the field would now be softened even more so when he returns to try to make time with his wife and daughter. He would extend his bear claw of a hand to the baby as she would grip his finger, smile, and giggle back at him.

Raising a family in the military has many advantages. Few things result in presenting a young couple with the true melting pot of what America is than what is realized in the U.S. military. Soldiers on base have spouses from all over the world: Asians, Germans, black, white, and Hispanics are the makeup of what is the United States Armed Forces. Friends from all over the world enter their circle. Different foods, cultures, and lifestyles abound in this microcosm of base life. Moving from place to place and country to country will allow his family to have experiences rarely captured by most American families. In a way, a better growing experience than this is hard to come by. One does not get rich in the military, but the perks can be without measure. There is a trade-off, but fortunately there are those who will take this life on and make it their own.

Ray, having survived the battles of the coldest environment that any U.S. military personnel had ever fought in, has become hardened. Leading men that were six to ten years older than he was as reservist and regular army in Korea, had laid the groundwork for the soldier that he was becoming. Dealing with soldiers that were under his command from foreign entities taught him how to work around communicational issues as well as leadership issues. He had become well-groomed for the position that he now holds.

In the late fall at Fort Riley, while on a routine training mission on the firing lines, Ray was busy getting soldiers familiar with their rifles. Word had been sent out to the rank and file that a general was to come to base to make an inspection. Ray was always a forward-thinking individual. To be a good soldier is to plan ahead to prevent issues coming to him as he moves forward. Plan for the worst, but expect the best. Being one step ahead of the issues is to be one step closer to victory. As he walks the gun range, and the soldiers fire off their rounds, he realizes that his platoon does not have the shoe packs that he had requested a month earlier from the supply depot on base.

Considering the general's visit, this was not acceptable. He realized that he had to do something about it. At the very least, he should see what the holdup was. When he walked into the building, he approached a long countertop separating it from the supplies in the rear. Just behind this countertop, he spied four men sitting at a table playing poker. As he looks to his side, he sees shelves of shoe packs. These were the shoe packs that were to be delivered to his men. This is really disturbing to Ray.

He calls back and requests, *"Who is in charge?"* A platoon sergeant, who had his back to him, turns around from his game and takes a long look over Ray. This man believes that this is a boy in men's clothing, and since Ray is not of a higher rank, this sergeant thought it would be cool in front of his underlings to talk Ray down. Unfortunately, he didn't take time to notice that they were both of equal rank or that under his winter coat that there was a combat pin on his chest. Perhaps he should have. He replies to Ray, "*That would be me, son.*" A cold chill slipped up Ray's back causing the hair to raise in the nape of his neck. Upon hearing this response, Ray responds professionally, "*I ordered shoe packs for my platoon, and I need to know when they are going to get issued.*" Ray knew that the shoe packs were available, and he also knew that they should have been delivered by now, but were not. The sergeant says in a very belligerent fashion, "*They're here. I will get around to getting to it sooner or later.*"

Ray is a man of action, and this attitude didn't sit well with him at all. The sergeant turns his head back to the game as if Ray's request was irrelevant. The four men return to their play. Ray's blood begins to boil, but his calm control of a heightened situation takes over. Compared to the dramas of combat, this was a problem that was easily rectified. He notices that there is an opening to the backroom from the countertop. He moves off and away out of sight toward the opening in the counter. He moves around the counter and follows the wall behind it to the back room. This put him on top of the sergeant. Before anyone notices that he is there, Ray's right hand strikes the man squarely on the side of the head, knocking him to the floor. He immediately mounts the man with a knee in his chest, a grip on his throat, and his right hand ready to strike him again. "*Understand this, I am not your son, and you will never speak to me in that manner again. I am a sergeant just like you, and you will address me accordingly. My men are out there in the rain and mud and need those shoe packs now. You need to get up off your collective asses and get them there. The general is on the way for an inspection, and I am not going to pay for your laziness. If you feel that you need to report this, we can head over to the commander's office right now. I will walk with you. What's it going to be?*" After a tense moment, the sergeant gurgles out, "They're on the way!" [4] Nothing more on the matter comes out. The men receive their materials as the first snows of winter begin to fall. Mission accomplished.

By the summer of 1953, as the peace agreements in Korea are approaching the end, Ray is up for reenlistment. A soldier accrues thirty days leave per year of service. He thinks to himself that he could make a little extra cash for reenlisting. By going to another duty post straight away, he would get extra cash for not using his leave time. Getting two months of extra pay is a pretty good deal to him and his young family. It was not that the military held any great sway on him for staying in, but he could handle what it offered, and he had to be responsible for not only himself now but for Lovey and Brenda as well. There were worse things in life than having relatively decent pay and providing for his family in the military while doing something that he is actually pretty good at.

Ray with a childhood friend Sonny Stevens circa 1955. Stevens and Ray entered the military at about the same time but he couldn't get over how fast Ray had advanced in rank.

Upon this reenlistment, his new duty station would be in Baumburg, Germany. This would take him out of Fort Riley, family and all. He would go first and set up housing for Lovey and the baby. She will arrive six months later after returning home to Richmond. Lovey would be required to travel on a very uncomfortable military transport ship with the newborn Brenda in swaddling clothes. While Lovey was still young in years, she was cultivating a strong control of her personal self and becoming a dutiful wife to her husband. The travel to Germany was no easy task for her, but she, like her husband, soldiers on. Adjustments had to be made and she was equipped to handle it.

Ray's orders are to join up with the 1st Division 26th Infantry. The role of the Twenty-Sixth Infantry is an occupation mission. They would train other infantry with the armored divisions as a joint task force. When he is not in the field training, they are on rotating watches as border control. Germany was being occupied by the communist forces to the north, and several other countries to the south. Berlin was landlocked in Russian-occupied territory. France, the UK, and the United States make up one side of the occupational forces, while the communist Russian Army occupies the other. The training facilities were jointly managed by the United States and France. Unfortunately, the French only trained about 10 percent of the time. This required the Twenty-Sixth to train in the fields a majority of the time. Evidently, the French were not so motivated, leaving the training task to the United States. This enlistment would keep him and his family in Germany until 1955. The supposed enemy of the future was always understood to be the Russians and other communists.

Is It a Sidewinder?

As part of Ray's training programs for his soldiers, he is required to run them through the rigors of firing the S10. This armored mobile missile unit can send a warhead down the line via a towline. As a culmination to the training exercises, a photo op was set up where his team would be in the field using the equipment that they were trained on. It would be a show of technical superiority to all those in attendance and a realization of all the hard work that brought these men to this point. He was in a position above the working team as the platoon sergeant. It required him to signal to the fire team to launch. The fire team was located below him in a ravine firing away from the dignitaries and military brass above. High-ranking individuals from different countries were in attendance.

It was a striking conglomeration of people, but it was not uncommon for Ray to see such pageantry. A tent was set up above Ray's position alongside the bleachers where the attendees were placed. The opening to the tent revealed the tactical operations center. This mechanized weapon required the pulling down of a lever from its safety position to fire the warhead. When the lever is in one position, it is locked onto a bolt at the end of the encased projectile. This keeps it in a safe position. In the firing position it clicks up, releasing the bolt and allowing the towed projectile to fire. Radio approval from Ray in his position would signal when to release. As Ray called down the ordering sequences to prepare to fire the weapon, the men manning it go into their motions, checking the bubble targeting site to ensure that the weapon would hit a tank loaded with dynamite. All is set, and the order to fire is sent. The soldiers hit the switch, but the projectile does not come out. It is burning in the tube. The soldiers begin to scurry. This can't be good. A few seconds later the booster rocket on the projectile kicks in, tearing the mount from the back of the jeep. The projectile releases from the tube and bounces in front of the jeep. It springs skyward and does a complete 180. Like a bottle rocket, it is now heading toward the crowd on the bleachers who are trying to make their way to the tent for cover. But the warhead is spinning out of control and heading for its new unapproved target: the tent. It goes right through the opening. Because the projectile is turning end over end, it grabs the tent and pulls it down the field, shredding it as it goes. Everyone is scattering in the shock and awe of the event. Fortunately, the S10 was not armed with an explosive warhead. It was only a training projectile. No one is injured short of a few cuts, bruises, and one officer suffered a broken rib. The broken rib was a result of the fin of the projectile nicking the officer. All other injuries were a result of fearful people getting out of the way of the fired missile.

Copy of passenger list from USNS Gen. William O. Darby (T AP 127) from Lovey and Brenda's trip home from Germany. [1]

Photo of the Royal Guard. Note the pointed metal helmets.

After the ensuing chaos, Ray's commanding officer approached him and demanded to know what happened. At a loss for words, he offers that the issue must be with the unit. *"We followed all protocols and procedures."* His commander informs him that he will get to the bottom of it, but he was satisfied that Ray and his men did not create this mayhem themselves on purpose. As he walks away, Ray starts to cackle in laughter. The commander turns around and wants to know what is so funny. He informs him to look on the back of his raincoat. His commander removes his coat and inspects the muddy footprints that track up the back of his coat. He begins to laugh out loud as well. As they look around there are several of the Palace Guard's hats all over the ground like someone was playing a game of yard darts with no specific target.

The S10 unit was taken off the field and locked up for inspection. Teams of investigators would look over the unit for weeks. Ray had discovered the issue before they could make their assertions. The investigators make no clear understanding for themselves as to why the unit acted in this manner. Ray approaches his commander and discusses with him what he thinks actually happened. He determines that after all the protocols were met in preparation for firing the unit, a particularly smaller fire team member had his hand relock the projectile to the firing tube. His unique height created the opportunity for this to happen. Right before the firing order was issued, this soldier had grabbed the locking/unlocking lever to pull himself up high enough in the rear of the jeep from the ground to sight the weapon on target. The sights on this weapon are a bubble sight designed to work off gravity for direction. Just before firing, he had inadvertently relocked the missile down when he pulled himself up. It was an unforeseen action and an accident. He determined that the soldier was in no way consciously responsible for the accident, but it was actually a design flaw of sorts from the drawing board itself. The manufacturers had to go back to the lab and create a retrofit scenario to prevent this type of error from reoccurring in the future. No charges were filed against Ray's soldiers, and it shows much credit to his commitment to both his men and to the mission at hand. A bulletin regarding this possible hazard was sent out to all bases and units worldwide that were using this weapon. It was to ensure that this would be accounted for in the future. But the memory of a scurrying entourage running for their lives will always be imprinted on his mind. It would offer many chuckles in his future.

However, the day's events did not end there. After the misfiring of the S10, the crowd was directed to another part of the field to watch another tactical unit being displayed and fired. Unfortunately, that unit too would misfire, but with much less drama and fanfare. The wary audience had a day to remember. The U.S. military had to take this day on the chin. It was determined later as well that the cause of the mishap was manufacturing related. An O-ring had worn out and caused the gun to fire as soon as the breach closed, causing the firing pin to strike and fire the projectile. Another bulletin would be sent out, military-wide, to look for failing O-rings and to maintain these as needed. Again, Ray and his men would discover the issue before the manufacturers. No one was seriously injured in either event, but it was a bad day for the military industrial complex. Ray would be congratulated for discovering the issues and for his involvement in resolving them to prevent the repeat of it all in the future. Mishaps such as these are not acceptable under any condition in a warzone.

Meanwhile

Back in the states, Sen. Joseph McCarthy is a leading member of a subcommittee committed to addressing the subversions of communism within the United States. Investigations supported by information from J. Edgar Hoover's reign over the FBI kept the country on its toes with case after case of spying and communist/socialist infiltration within the states. Members of the Hollywood community along with government officials at the federal, state, and local levels were put on trial and presented before the congressional hearings on the matter. Many of these people were singled out for their leftist views. Most were released because of the unconstitutionality of the charges with others released for lack of evidence. Some spies were prosecuted to the highest level though. An uncomfortable feeling could be noticed within the citizenry because of these actions. Mistrust of the government, neighbors, and friends kept many people nervous. This was the beginnings of the Cold War. Militarily speaking, the joint chiefs held the perception that the next war would be a conventional war between the democratic west and the communist, socialist, and Islamic countries of the east.

Ray had settled well into his military life at this point. He had many acquaintances, including Command Sergeant Major (CSM) Dobel. Being with the 1st Div. 26th Inf. changed his aspect on the army. The First Division was different than the other sectors of the army that he had served in before. They were better equipped, better trained, better managed, and held a higher level of discipline than any other battalion with which he had been associated. While here, he developed a connection with his NCO CSM Dobel. Major Dobel was the first ever CSM in the U.S. Army. When the army began elevating NCOs to the level of E9, SGM Dobel received his title one day before anyone else.

Within the Twenty-Sixth Infantry, another member would make CSM. It was William O. Woolridge. While in his position, the military would make another elevation for the non-commissioned officer. This title is sergeant major of the army (SMA). It requires this person to report to the Army Chiefs of the Government. One of the tasks of an NCO SM is to manage the affairs of the enlisted and to report to the commanding officer on the esprit de corps of the troops. He is the go-between of the officers and the enlisted. Dobel and Woolridge become friends of Ray as his military career progresses. These friendships start in Germany.

In November 1955, the Twenty-Sixth Infantry is routed to Fort Riley, familiar territory for Ray and the family. His position of platoon sergeant (PSG) in the Twenty-Sixth Infantry Division would be put on hold by late January of 1956. It was at this point that he entered the NCO Academy at Fort Riley. While it offered no increase in pay, it would afford him the opportunity to move up. He is assigned to the Fifth Army NCO Academy. It is time for him to go from teacher to student. Ray appreciated training. He would be quick to pick up on anything that would make him a better leader. Knowledge and abilities are what separates him from the rest of the pack. He is quick to take advantage of whatever the military was offering. Half of his time so far in his marriage was split between being away from Lovey overseas or in the field, and on base when he could come home and be with her at home. This school would allow him at least some quality time with the family.

When he graduates in March, he returns as PSG of Co. C 1st BG. within the 26th Inf. The next year would be business as usual for him. Things have settled into place for him and his young family. His reenlistment in 1956 would keep him in Fort Riley until 1959. While his reenlistment would keep him attached to the Twenty-Sixth, his orders would move the division back to Germany. They would take up residence in Baumholder. A political agenda had been raised by the USSR. This geopolitical/military issue was over the occupation of Berlin in the west. The Soviets wanted all the U.N./U.S. forces out of Germany and to take control of the entire city. Because of the agreements made after WWII, the West was not about to cede its occupation. Ray was right where he wanted to be: where the action was.

During the Berlin Crisis, Russia held the Twenty-Second Congress of the Communist Party of the Soviet Union. This congress would be the last one attended by the Communist Party of China. The meetings were held in Moscow in 1961. This would be the first sign of the break between the ideologies of the governments of the USSR and the Chinese. Since WWII, these two countries shared intelligence and common goals. Their joint participations in Korea was proof of that. The threat of communism, whether real or perceived, were based on this alliance. Russia had obtained a nuclear bomb by this point, and China was only three years away from their first detonation. Russia perceived the bomb as a deterrent against aggressions from the United States, but China perceived the weapon as a deterrent from aggressions from both the United States and Russia. It would prove accurate of the joint chiefs with regard to the next "Big One" being between the Soviets and the democracies of the West.

For Ray, he is part of headquarters of the Twenty-Sixth Infantry Division in Baumholder. From this position, a closer relationship with CSM Dobel and SM Woolridge would develop. Both men had served since WWII and had played a part in Ray's life as role models. As part of headquarters, he would have increased responsibilities. His understandings of the inner workings of the army would be heightened as well. While in Baumholder, Ray takes on the three weeks' training course as a "pathfinder." This training would qualify him for first insertions into combat areas. This is Ray's kind of action. A "pathfinder" team was required in every battalion. Their mission was to jump into hostile territories and set up landing zones (LZs) as a first-response group. Once inserted, they would signal fire and directions for helicopters and planes. Part of the training for this group was to make one night jump and two day jumps over a five-day period. Because of bad weather, a day jump and night jump were done in the same day. It was an effort to get the training completed. The remaining day jump was the next day. These are elaborate and tiresome operations.

In April 1961, 1,400 Cuban exiles were trained up and put into an invasion in Cuba. The lack of support from the United States and others led to a failed event. It is believed that fear of war with Russia was the final say as to why the Bay of Pigs invasion didn't meet their expectations. The absence of a democratically controlled government found the rebels of Fidel Castro still in power after the incident. Castro was heavily supported by the USSR. Up until the point of Castro seizing power, Cuba was a friendly country to the United States. It was a vacation destination for many in the United States and abroad.

October 14, 1962, and Those Pesky Russians

It is from here that Ray would launch yet again a rise in the army. In September 1961, he was assigned to Fort Bragg. Russia's communist expansion was the call of the day. America would combat this at every possible turn. From Fort Bragg, he would be routed to Fort Gordon, Georgia. This location is the training facility of the Signal Corp of the Army. One of their many tasks is the training of occupying forces. Ray is the 1st Sgt. of Co. C. 32nd Inf. This company is a missile command group.

Russian aggression was escalating vis-à-vis nuclear weapons being acknowledged in Cuba at this time. The United States had installed Jupiter nuclear missiles in range of the Soviet Union in Turkey and Italy. In response, and upon request of Fidel Castro, Russian Premier Nikita Khrushchev had started sending short- and midrange nuclear missiles to the communist regime in Cuba. These were identified by a U2 spy plane. A blockade had been formed by the United States to prevent further shipments to the militarily controlled island ninety miles away.

Cuban missile sight 1962. The small island country was surveyed by U2 spy planes during the era. U2 reconnaissance photo. [3]

John F. Kennedy had been elected in November of 1960, and upon receiving the Office of President, was immediately strapped with the Cuban situation. Pres. John F. Kennedy addresses the country on national television. The next thirteen days would be considered some of the most intense that every citizen would ever be a part of since WWII.

Ray was about to be immediately strapped with the same problem on a more direct result as well. Support of an antisocialist Cuban military insertion had failed in the operations of the Bay of Pigs. On the night that President Kennedy spoke to the people, Ray's command group was immediately transported out from the base. Fort Bragg was put on lockdown, and all was hush-hush amongst the family members left behind. Lovey had no idea where Ray was going, how long he would be gone, or when he would be coming back, if at all. This would present another problem as well. Lovey was pregnant and about to give birth to her second child, Ray Hooker Cottrell, Jr. Most Americans were on pins and needles as well, in what would be called one of the most anxious moments in U.S. history. The possibility of a full-blown nuclear war was coming to a head.

The army, on the other hand, was proactive in their operations. A team of engineers had been put to work in Fort Everglades, Florida. Their job was to build three separate quarantine areas for POWs expected to be realized from the conflict expected in Cuba. One would hold government officials, another to hold the military captured, and yet another to hold officers.

Ray was put with a military police task force that was sent to the newly built Yankee Stadium baseball practice facility south of Homestead, Florida. He is assigned via teletype. Ray recalls the rental agreement between the Yankees organization and the armed forces offered only one limitation. No one was to get on the field of play. *"Stay off the grass!"*

When the unit arrived, they only had sleeping bags and MREs. Short-range nuclear missiles would become part of their oversight during this operation. Three different airborne groups would be attached along with two armored divisions. Because of the low preparation and fast actions of the move to Florida, Ray's job is in high gear. The nature of the event required many aspects of preparation. The possible ensuing battles required him to be involved in many different assignments and tactical awareness of the overall mission. The government, as a means to an end, offered credit cards to the unit to obtain anything that would be needed in this makeshift base. They would go out into the civilian population for anything that the military had not provided. Bedding and sheets would be obtained from places like JC Penney while food supplies were bought from Safeway. Doctors, nurses, and medical supplies were rushed into the makeshift base almost immediately. Many were called up and put into action in the area from Fort Everglades to Homestead. As an MP battalion, jeeps and vehicles were quickly shipped in along with firearms and support material. The quick buildup was unprecedented. Ray's unit was required to secure the area along with other normal functions of an MP unit in wartime.

One interruption to the escalating events would be a welcomed break from the rigorous routines of the camp. Lovey had gone into labor. Ray drops all of what he was doing to make a beeline to see his wife. His company commander had issued him a temporary leave, and that would allow him to get to Lovey. He acquires a vehicle in short order and begins an 800-mile drive to Fort Bragg. It is an arduous road trip that would have little time for breaks, but a small price to pay to be present for the arrival of his son. The thought of Lovey not having him at his side constantly plays on his mind as he drives. Anticipation and hopes of getting there on time rumble through his head. This is a long and tedious thirteen hours. He is comforted by the thought that even if he didn't make it on time, he would at least be afforded some time to see his growing family.

As the acting SGM, Ray is privy to the overall plan being put into play by General Howell which was approved by the Kennedy administration. Two landing parties of armored divisions would make landings at different beaches. The air force would take immediate control of the skies while three different divisions of airborne groups would make jumps into the small communist-controlled island. The 82nd, 101st, and 173rd airborne groups were set to launch at a moment's notice. Each group had their own set of missions working in collaboration with the air force and naval ships already creating a blockade of the country. From Cuba, Russia could reach DC and a large majority of tactical sites within our borders. Fort Knox would be available as a target as well. Few Russian military units were on-site in Cuba at this time. A provisional government had been put together and was ready to go once the fighting ceased. Ray believes this was the best military operation that he had ever seen. He tells Captain Dillon, a fellow soldier on-site in the stadium, *"The U.S. forces would go through Castro's forces like shit through a goose. I don't see how it could fail. If this gets implemented, the only trouble would be small bands of guerillas in the mountains. They will not last long."* [4]

The army was to bring in the armored group with LSTs to the two beaches. Because the Cuban government had no air support, these LSTs would remain on site to transport POWs back to Fort Everglades detention camps and then return to Cuba to bring back the armored group that they had just delivered. Landing parties in the airborne groups would also be transferred back to the mainland once all was secured. Special forces groups would remain until the guerilla groups were rounded up and brought in. The expectations of the operations were to run from 72 to 84 hours. Other military groups that were battle-ready were also put on notice and ready to go should an expansion of the mission require it.

President Kennedy, in a surprising show of strength to Nikita Khrushchev, issued ultimatums. If the USSR would not remove the missiles, a full-scale war could be expected. The premier once believed that Kennedy was weak as a leader and could be manipulated through a show of force. But Kennedy did not back off. Within three months of Kennedy's national announcement on television, the entire operation was being drawn down. Ray's job now required him to help manage the transfer of all these things put into play back to where they came from.

As it goes, these assigned troops, special forces, doctors, nurses, and equipment had to be shipped back to where they came from. A SNAFU would be quickly realized. As troops and support staffs move out, Ray's MP TF is left holding the bag for the leftovers. A supply of handguns was left behind and put into his charge, along with a large supply of drugs that had been left behind by the medical staff. When he contacted Fort Bragg about the drugs, the base commander said that they would not take them back to that base. What to do with them? It was debated that these drugs could not be returned. Some of them were dated materials, but Ray is no drug dealer. He had made quite a name for himself in getting things done, but this presented a special type of problem. Army bases didn't need a supply of such things on base. He knew this, but the problem would still have to be resolved. Destroying the cache was not acceptable to him as well. He contacts Washington and gets in contact with the army there. Upon discussing the problem with them, a man was sent out to inspect the materials. He was informed to ship the drugs to a hospital near Fort Bragg. Situation resolved.

In a conversation with his newly made friend Captain Dillon, Ray tells him, "*I hear that things are heating up in Indochina.*" It is the only place that he knew of where there were actual military actions with the United States. The captain discusses with Ray saying, "*I would be interested in doing some time there. It would help me in my career, but I don't think you have any sway over that.*" Ray tells him, "*I think I can get us there if you want to go. General Rawson is a friend of mine, and I think I can get it cleared through him.*" The captain, not believing that Ray had such abilities, tells him, "*Go ahead and see what you can do.*" [4]

Ray contacts General Rawson, a person who he served with as VP of the AUSA in Germany. He tells Ray, "*I can send you, but you will have to go to special forces training at Fort Bragg.*" Ray says, "*With all due respect, general, I have my jump wings and have been trained in artillery, armor, and infantry. Am I not qualified enough?*" General Rawson tells him, "*I cannot in good conscience send you without some extra training. You will have to take some special forces training. Part of that training will require you to have some medical experience in the event you or one of your men get injured. You may be the only medical help that is available while you are there.*" Ray agrees and awaits his assignment. The general goes on to say, "*Your papers will be ready for you when you get back to Fort Bragg. For Captain Dillon, his papers will be ready tomorrow.*" Tomorrow comes and Captain Dillon has a look of surprise on his face. He didn't think Ray could do it. The captain tells him, "*This just turned my life completely upside down.*" He neither had expectations nor desire to go to Vietnam, but the need for captains in the small Asian country were immediate. A plane landed that day to pick Captain Dillon up. He was to go straight away. Ray would never cross this man's path again. [4]

January 6, 1963

Special War School, Fort Bragg

After many nights of being alone with two kids to raise, Lovey is relieved to see her man walk through those doors. He was home. He was safe. For a short period, all is right within the Cottrell house. They were able to share a Christmas together and even ring in the New Year with friends. The homecoming would be short-lived though. As General Rawson had said, his orders would be waiting for him when he returned to Fort Bragg.

From January to March, Ray is engaged in some of the most intense training that the U.S. Army has to offer. This training will introduce him once again to jumping out of perfectly good aircraft, treading through rough terrain, and getting a deeper understanding of management of both himself and the ones under his command. It is rigorous and exacting. Once again, his time in the field will separate him from his family back on base. He learns to live off the land; what to look for in the wild for sustenance. Plants, animals, bugs, how to find water, all these things would fall into his training. What to drink and eat and when to do it. He would be tested and tested again. The training would take him to his limits and bring him back again. Maintaining his wits and self-reliance under pressure is the root of this education. It was not unusual to come to the mess hall and be introduced to such delicacies as monkey and snake meat. He purified his own water while in the field. This was not training of convenience but preparation of handling any and all aspects of survival in the field. General Rawson was right. He would need it in the days to come.

At the end of his training, he is given a few days to spend with his family once again. His orders were cut. Ray would become one of the first 350 advisors sent to a small Asian country in Indochina known as Vietnam. One does not just waltz into Vietnam and say, "Here I am." The government of Vietnam only allowed these men by invitation. That invitation was granted by a commitment from the U.S. government under J. F. Kennedy with the president of Vietnam. Ngo Dinh Diem,

President of Viet Nam, was currently engulfed in a few issues. One such issue was the Buddhist crisis within the country.

President Ngo Dinh Diem was a member of the Catholic minority of the country. The Buddhist community comprised roughly 80-plus percent of the population. Under his administration, many political posts were given to Catholics and failed to meet a true variance of the country's population. The Catholic minority also received favors in tax exemptions, land grants, along with many military post assignments. The Buddhist majority of the country found little support from the biases of Diem's administration. Buddhist monks led upheavals and peaceful revolts were realized because of the decisions of Diem.

The Catholic Church was the largest landowner in the country, and the "private" status that was imposed on Buddhism by the French, which required official permission to conduct public activities, was not repealed by Diem. The land owned by the church was exempt from land reform, and Catholics were also de facto exempt from the corvée labor that the government obliged all other citizens to perform; public spending was disproportionately distributed to Catholic majority villages. Under Diệm, the Catholic Church enjoyed special exemptions in property acquisition, and in 1959, he dedicated the country to the Virgin Mary. The Vatican flag was regularly flown at major public events in South Vietnam. [5]

A rarely enforced 1958 law—known as Decree Number 10—was invoked in May 1963 to prohibit the display of religious flags. This disallowed the flying of the Buddhist flag on Vesak, the birthday of Gautama Buddha. The application of the law caused indignation among Buddhists on the eve of the most important religious festival of the year, as a week earlier Catholics had been encouraged to display Vatican flags at a government-sponsored celebration for Diem's brother, Archbishop Ngô Đình Thục, the most senior Catholic cleric in the country. On May 8, in Huế, a crowd of Buddhists protested the ban on the Buddhist flag. The police and army broke up the demonstration by firing guns at and throwing grenades into the gathering, leaving nine dead. Diệm denied governmental responsibility for the incident. Instead, the president blamed the Viet Cong for the event. Diệm's Secretary of State Nguyễn Đình Thuận accused the Viet Cong of exploiting Buddhist unrest and declared that Diệm could not make concessions without fueling further demands. The Vietnam Press, a pro-Diệm newspaper, published a government declaration confirming the existence of religious freedom and emphasizing the supremacy of the country's flag. Diệm's National Assembly affirmed this statement, but this did not placate the Buddhists. [5]

On May 30, more than 500 monks demonstrated in front of the National Assembly in Saigon. The Buddhists had evaded a ban on public assembly by hiring four buses and filling up and pulling the blinds down. They drove around the city before the convoy stopped at the designated time and the monks disembarked. This was the first time that an open protest had been held in Saigon against Diệm in his eight years of rule. They unfurled banners and sat down for four hours before disbanding and returning to the pagodas to begin a nationwide 48-hour hunger strike organized by the Buddhist patriarch Thich Tinh Khiet. [5]

A second issue for this seven-year president was the Viet Cong.

*The **Việt Cộng** was the name given by Western sources to the **National Liberation Front**, a political organization with its own army in South Vietnam and Cambodia - People's Liberation Armed Forces of South Vietnam (PLAF). It had both guerrilla and regular army units, as well as a network of cadres who organized peasants in the territory it controlled. Many soldiers were recruited in South Vietnam, but others were attached to the People's Army of Vietnam (PAVN), the regular North Vietnamese army. Communists and anti-war spokesmen insisted that the Việt Cộng was an insurgency indigenous to the South, while the U.S. and South Vietnamese governments portrayed the group as a tool of Hanoi. Although the terminology distinguishes northerners from the southerners, communist forces were under a single command structure set up in 1958.*

North Vietnam established the National Liberation Front on December 20, 1960 to foment insurgency in the South. Many of the Việt Cộng's core members were volunteer "regroupees," southern Viet Minh who had resettled in the North after the Geneva Accord (1954). Hanoi gave the regroupees military training and sent them back to the South along the Ho Chi Minh trail in the early 1960s. The NLF called for southern Vietnamese to "overthrow the camouflaged colonial regime of the American imperialists" and to make "efforts toward the peaceful unification." [6]

As a senator, President Kennedy, had spoken out before of his concerns of interventions in Vietnam, but the resolve of his opinion would be put to the test as a U.S. president facing USSR expansionism when the democracies of the West were trying to do the same thing. It was a precarious position to be in as a world leader of a country that was predisposed to mistrust of Russia and communism.

There had been some changes in the how we look at war, and this has been evolving since the Korean conflict. The United States, along with other free countries, had started to send reporters into the field that can take moving pictures of the ever-changing battlefields. The media had technologically evolved. It is a critical concept to remember when looking at wartime engagements involving the United States. During the Vietnam War, Joseph L. Galloway was one such reporter. His actions in Vietnam went way past the normal functions of news reporter. In the first major engagement with U.S. troops in Vietnam, Galloway was embedded with the troops, a rare concept for reporting of the time. He was perhaps the first newsman on the ground in that capacity during these years. His actions in this first engagement of helping the soldiers preserve the integrity of the fighting lines, and for helping the wounded, would get him the Bronze Star by the army. Not only was he able to capture the actions of these brave men; he was able to articulate to the civilians back home what war was like from a civilian point of view.

The soldiers and citizens of WWII are referred to as the "greatest generation," an accolade bestowed upon them by the generations that followed. It is a title that still holds today. For Joe Galloway, that concept would be expanded upon in the documentary *Viet Nam in HD*, directed by Sammy Jackson. Joseph Galloway would come to understand something more. If it was fair to call the generation of WWII as the greatest, then it was also fair to say that *"anyone who serves in the military should be considered the greatest of THIER generation."* Galloway had been dropped into a landing zone that was not only a major bloody battle but also overrun by the enemy. The situation was so bad that "Broken Arrow" had to be called.

When "Broken Arrow" is issued and confirmed in a battle zone, all available attack ships, aircraft, helicopters, etc., are immediately put on alert and guided to the battle zone to either drop ordnance, use their firepower, or offer aid to the troops on the ground. This was Joe Galloway's first event in reporting on the front line. It also puts our soldiers at high risk because of the close proximity of airpower being utilized there. Front line soldiers can and have been injured and killed by friendly fire under such conditions. Galloway's story can be captured in the movie *When We Were Soldiers*.

It is important to understand that there are several reporters on the ground in the Vietnam conflict, each working in different capacities and offering different takes on the actions that they see. Reporting is a double-edged sword. It allows the news to be delivered to the folks back at home so that they can postulate their own opinions on the matter being discussed, but it also can offer insights to the enemy on the national point of view of the United States. With that type of information, the enemy can direct their troops. These reporters can even divulge to the enemy how the war may be fought or is progressing. The last thing a military commander wants is for the enemy to ascertain any intentions or actions. The reality of reporters on the ground creates a unique situation for these commanders and as such create more complicated procedures because of it. The degree of reporting, while advantageous to the citizenry, is somewhat troublesome to the commander. A large number of current and ex-military hold the opinion that we have not won a war since WWII and cite the failure to do so as a direct result either in whole or in part to the newsmen on the ground.

This is just a small insight into the atmosphere and geopolitical world that Ray has to operate in. As he comes up to speed on the situation, he takes notes and reflects to himself, *This could get interesting.* For Ray, working on the front lines is what he is geared for. He is directed to Saigon. From there he will be moved just north of town to a training location designed to prepare the South Vietnamese regulars for the defense of their country.

CHAPTER 8

May 21, 1963

AFTER FINISHING THE special forces training at Fort Bragg, Ray finds himself in the southwest portion of Vietnam. His first assignment is to train Vietnamese regulars to become useful soldiers in their fight against aggressors to the government of Vietnam. It is not an easy task, although he seems well settled in to his new position as an E7 sergeant first class. Ray is part of the president's commitment to put advisors into the country. This was an ideology that was put into play before the Kennedy administration took control. He is one of the first 350 advisors sent by the U.S. Army into the country at the time. In the '50s, 128 men were sent as part of an assistance program by the U.S. government by request of the Vietnamese and French governments. As is consistent with his desire to be on the front lines, it is not quite up to speed with being there. Ray has made his mark in the army as a very proficient leader, trainer, and organizer. His talents, proven in the field, along with his contacts and personal motivations, have landed him right where he wants to be: in the thick of things.

He is assigned to the Military Assistance Advisory Group, Vietnam (MAAGV). The advisors in this first wave of army personnel have many missions. Some are in command. Some are direct advisors to the existing governmental officials of the country. Ray's assignment is not that glamorous though. He is placed in a small town north of Saigon at the perimeter of the town is a training base. Its job is to prepare the new recruits of the Vietnamese army in the use of guns, mortars, etc. Along with that task, he is responsible to teach these young men on the process of field operations.

These soldiers are so raw and the training process is so complicated that the task seems impossible. Few of these soldiers have any understanding of war and what it takes to wage it. The whole process is complicated even more so by the language barrier that Ray must also overcome. These men are there because they are hungry. It is a paying job. Cultural differences show themselves to Ray at virtually every turn and with every lesson. Ray discovers quickly that even the most basic of issues must be resolved. He quickly discovers that these men would just relieve themselves anywhere and at any time on the base. The very basic need of controlling latrine issues would have to be taught. He organizes a pit to be dug and covered. Toilets were brought in to fill out the facility as well as directions on how to use them. Fundamentals on sanitation had to be explained. Much of that education fell on deaf ears. Some issues had to be managed, but other issues such as these just had to be tolerated. He realizes that, even with latrines put into action, it didn't mean that they would be used properly. Shit would be found all over the place. The proper use of toilet paper would never be realized here. They had been defecating all over the training areas, but at least now it was more focused but not contained.

The task of organizing and training still had to be continued. Getting troops to stand in line or at attention was no easy undertaking either. The proper way to handle a rifle was explained. Issuing of the simplest of orders was complicated not only by language but by attention span. These were boys fresh out of the rice patties, fields, and villages of this Third World country. They had been brought up to be the way they were, and to alter some of that thinking was going to take a lot of effort. These boys knew that they could eat better than they had in months and oftentimes didn't really care who was in charge of them. They would follow their leaders. For most of them, though, they had no true alliances to the country that they lived in. They were just not brought up to think like most Westerners. That is not to say that they wouldn't get there. Some would distinguish themselves highly once certain concepts were explained completely.

On a hot and especially humid morning, Ray had collected his troops and proceeded down to the mortar range. Today's task would be about firing mortars properly. He knows his indirect firing business from his years in artillery. He knows the nomenclature of all that he has been trained on to the highest of levels. If he was using a 150 howitzer, he could disseminate the exact recoil of the gun when it fires, what the range is on the projectile, the weight of the projectile, the cleaning processes of the gun, and most importantly how to aim it for its most effective use. These are the things that a first sergeant is supposed to know. He knows it down to a T. So it is with the mortars.

Upon reaching the field, Ray organizes the men into teams. Some of the men would be firing, while other teams would learn the directions and await their turn with the weapon. Ray takes his time to explain the basics of the mortar tube and how to set it up for proper use. A detailed explanation of how to target the weapon is also explained. With the first set of men, the process is rather simple but somewhat time-consuming. He shows them how to handle the mortar itself and what it takes to set it in the tube once the aim had been set and the unit is ready to fire. He has to be careful here. The mortars are live and can easily kill someone if not properly handled. He pays close attention that no one does anything out of line here lest they incur casualties. Practice mortars are not well stocked for these recruits. A specific peculiarity of the device is that it is not intended to be aimed at anything less than twenty yards away. If the sights are properly used, the weapon should not be used in such a short range for safety purposes.

The men are working as trained and all is progressing well. Targets had been set up and a few of the men had actually landed their rounds within feet of its intended mark. Ray starts to get the feeling that perhaps there is hope for this ragtag group of soldiers after all. He walks the line of men and each team seems to be progressing.

One issue with new recruits is that there is no time or tolerance for free thinking. Everything seems to be progressing, but as he makes another pass of the firing teams, he quickly discovers that some of the men had found it necessary to take the targeting portion of the mortar tubes off the weapon or they were totally ignoring the targeting process altogether. It seems the men thought it was only necessary to fire off a round and play the guessing game on how to aim it. This is totally unacceptable for Ray, but his hands are basically tied by means of discipline. These men are not in his army. They are under his tutelage but not under his ability to reprimand as he is accustomed to. He was sent out here to be self-sufficient, proactive, and self-contained. His hands are not only full but also tied behind his back.

After three months of this, Ray realizes that he is not gaining much traction. He is beating himself up over a project that is not moving anywhere near the speed that will be required for his satisfaction. In the states, he would and could mold men for battle in just a few months. This was never going to be the case for him with these men here. He contacts MAAGV HQ and puts in for a transfer. His commanding officer suggests to him to hang in there for just a few more months and that he will make things right for Ray if he will. Ray cannot hold to it. He understands his abilities and when something is untenable.

MAAGV headquarters, Saigon. Photo taken 1961. [1]

By June 1, 1963, Ray had traveled back to the states and reassigned back to Vietnam. He would be working under MAAGV again, but this time his abilities are better utilized by the army. He is assigned as an advanced infantry and light weapons training advisor to a brigade of

ROBERT BROOKS

the Army of the Republic of Vietnam (ARVN). The ARVN is growing under the financial assistance of the United States as per the support of congress on the president's request. The intent was to prevent the spread of communism. Because of French military intervention and strife between the French and the Vietnamese, the U.N. and NATO groups had gone to work to bring a diplomatic solution to the problems in Indochina. The Geneva Accords had brought the country's status to this point. An active participation in Laos and Cambodia had been realized up to this point as per the Geneva Agreement. That agreement had been ratified back in 1955, but the two sides of Vietnam could not come together. The Geneva Accords were a peaceful agreement to separate North Vietnam from the south. The situation had effectively returned the status of Vietnam back to the state that it was in almost two thousand years ago when the Chinese would use Vietnam as a prefecture of China. It could barely manage the north of the country as it was. The control over the south, using its feudal system, was doing little to prevent the indigenous people of the south from looking toward emancipation and independence for themselves.

Why Are We in Vietnam?

By 1957, what few had expected to see in South Vietnam-political stability-had been accomplished. The economy was on a sound basis and improving. The armed forces had defeated the dissidents. The achievement obliterated Communist expectations of a take-over more or less by default. President Diem's (of South Viet Nam) refusal to allow a referendum in 1956 apparently had deprived the North Vietnamese of a legal means by which to gain control of the south.

In 1957 the Communist North Vietnamese Lao Dong Party therefore decided on a change of strategy for winning its objective. The strategy was not new; it was a revival of the Viet Minh insurrection against French domination, and the tactics were those of guerrilla warfare, terror, sabotage, kidnapping, and assassination. The goal was to paralyze the Diem administration by eliminating government officials and severing contact between the countryside and Saigon. At the same time, the Communists would usurp government control, either openly or surreptitiously, depending on the local situation. The new insurgents became known as the Viet Cong, and their political arm was the National Liberation Front, proclaimed in December 1960.

The first, faint signs of a change in Communist strategy, from the plan to take over South Vietnam through political means supported by external pressure to a policy of subversion and insurgency within the country, began to be noticed in 1957. The following year, the Viet Cong intensified and extended their political and guerrilla operations to a point where they created serious problems that threatened South Vietnamese government control in the countryside. Prodded by General Williams and faced with an election, President Diem belatedly ordered countermeasures in 1959 and committed more forces to internal security. But after the elections, in the fall of 1959, the Viet Cong began to gain the upper hand. Government control was eroding, the countryside and the cities were being isolated from one another, and the economy was suffering.

The crisis called for a re-evaluation of the U.S. effort. In March 1960 General Lyman L. Lemnitzer, U.S. Army Chief of Staff, visited South Vietnam. He reported to the Joint Chiefs of Staff that the situation had deteriorated markedly during the past months. President Diem had declared the country to be in a state of all-out war against the Viet Cong and requested increased U.S. Assistance in materiel and training. General Lemnitzer supported the request and recommended that the training and organization of the Vietnamese Army should be modified to shift the emphasis from conventional to antiguerrilla warfare training. He offered U.S. Army personnel, in the form of mobile training teams, to help achieve this objective. In April the Commander in Chief, Pacific, recommended that a coordinated plan be developed for the over-all U.S. Effort in support of the government of South Vietnam. The Departments of State and Defense sanctioned this recommendation.

In Saigon the U.S. Ambassador, the chief of the advisory group, and other senior officials, constituting what was known as the Country Team, drew up a planning document that dealt with the political, military, economic, and psychological requirements for fighting the Communist insurgency. This Counterinsurgency Plan for South Vietnam contained significant reforms, many of which had been proposed to the government of South Vietnam for some time but had not been accepted. Among the prominent features of the Counterinsurgency Plan were the reorganization of the South Vietnamese command and control organization; an increase in Vietnam's armed forces from 150,000 to 170,000 men; and additional funds of about $49 million to support the plan. The Counterinsurgency Plan urged the Vietnamese to streamline their command structure to allow for central direction, to eliminate overlapping functions, and to pool military, paramilitary, and civilian resources.

The Military Assistance Advisory Group was also eager to provide more advisers at lower levels of command. At the beginning of the U.S. Training effort, advisers had been limited to higher commands down to the division level, and to schools, training centers, territorial headquarters, and logistic installations. Only on a very small scale and on a temporary basis had U.S. Advisers been attached to battalion-size units. The new emphasis on counter- insurgency training early in 1960 changed this situation. In May 1960, the MAAG chief was authorized to increase the number of personnel assignments to field advisory duties at battalion levels. These assignments remained temporary, however, and were still made selectively-mainly to armored, artillery, and marine battalions. Toward the end of 1960, the government of Vietnam transferred the paramilitary forces of its Civil Guard and Self Defense Corps from the Interior Ministry to the Ministry of Defense. Both organizations, vital to the maintenance of security in the provinces and districts, thus became eligible for MAAG training and assistance. In addition, U.S. Special Forces teams began training the newly established, 5,000-man, Vietnamese Ranger force by the end of 1960. Clearly, the U.S. Commitment in Vietnam was growing. At this time, General Williams ended his almost five-year tour as MAAG chief. He was succeeded by Lieutenant General Lionel C. McGarr on 1 September 1960.

In Washington the Eisenhower administration was replaced by the Kennedy administration. Among President John F. Kennedy's first concerns was the situation in Vietnam. At this crucial time, the Country Team's proposals for countering the Viet Cong insurgency arrived in Washington. Subsequently, the President decided to continue U.S. support for South Vietnam and increased both funds and personnel in support of the Diem government. On 3 April 1961 the United States and South Vietnam signed the *Treaty of Amity and Economic Relations* in Saigon. One week later President Diem won re-election in his country by an overwhelming majority. To strengthen U.S.-Vietnamese ties further, President Kennedy sent Vice President Lyndon B. Johnson to Saigon on 11 May. In a joint communiqué issued two days later, the United States announced it would grant additional U.S. Military and economic aid to South Vietnam in its fight against Communist forces.

These measures, taken by President Kennedy, were based on preliminary surveys and consultations and on the recommendations of a temporary organization set up to deal with the crisis. In January 1961 the Secretary of Defense, Thomas S. Gates, Jr., had dispatched Major General Edward G. Lansdale to Vietnam. On the general's return, the Deputy Secretary of Defense, Roswell L. Gilpatric, was put in charge of an interdepartmental task force, subsequently known as Task Force, Vietnam, which identified and defined the actions the new administration was about to undertake. In Saigon a counterpart task force was established, its members taken from the Country Team. In addition, General McGarr, the MAAG chief, was brought to Washington in April to give his advice.

Washington had also accepted significant points of the Country Team's *Counterinsurgency Plan*, including support by the Military Assistance Program for a 20,000-man increase in the Vietnamese armed forces, for a 68,000-man Civil Guard and a 40,000-man Self Defense Corps, and for more U.S. Advisers for these additional forces. In May President Kennedy appointed Frederick C. Nolting, Jr., as Ambassador to South Vietnam, replacing Elbridge Durbrow. An economic survey mission, headed by Dr. Eugene Staley of the Stanford Research Institute, visited Vietnam during June and July and submitted its findings to President Kennedy on 29 July 1961. Later, in an address to the Vietnamese National Assembly in October 1961, President Diem referred to Dr. Staley's report, emphasizing the inseparable impact of military and economic assistance on internal security.

Soon after the return of the Staley mission to Viet Nam, President Kennedy announced at a press conference on 11 October 1961 that General Maxwell D. Taylor would visit Vietnam to investigate the military situation and would report back to him personally. Dr. Walt W. Rostow, Chairman *of the Policy Planning Council, Department of State, accompanied General Taylor. Upon its return, the Taylor Rostow mission recommended a substantial increase in the U.S. Advisory effort; U.S. Combat support (mainly tactical airlift); further expansion of the Vietnamese armed forces; and support for the strategic hamlet program, an early attempt at Vietnamization.*

Subsequently, the military effort was directed primarily at carrying out these proposals. The task was more than the MAAG headquarters in Vietnam could handle. In November 1961 therefore President Kennedy decided to upgrade the U.S. Command by forming the U.S. Military Assistance Command, Vietnam (MACV), and selected General Paul D. Harkins as commander. General Harkins had been serving as Deputy Commanding General, U.S. Army, Pacific, and had been actively involved in the Pacific Command's contingency planning for Vietnam. Following an interview with President Kennedy in early 1962, he went to Saigon and established Headquarters, Military Assistance Command, Vietnam, on 8 February 1962.

From 7 November 1950 through 7 February 1962 a single headquarters provided command and control for the U.S. Military effort in Vietnam. The number of authorized spaces increased from the original 128 in 1950 to 2,394 by early 1962. It would take some time to get these numbers up.

The responsibility for directing and controlling military assistance programs lay with both the legislative and executive branches of the U.S. Government The Mutual Defense Assistance Act of 1949 provided the basis for these programs in Vietnam. Within the executive branch, major assistance duties were performed by the Office of the President, the Department of Defense, and the Department of State. Policies and objectives of military assistance to Vietnam from 1950 to 1962 were based on decisions made by three different administration.

In the Department of Defense the joint Chiefs of Staff' determined the military objectives. The Assistant Secretary of Defense for International Security Affairs coordinated the broad political and military guidelines established by the White House and the Departments of State and Defense. The Commander in Chief, Pacific, provided specific guidance and direction to Headquarters, Military Assistance Advisory Group, Vietnam.

As the President's personal representative, the U.S. Ambassador to South Vietnam was charged with over-all responsibility for the co-ordination and supervision of U.S. activities in Vietnam. On political and economic matters, he was guided by the Department of State. The chief of the Military Assistance Advisory Group in Vietnam (MAAGV) was responsible to the ambassador for military matters under the Mutual Security Program and, as senior military adviser, was a member of the Country Team.

The MACV (Military Assistance Command Vietnam) was created on 8 February 1962, in response to the increase in United States military assistance to South Vietnam. MACV was first implemented to assist the MAAG Vietnam, controlling every advisory and assistance effort in Vietnam, but was reorganized on 15 May 1964 and absorbed MAAG Vietnam to its command when combat unit deployment became too large for advisory group control. MACV was disestablished on 29 March 1973. [3]

Understanding the Enemy

By this time, the North Vietnamese Army was for all intents and purposes a regular army. Fairly well trained and identifiable by their drab green uniforms, and well supported by both the Chinese government and the Russians in no small degree, these units were well engaged and prepared. Russian support to the NVA was verified when machine guns, issued to Russia only in WWII, started showing up with the captured NVA components. Serial numbers on the guns were tracked back to their origin. In this case, it was the United States. While the guns were antiquated in terms of modern warfare technology, that didn't alleviate the effectiveness of the guns in combat. These machine guns could, and did, kill. Information of this kind trickling back to the citizenry of the United States gave the people a suspicion of governmental and/or corporate conspiracy theories: that both sides of the disagreement were being funded by the same people.

A more organic form of aggressors to the South Vietnamese were the Viet Cong. They were their own political party with their own army. Holding to the belief of a free and independent Vietnam of both the communist and the western cultures is the best description as to why this group came to be. Operating in both South Vietnam and Cambodia, this group was self-proclaimed as a liberation army, but the United States and South Vietnamese governments looked at them as insurgents. They had a conglomeration of plainclothes infiltrators of peasant sympathizers to the North.

The French had been in control of Vietnam for a century at this point. They believed it to be a country that was a key to Asian trade routes and business. With so many advancements in roads, buildings, and commerce, it was once hailed as the Paris of Indochina. Only about 10 percent of the Vietnamese people truly enjoyed the benefits of this resurgence into the modern era though. The children attended French-speaking private schools. The adult group was made up of teachers, journalists, government officials, and business owners. The other 90 percent were an agrarian society where each family could self-sustain on their own parcels of land. As taxation came into play, these small farmers were forced to sell out in most cases and take jobs at the docks, farms, and rubber plantations. The influx of government control and taxation created an unprecedented level of poverty upon the peasants. It was reported that a job at the rubber plantations would result in a death rate of 25 percent. Once on these plantations, escape was rarely realized in the '40s and '50s. It was not unheard of to see a hanging. They were run more as slave camps than anything else. A growing dissention between the two classes laid the groundwork for the creation of the Viet Cong, who were heavily supported through Cambodia.

The PAV soldiers of the north, the Viet Cong, and the peasant sympathizers of the south had infiltrated and been given positions within the South Vietnamese Army. The Viet Cong could usually be identified by guerilla actions in the jungles through their typical but nonregulated black dress. The South Vietnamese government and the United States held the belief that the Viet Cong were pawns of the PAV from the north. They were right to think so to an extent. The conglomeration of a regular army, Viet Cong, and peasants all fell under command and control of the northern communists. Some of the peasants were forced into supporting the Viet Cong and the PAV for lack of self-defense. These units would take over their barns and stores as a place to hide weapons. To speak out or fight against this action would result in death.

Doing the Job

Ray is working in the field with a battalion of the AVRN. His assignment is to advise in all operations to complete the task of the group. He is directly working with a colonel of the AVRN and doing so in much the same way as he did in the states as an NCO. Their mission is to patrol and remove all Viet Cong as they are discovered.

In the summer of 1963, while on a reconnaissance mission, the men are on a long traverse through sharp-edged elephant grass and hilly terrain. After several miles of terrain, the commander calls the men to halt. It is a welcome respite to a long hot day in the sun. Ray is afforded a little time under the shade of a tree at the top of a hill. The hill was chosen for its strategic value as the site to rest and eat. During the break, he has fallen asleep from the excessive heat of the day. When he awakes from the short nap, he finds himself alone in the wilderness. The colonel had moved off with his men, leaving Ray behind. He is now forced to make his own way back to the post. He no longer has the protection of the group and will have to move back to safety while remaining unnoticed by any guerillas in the area. The value of special forces at Fort Bragg is now a necessity. He is given plenty of time to think about his position and how the friendly forces that he is assigned to really think of him. The situation verifies his belief in the alliance of the AVRN and the United States, or at least as far their allegiance to him.

For months now, the situation is the same. He gives his best in defining the role of the AVRN group that he is assigned to while adding his experience on what to do as situations arise. It is a complicated situation wrought with danger and insecurity. Communications with MAAGV are also complicated. While there is an interpreter to work with, the radioman of the unit is not compelled to share all information coming to his unit through him. The AVRN general is not always forthcoming as well. The unit was fairly effective but prone to withdrawal from contact with the enemy.

On one specific mission, the radioman was left behind the forward-moving group. Ray had noticed that there was a U.S. Army helicopter flying overhead. Ray had commandeered the radio to make contact with the craft. He was going to ask the pilot to radio back on possible enemy movements ahead as he was flying over. He identifies himself to the pilot as the unit begins to engage in enemy forces across a riverfront with mortar and rifle fire. When the pilot discovers that Ray is part of MAAGV, he informs Ray that he is not even supposed to be there. Orders had been sent to Saigon from the U.S. command to recall him. Ray discovers quickly that he was being withheld from returning to HQ because the general had failed to relay the information to him. He was basically being used. The pilot of the airship tells him to move back behind the encounter to a safe location for him to be picked up. He should have returned to Saigon over a week ago.

Ray gives the pilot logistical info of a clearing about a quarter of a mile back from his current location. The short trip back could have the potential to be lethal. Had the enemy forces outflanked the unit, Ray could find himself in the hands of the Viet Cong if he didn't get back there safely. He emerges from the tree line at the edge of the clearing as the helicopter starts to make its descent. After a quick sprint to the craft, he jumps on board as the chopper touches down. They are only on the grass for a few seconds before the pilot takes him skyward. Had Ray not acted quickly, he could have found himself overrun by the enemy. Orders were orders. He had no ill will toward the unit and his commander but was grateful for the off chance to make the discovery of the pilot's intelligence. Had he stayed with the battalion, he may have never made it back. They certainly showed no great concern for his welfare in the past.

A short stint in Saigon was just what the doctor ordered. A chance to recoup, collect himself and unwind was in order. While basically tied to the post in Saigon, he is given the opportunity to catch up with his commanders for some face time. Other advisors were also here, and the group was afforded the time to make notes of each other's experiences and how to best move forward. It was warranted and necessary. Things are really heating up in this god-awful confusion. There were dramatic changes in the government. Officers in the military were moved out and other officers were moved up. Key officials in the government at this time were also replaced. The MAAGV command was being consumed into the new operational control under the heading MACV. The ever-increasing issues of command structure expansion, and with many more advisors coming into play, facilitated the need for the restructuring of the command. It would not be long before Gen. William Childs Westmoreland would be put in control over MACV. He would be taking over in January of 1964. Former control over MACV was under the command of Gen. Paul D. Harkins.

This engagement has many perspectives. It is like driving a car while looking through an adjustable scope. If the focus of the scope is in one position, only the dashboard of the car is visible. Turning the focus knob slightly allows for ten feet of vision in front of the vehicle. A slight turn of the knob again shifts the focus to a quarter mile down the road as the vehicle continues. One more turn of the knob transfers all vision to the horizon, losing all sight of the road.

So it is in Vietnam. The generals in Washington see the war through maps and intelligence reports. They work from the motivations of the president and congress. The commanders on the ground see the mission statements of the generals and apply it to the terrain of the objectives. The sergeants and platoon leaders see the quarter mile down the road, while the infantrymen see the ground in front of them. It was once argued by a veteran that *"one's aspect of the Vietnam engagement was relevant to that person's position. If you were a pilot you held one view point. If you were a 'tunnel rat' charged with going deep into underground bases and supply depots you had another view. If you were a citizen back in the states, you held another view of it all. Perspective is everything."* [4]

As a military advisor working in the lowlands of the country, Ray's tasks are multileveled. While militarily advising generals and captains, he is also required to go out into the villages and make contact with the locals. Winning the hearts and minds of the locals was just as important as performing at his peak as an advisor. Having the Viet

Cong maneuvering and controlling the local villagers will not be acceptable to a country trying to find its identity. Ray is tasked in this area as not only an advisor but also a confidante and possible supplier of information and goods to the people.

The villagers would have to be supportive of the actions of the current government and the U.S. support. Without faith in these two entities, success in the country could never be realized. A mission had come up for Ray. He was informed by the locals that a Viet Cong soldier had been visiting the village trying to get supplies and support for their

> On the issue of Indo China, JFK spoke, "I am, frankly, of the belief that no amount of American military assistance in Indochina can conquer an enemy which is everywhere and at the same time nowhere, 'an enemy of the people' which has the sympathy and covert support of the people." **United States Senate, Washington DC, April 1954**

side. A village elder had gotten word to Ray of his presence, and Ray was charged with acquiring the insurgent and removing him from the area. Ray had been tracking enemy movements for weeks in the area, but this man had become very elusive. Ray had managed to garner the trust and confidence of the village. This man stood against all that had been created. It was explained that the man was using intimidation and fear to get what he wanted.

Patterns of his presence in the village had been discovered. It was up to Ray to be there during this man's repetitive arrivals. Timing would have to be everything. Ray needed to apprehend the guy. Timing was all he had to go on. Pictures did no good. It wasn't like he could give the villagers a camera and have them shoot a picture of the guy. Technology such as a camera would never be owned by a civilian way out there. Ray would have to calculate when to go into the village and hope that no one in the village would be given up as a U.S. sympathizer. This could result in various penalties for these peasants had the enemy come to that conclusion. It was a touchy situation.

An optimum day had arrived. Ray would dress in plain clothes so as not to arouse suspicions of the VC. He could be explained away by the elders as something other than a U.S. soldier had he been seen talking to the villagers. Ray arrives with a few locals and moves about the huts as if to be surveying the area. He starts taking pictures randomly about the area but ensures that he covers as much of the village as possible while making it look like his photography is random in nature. He is armed and prepared, but that little surprise cannot be seen by anyone. After speaking with the elders on subjects not related to his current presence there, Ray is forced to move off. Evidently his timing was off. The man is not present. He returns to HQ.

Before speaking with the commanders and others at HQ, he had sent the film out to be developed through the military. Military film such as this is not developed by an outside source. When the pictures are returned, he sets a meeting up with his commander. The now-developed photographs were put onto the table as Ray explains what he was doing. He explains why he did it in that fashion. At this point the pictures had no significant value other than to give a visual of some of his area of operations. He explained that he timed his visit to coincide with the VC's visit, but alas, as far as he could tell, his timing was off. As the two speak to each other, his commander takes a second look over the photography. A curious thing has been spotted. As they looked at one of the roofs of the grass huts in a particular photo, they could see a human leg and foot hanging out in the open. The man was there. He could clearly be made out in the photo hiding in the grass-covered rafters of one of the structures. Ray could have easily been taken out with a well-placed shot had the insurgent decided to fire.

No one in the village slipped him a note to say where the guy was. No one signaled to him or his men of his hiding place as well. This created another problem. It was not unusual to find villagers playing both sides of the fence to improve their own personal standings. This would now have to be calculated into Ray's thinking and actions. He would now have to calculate the accuracy and sincerity of the ones he was dealing with from here on out. The soldiery of the ARVN had put him on this path early on. Now the peasants would have to be looked at in the same way. His decisions would have to ensure that things went as planned even if the trust levels were false. That would prove to be no easy task. Almost everything he had done up until now would have to be recalculated into his planning going forward. For Ray, the mission would still come first, but mission 1A (protecting your men) would become more complicated in the days ahead. Fortunately for him, at this point, it was only himself who made up mission 1A.

Ray, serving as first sergeant, kept him close to the commanders back in Saigon. This allowed many opportunities to have input. Some of that information was field-related. Some of it would be in communications or even managerial input to decision-making. No war is complete without propaganda as well. In Vietnamese society, propaganda took many forms: leaflets, radio, newspapers, and in some areas even television. A unique situation came to bear in this front. Vehicles with speakers and even picture shows were circulated throughout the country. The United States had been employing the Willy jeep/truck as a multipurpose vehicle. Behind it, a wagon could be towed, supporting all the propaganda material needed to spread the word. The Willy jeep was a tough vehicle. It was well used in Korea and the jeep itself still had very plausible value here in Vietnam. However, it did hold a setback, a negative value that Ray could not resolve.

A four-wheeled vehicle, whether it be a truck or jeep, was not a valuable tool for spreading the word to villages that could only be reached via two-wheeled vehicles or light bikes. Ray took notice of this. Many of the locations that he worked in and out of required something more versatile than even a jeep. That something lighter came in the form of a French made vehicle called the Lambretta, more specifically the Tri-Lambretta. This little gem was more adaptable to the situation. It was much lighter. Speed and agility was as not much an issue as maneuverability. Its light weight allowed it to be pulled/pushed out of situations that would require more manpower for the Willy. He had also accounted for a major cost savings for the army as well. By employing these units for that task, repair and maintenance could be obtained in country, whereas parts for the Willy had to be shipped in. The Lambretta could be taken to local repair shops where parts were readily available. This was a vehicle of the people. Propaganda would also be more readily received without using a foreign vehicle. All this was taken into account when Ray made these suggestions to the upper command. It was well received. In fact, it was very well received. He was honored with distinction yet again with a commendation. This award was issued with a sign-off and letter of appreciation from Col. Richard Stillwell. Ray was already a military man. He is now becoming a military man's man.

A 1950's Willy jeep. Ray's Rat jeeps would have two rear-mounted M60s. This jeep is dated as a Vietnam restoration and part of Ray's personal collection. It sits in his car dealership in Kentucky. The mounted gun is an Airsoft replica. [6]

The Tri-Lambretta. It is more of a bike/motorcycle than a jeep. [7]

MACJ 34   11 Mar 1964

SUBJECT: Field Testing Tri-Lambretta Audio/Visual Vehicles

TO: Commanding General
          Military Assistance Advisory Group, Vietnam
          APO 143, San Francisco, California

1. Tri-Lambretta Audio/Visual Vehicles were recently received in Vietnam for field testing by the Army Concept Team to determine their capability to support the Psychological Warfare/Civic Action Program.

2. It has been brought to my attention that a member of your command, SFC Raymond M. Cottrell, Operations Sergeant, 9th Infantry Division Advisory Detachment, has made several useful modifications to this vehicle. These design changes have significantly increased the Tri-Lambretta's capability and will be included in the final test report prepared by ACTIV. SFC Cottrell's suggestions will be extremely helpful to both U. S. Advisors and their Vietnamese counterparts in obtaining maximum performance from the Tri-Lambretta in field operations.

3. I wish to commend Sergeant Cottrell for this performance of duty which reflects personal initiative and imagination. It is this type of performance which makes the American non-commissioned officer unique in the military world. I am sure that Sergeant Cottrell's future service will continue to reflect this superior performance of duty.

                              /s/Richard G. Stilwell
                              /t/RICHARD G. STILWELL
                              Major General, USA
                              Asst CofS, J-3

TRUE COPY:

ALAN B. CAMPBELL
1LT, Armor
Adjutant

[6]

MAJAR-CH (11 Mar 64)   2d Ind
SUBJECT: Field Testing Tri-Lambretta Audio-Visual Vehicles

HEADQUARTERS, US ARMY SECTION, MAAG, Vietnam, APO 143, US Forces

THRU: Senior Advisor, Advisory Team Nr. 96, APO 15, US Forces

TO: Sergeant First Class Raymond H. Cottrell, ████████
        Advisory Team Nr. 27, APO 38, US Forces

I wish to add my own appreciation to those expressed by Major
General Stilwell and Major General Timmes. My congratulations for a
job well done.

                        /s/Delk M. Oden
                        /t/DELK M. ODEN
                            Brigadier General, USA
                            Chief

MAJTN-IVC-SA (11 Mar 64)   3rd Ind

HEADQUARTERS, US ARMY ADVISORY GROUP, IV CORPS, APO 15, US Forces 6 Apr 64

THRU: Senior Advisor 9th Infantry Division, APO 157, US Forces

TO: Sergeant First Class Raymond H. Cottrell RA ████████

It gives me great pleasure to forward this letter of commendation
from Major General Richard G. Stilwell and to add my personal commendation for the actions which prompted such recognition.

                        /s/Sammie N. Homan
                        /t/SAMMIE N. HOMAN
                            Colonel, Infantry
                            Senior Advisor

TRUE COPY:

ALAN R. CAMPBELL
1LT, Armor
Adjutant

AIBKAC-PA (11 Mar 64)   5th Ind

SUBJECT: Field Testing Tri-Lambretta Audio-Visual Vehicles

HEADQUARTERS, US ARMY ARMOR CENTER, Fort Knox, Kentucky, 23 April 1964

THRU: Assistant Commandant, US Army Armor School

TO: Sergeant First Class Raymond H. Cottrell, ▓▓▓▓▓▓, US Army

It is a distinct pleasure to note and forward this letter of
commendation from Major General Richard G. Stilwell, Assistant Chief
of Staff, J3, US Military Assistance Command, Vietnam, and to extent
my personal congratulations for this exemplary performance of duty.

                              /s/J. K. Bastion, Jr.
                              /t/J. K. BASTION, JR.
                                 Major General, USA
                                 Commanding

TRUE COPY:

ALAN R. CAMPBELL
1LT, Armor
Adjutant

[6]

[7]

When the Tri-Lambretta was put into action, it could finally reach the peasants as well as the affluent. As with everything, there is always more to the story. Every military man can attest that there is a comical side to being in the services. One does not give up two to four years of his lives without coming across a little humor. Sometimes it takes the form of a private being embarrassed because of his lack of knowledge on a subject, or a sneak attack on the secretary of state. It had been reported that Secretary of State Henry Kissinger would often be sabotaged while presenting crucial information to the president. An unknown assailant would put pornographic photos in his briefs while he attended cabinet meetings. He would be flipping through his documents as he reported to the president, and lo and behold, he would turn to a picture of a naked woman in the middle of his dissertations. This would cause him to freeze up and require him to pause and choke up while rethinking his position.

This early Vietnam experience would also avail the conscious soldier some comic relief. When working in highly stressful situations, a little humor could go a long way. It was nothing for a soldier of the highest level, or even the lowest level, to seek out something fun to do. The job of the Tri-Lambretta was to deliver audio/visual propaganda to the people of the country. On one occasion, a particular unit was sent out to give audio loudspeaker taped recordings throughout a specific area of operation. During the normal process of deployment, an officer would give the statements to be recorded to bilingual Vietnamese personnel. They would translate and record the qualified message to be transmitted through the audio devices of the Tri-Lambretta units. An unknown individual had managed to take over this recording. Using his own words, what was supposed to be an approved message, had been translated into something completely unapproved. **STOP HERE! Author's note: If you are easily offended, skip to the next paragraph.** The message that was put out said, "Ho Chi Minh will be fucked by a water buffalo and die." This transmission would reverberate for almost two weeks before the U.S. military would realize what was being said. It was quickly addressed. No one ever said that their humor couldn't be dark.

A Sense of Normality

Because of his accomplishments, officers of rank had picked Ray to be a part of the training programs starting to get into high gear back in the states. This was good timing. He was up to reenlist anyway. He was picked to support the training programs back at Fort Knox, familiar ground for him. Elevated above the level of training recruits, his services were now needed to train officers. He would be assigned to the Company B Third Battalion School Brigade for armor schooling. It is now February 1964.

From March of 1963 to February of 1964, Ray had become quite an effective and proficient soldier in the U.S. Army. He learned the ways of the enemy. He had learned the ways of the brass and how they thought and saw things. Because he had become so adaptive to his ever-changing situations, and his ability to adjust to environments on the fly, he got noticed. His attention to details with the commanders showed itself to them. Because he showed foresight and a proactive initiative, he had gotten awarded. This was valuable to him. When the U.S. Army was downsizing in the 1950s, he had started his journey. He hit the ground running in 1950. He hit it hard. He was put in environments never realized by the average infantryman and was awarded the Silver Star for his efforts. A level of excellence and productivity had become a standard for him. From the frozen rocky landscape of North Korea to the rainy hot jungles of Vietnam, range had become part of his moniker. Because of his many accomplishments, he had been selected to move out of the jungles and back to the real world.

Ray had been able to quench his thirst for the front line for the time being. His education level had grown exponentially up to this point, and his talents were needed back home. Lovey and the family were still back in the states, and it wasn't prudent to stay any longer in Vietnam than what was necessary. The family needed him back home.

Making the transition from the jungle to spit shines is not a comfortable event for most servicemen. They become acclimated to either one or the other. For most, it will either be one or the other. It is not that way for him. He made that transition coming home from Korea and yet again in Germany.

The family is now in base housing. He has been gone too long for Lovey's taste. She is relieved to be reunited with her husband from a long overdue connection. He had a role that needed to be filled for the family's sake as well. She could not be expected to do everything by herself all the time. The kids needed their father. They were availed the opportunity to spend Christmas together. His daughter Brenda has grown up quite a bit in his absence. Ray Jr. had spoken his first words and began to walk while he was gone. There was so much to get caught up on. Lovey had missed him, but her concerns were lifted when he made his way to the house back in December. This is the life of the military front line: fleeting moments of family surrounded by the call of duty.

Family viability is tied to his career. Every few years he is tormented in no small degree with reenlisting or getting out. With every end to every cycle, he is forced to rethink his position. Stay in or get out. Every time the issues are weighed against family, timed served, and financial need. Every time, he finds himself recommitting to another cycle. Every cycle had availed him much with awards, commendations, and pay raises. Every time he reenlisted, he got a bonus. Every bonus came with a little time off, but a few extra months in pay are delivered to him in the mail. It seems every time he got that bonus, that check was sorely needed. He is a doer. A worker. He must work.

It is below freezing today. Just a few weeks earlier it was one degree Fahrenheit. Outside, it is snowing lightly. It is 4:00 a.m. when he rolls out of bed. He has to ready himself for the day and make it to the training facilities before the men can be awakened. They will feel like they are in boot camp again when he walks through those doors. Making his way onto the base requires a little concentration because of the weather conditions. The base is starting to come to life. He drives through the main gate. The check-in with the guards is normal procedure. They don't know him from Adam. But they will. It will be weeks before they get used to seeing his face twice a day.

He slips his vehicle into the assigned parking space. As he steps out of the car, he leans back in to get his notes and training materials. His galoshes keep his shoes dry. First appearances to recruits are important. That is heightened to a new level now that he is taking on the training of officers. Setting good examples is paramount.

The walk to his office is short, wet, and cold. A little of that time is used to reflect on his way in. He has been here a few times before. His first experience was almost fifteen years ago. A note is taken on how some things change, but some things are still the same. Two months earlier, he was treading through the jungles of Vietnam in unbearable heat and never-ending rain. A decade and half later and here he was again, traveling the roads and sidewalks of where it all stated back in 1949. He drove past the barracks where a drunk and overzealous officer had tried to get him to tie his boots when he was a PFC. That event cost him two weeks' pay, but slugging him in the mouth was well worth it. He takes a second to measure just how much he has changed since those days as he approaches the door. When he reaches the top step, he pauses at the door and looks back around to take in the view. Enough of that. Time to get busy.

[8]

CHAPTER 9

Off to Class

A NEW SET of parameters are now in play. As an instructor in the school brigade, the men that he is working with are attempting to get commissions as officers relative to the countries where they wish to be deployed. Some would be heading to Germany, some to Vietnam, while others are shooting for spots in other countries. It is a grueling twenty-two-week course designed to test the men of their mettle. No one entered this training with the expectation that it would be easier than any other training before. If they did, those thoughts would be immediately removed. Long marches, tests of endurance, and tolerance tests of psyche would all so be employed. Ray was tough. He had to be. These men would come to terms with that concept quickly.

While in the OLTC (officer leadership training course), Ray's objective is to prepare men for leadership in the companies that they represent. There is some wiggle room here in OLTC. These men come with their own cadre of officers, so the full extent of management and control is not completely under his jurisdiction. If for example, a cadet, wishing to get an officer's position in France, would have his French officers issue any type of reprimands should it be required. For the men at Fort Knox, under U.S. control, it was a simple pass/fail scenario.

Ray could be tough on these guys, but it was limited. That doesn't mean that Ray was merciless. He would become well aware of each of his students. He needed to know what motivated them, what made them tick, and what their breaking points were, if they had any. These leaders are being trained up to be just that, leaders. It does no good to have a lieutenant break down under pressure in the height of combat. In that logic, it is also fair to say that a good trainer should go out of the way to remove the barriers that prevent that student from being the best that he can be.

In one particular case, one of his candidates had gotten involved in a very messy divorce. That individual had to be called away to resolve the issue in midtraining. Since the man was required to finish the training uninterrupted, it would not do for him to leave midstream. Going AWOL is not relevant. To drop out or be dismissed from the process means he would be done with no exceptions. This man had already accomplished much as an enlisted man and worked very hard to get himself in the position to transition from enlisted to officer. At the same time, he could not function properly as a candidate, much less an officer, if he didn't get out of there and resolve the pressure coming from home. In the end, he left. In light of the circumstances, Ray went out of his way to get the man back into class after all was resolved. It required him to restart the cycle from where he left off. This option is way out of the norm. Ray felt the man deserved a second shot, and at his urging to his superior officers, the man was reinstated to do so. A lot of time, money and sweat had been for and by this man so far. Ray found it only fitting to work as hard as he could to get the man a second chance. A rare event indeed.

All movements of a company of men are well planned. A simple day in the life of a soldier in training has many requirements. Training is only part of the routine. The goal is to set parameters that the men will use personally for themselves and for the men that they are to lead. A correct coerciveness is the paramount goal. They think as a unit. They move as a unit. They learn as a unit. This logic and process has many advantages and is considered a streamlined process of the highest order. Processes have to be in place to make all this work out. Their sleeping quarters are defined and organized. They are checked regularly and looked over with a white glove level of cleanliness. Their sleep schedule is defined per their training requirements. Their dress code is predefined based on the training of the day. No man should, or ever want to, come up short in terms of gear for the required issue at hand. If the men were scheduled to go to the firing range to shoot, a plan had to be made to ensure that they had their rifles cleaned, inspected, and prepared for the event. Ammo had to be delivered to the site as well. So it goes for all their training.

It is not unusual to have a monkey wrench thrown into one's expectations when in training. A two-mile run can turn into five within a blink of an eye. If one man lags behind, mileage can be added. If a man falls and no one helps him to his feet, mileage can be added. If a question is asked and the wrong answer is stated, another mile can be added. Basically they have sold their souls to the company store. They are the property of the U.S. government. They are GIs (Government Issue). A master sergeant can and will look for any reason whatsoever to push the men a little further. Sometimes they will add more to the task just because they are feeling chipper that day and want a stronger workout for themselves. This, of course, adds more to the existing challenges for the students.

Today's events have been no different than those of an enlisted man's basic training. Hard work and hard training are always the call of the day.

These men have accomplished more in the wee hours of the morning than most men will do all day at their jobs. While a private citizen might be enjoying his first cup of coffee, they may have put in a full day. Ray is there before it starts and stays with them until "lights out" in the barracks.

It is not like these men are on vacation down in Cancun. The men know that they had better not bemoan anything during their training process. In their world, it's not what it said but who hears it said. One wisecrack, or even a begrudged smirk, could result into more calisthenics for that person, or worse yet, for the whole platoon.

A blanket party defined: The sleeping subject is surrounded by his fellow men. Some of the men will be tasked with pulling down of your blanket from all four corners. Meanwhile, others will hit you with a sock filled with a bar of soap or some other type of load. The actions happen all at once and during your sleep. Some men hold down the blanket to prevent you from exiting the bed as if you had been sewn into it. The other men beat you with their loaded socks until they feel they have made their point. Generally speaking, those who are not taking part in the mugging will do nothing to stop it lest they find themselves on the receiving end of the same treatment. [1]

Lessons had to be learned. An individual's actions always represent the whole unit. No one ever wants to be the cause of an unpredictably negative outcome for a fellow soldier. It is never a good thing to be on the receiving end of a blanket party thrown by the men as a result of your personal failings.

Ray had grown up with the knowledge of knowing what it was like to be hungry. Shit on a shingle was commonplace back home. The slightest complaint about a meal would easily convince him to act. He would go out of his way to teach the men respect and discipline. He had been through pathfinder training himself. If he could eat rats and bugs for sustenance in the field, these men better be able to stomach anything.

Sometimes the army creates surprises that even the best-laid plans can't overcome. Mother Nature has also been known to play a part in taking a normal day and disrupting it. Some would call this chaos theory. Basically it states what can go wrong will go wrong. Others call it Murphy's law. Nature can provide unexpected heat for the day or a torrential downpour. There is no day off for weather conditions short of a hurricane or tornado. These men have been trained to take what they are given when they are given it. They have been trained to not complain.

A New Launch

By April 1, 1965, after two grueling rounds of training, Ray finds himself moved from instructor to the first sergeant of the Third Battalion's school brigade. His high proficiency at the OLTC had provided this opportunity. It is a time of U.S. advancement not just for him but the country as well. The U.S. military is in expansion mode. Technological advances in the space program, thanks to the Kennedy administration, were starting to show its fruits. Sputnik launched in 1958, marking the start of the "space race." The first space flights of the Mercury program had already taken place. The resulting Gemini program followed. Its intent is to make a formal docking with two space vehicles. This test was needed to ensure that a flight to the moon could be obtained. By 1962, NASA was well on their way to beat the Russians to the moon. That year, they named a Korean War veteran pilot as the slated astronaut to be the first man on the moon. His name is Neil Armstrong.

It was intended that the space flight could be done by any citizen willing to make the commitment. Under President Eisenhower's urging, the final selection group would come from the 508 existing active U.S. military test pilots. Aside from physical ability and talents, a degree in engineering or science was also required. This automatically excluded women. It also cut out some noted names such as Chuck Yeager and Joseph Kettinger. Kettinger was a noted stratospheric balloonist. Their education levels kept them out. The numbers were dwindled down to just over one hundred. From there, the numbers are dropped to thirty-two.

On April 6, 1965, NASA had launched a Delta D rocket into space. It was the first geosynchronous communications satellite put into orbit. Intelsat I is the name of this satellite. Its name identifies its job. It is the first communications unit successfully launched into space for the United States. It would serve well in communicating with the up-and-coming Apollo program now in training. This type of satellite is the grandfather of what we use today for our cell phones and geopositioning tools.

Some notable events of the year included the first space walk by man. It was the USSR cosmonaut Alexi Leonov's honor to have. Gen. William Westmoreland is _Time Magazine's_ "Man of the Year." Manhattan was introduced to the very first TGI Friday restaurant. The Kentucky Derby winner is Lucky Debonair. In college sports, UCLA had just won their second of two in a row of NCAA Men's National Championships in basketball. The Green Bay Packers are the first NFL champion. The Beatles made their sixth album while The Rolling Stones got their first hit single. Martin Luther King was arrested in Selma, Alabama, earlier in the year but was working to get blacks registered to vote. India and Pakistan engaged in a border war. Forty tornadoes killed 272 people in the midwest while injuring over 5,000.

All that aside, Ray is now leading as an NCO in the OCS at the HQ/3rd BN School Brigade. It is a twenty-six-week training program that he will help oversee. For him, a lot of the bugs of the training program could now be worked out a little better. He had a keen eye for detail, and his experiences would guide him to better serve the BN in the weeks to come.

For this first class, a competition between companies was arranged at the sixteenth week of training. The game was basketball. It was a chance to let the men let off a little steam. The men had come along nicely in their training. They had no breaks up until now. In an attempt to reward the winners, a day of leave was offered to the titleholders. Under chaos theory, this too would devolve into something unexpected. But that surprise was not offered by Mother Nature. It would come in the form of discipline from Ray.

The games were played on Friday night and a winner was established. Rumors were circulating that all the men would be released Saturday at 1200 to leave the base until Monday morning. The original offering was for the winners and for Saturday night only.

Saturday morning comes and the mess hall reports to him that no one was there to eat the food that was prepared for the expected amount of men. It seems that every man in every company was making plans for the evening and decided to skip lunch because they expected to be on the road at noon.

That little tidbit of information started the wheels in motion that all these men would regret. Food had been prepared for five companies of men. Most of that will be wasted. Ray decides, if food is to be wasted, then wasted food will be the tool by which they learn. He requests that the mess hall make up large pans of peas. They didn't have to be well cooked, but they did have to be done. The food was to be set up at the training field on base. Ray informs the men that there was one more task that was to be completed before anyone was given leave. Rumors are loose lips, and these lips will be educated to pay attention.

The men head to the barracks and are told to prepare for a last-minute workout in the exercise yard. As the men get dressed and prepare for reporting, the kitchen has had enough time to get the peas ready and out to the exercise yard. The look of curiosity is overwhelming in the men's eyes. Ray is maintaining his standard stink-eye look as their platoon sergeants call them to the line. The orders are simple and direct: eat as much peas as they can, and do a four-legged monkey walk around the course until they throw up. Each time they completed a cycle, they were to return to the peas and eat more. This will continue until they lost their guts.

For Ray, the goal is to get them to follow explicit orders. He is being a hard ass, but it was time to be a hard ass. He was as explicit in these orders as he was in offering only the winners an opportunity for leave. The men are confused and anxious. No such order like this had ever been given to any of them. But they dare not question it. Mouths are starting to fill up. Bellies are becoming distended from the rare delicacy that is a bowl of peas with no flavors added. None of the men are catching on. None of them realized that they could eat until they were about to throw up before they started to run. In that way, they wouldn't have to run more than a few steps before they blew chunks. Ignorance is not always bliss.

Around and around they go like sheep to the slaughter. But these men were trained to be obstinate. They were geared to be winners. Each one was taught to overcome obstacles. Slowly but surely, the men are starting to fall off. Every few minutes, some peel off the track to clutch over and bow to King Ralph. As the clock ticks, the number keeps getting smaller and smaller. The cooks, who at first were enjoying the humor of the situation, are now starting to feel sorry for the men working their asses off to succeed. They want to be winners of a contest that was intended to have no winners. The light of wisdom never clicks in for the remaining few. They are strong-willed and motivated. They are the ones that are wanting to be the last one who loses it. As the clock ticks down, the last five men are stopped and told to stick their hands down their throats to cause the gag reflex to kick in. They will be the last to leave the field, but they have now all been taught. It is not a punishment as much as it is a lesson in following orders.

The First Mobile Phone

Ray has come into his own in several ways at this point. His experiences in the U.S. Army have separated him from the pack in many ways. By September 1965, he has moved to OCS. Now he will strictly be involved in the training of U.S. military personnel only. All his candidates will be drawn from the enlisted, college students, and ROTC personnel attempting to get officer status. As an E8 NCO, a few perks have come along with a pay increase. He is given an office just outside the commanding officer's (CO). He is assigned to the duty of 1st Sgt. Co. A OCS at Fort Knox. So closely tied to his CO, his input to the battalion is received almost instantaneously. He is the go-to guy not just for the enlisted and the candidates but also for the brass.

An insight to the respect that he has offered can be described very simply. On one occasion, he is at his desk. He is in the middle of chastising a candidate for issues unbecoming of his position, a mistake the candidate made that needed his direct attention. Every so often, officers of lower ranks failed to realize the importance of the work of the NCO within the military. These men need to be brought up to speed.

In Ray's place of business, his office is just outside of his commander. A lieutenant was invited in to have a sit-down meeting over some issue that pertained to those two members of the brass. At the end of their discussions, the lieutenant exited the CO's office. As he starts to pass the NCO's desk, he notices that Ray's phone is on the corner of the desktop. Ray is in full discussion mode with his candidate and pays little attention to the actions of the lieutenant. The lieutenant picks up the phone and starts to dial. In the middle of the lieutenant's phone conversation, Ray looks at his candidate and asks him, *"Will you excuse me for just a second?"* The lieutenant has the phone to his ear and his back turned on Ray as if to raise some semblance of privacy in such a short distance. Ray immediately grabs the phone line and yanks it out of the wall. He picks up the base of the phone and throws it out the open window behind his desk. This action ripped the phone cord from the base as it flew out. The lieutenant is left there with nothing more than a receiver in his hand. He stands there for a second in disbelief. Ray responds quickly to the blank-looking officer. In a loud and stern voice, he tells him, *"Can't you see that I am in the middle of something here?"* The tone and volume of his voice again shocks the young officer. The lieutenant tells him, *"Do you know who the hell you are talking to?"* Ray says, *"That, SIR, is not important, nor relevant!"*

This is the moment that the CO reacts. The door was left open when the lieutenant left him. This afforded a direct line of sight to the incident. By this point, the CO had made his way to the outer office. He is not a happy camper. Commanding officers do not desire to resolve such mundane issues. But he knows that he is the only one who can. He immediately informs the young lieutenant, *"Go back into my office and have a seat. Shut the door. I will be with you in a second!"* He watches as the LT follows the colonel's orders. When the door shuts, he turns to Ray. *"Don't worry about this. I got this. Carry on."* He returns to his office and shuts the door. In short order, Ray can hear his CO's voice raise a few octaves as he begins to berate the officer.

Ray is a little distracted by the conversation that he is having with his cadet and the words coming out of the colonel's mouth. The cadet is dummying up and only focused on Ray. Ray hears the CO saying, *"That is my NCO. You might as well look at him as an extension of me. He does what I tell him to do. He does his job well. You might outrank him on the sidewalk. That means something, but when you come into these offices, things are a bit different. Your rank is no reason for being disrespectful to one my subordinates. He didn't get this job because he is some kind of desk jockey flunky. Did you notice the bars and fruit salad he as on? That man has seen more action than you may ever see. He is why this office runs as good as it does."* The colonel carries on further and with each statement that he makes, Ray relaxes a bit more and returns his focus back to the cadet in front of him. Satisfied, he gets back to business.

Ray wraps up his conversation with the cadet and scurries him out of the office. A few minutes later, after the voices in the other room settle down, the young officer exits the CO's office. If Ray expected an apology, it wasn't forthcoming. The man does stop at his desk as he was leaving. Ray stands up from his seated position. In unison, they both salute each other. He returns to his seat and the lieutenant moves out. Nothing more is said. [1]

In the Classroom

Ray's involvement with his cadets takes many aspects in to play. Oftentimes, cadets would question him on situations that he was a party to. They would ask him about his time in Germany. How cold was it in Korea? What is it like in Vietnam? All these questions are easy to respond to. Being there makes a difference. But Ray takes advantage of these question-and-answer opportunities to teach. In one particular instance, a cadet asked him about friendly fire.

Ray explains, *"Friendly fire is a complicated issue. It represents many difficulties for many different reasons. It is virtually impossible to escape the inevitability of friendly fire in a war environment. When you put one million people in an enclosed environment, it should be a foregone conclusion that someone is going to die by accident. You could be working in darkness, or a triangulation given to a fire team might be misunderstood on the radio. Flawed munitions of a mortar team can create this. Weather conditions might put contaminants into a firing situation. A more common example would be something as timing.*

"In an example of something so innocuous as taking a hill could result in deaths by friendly fire. Let's take that example and expand upon it. Assume a commander makes plans to have two different companies take a specific hilltop. Company A is charged with aggressing the hill from the east. Company B is charged with aggressing to the top from the west. Both companies begin their attacks with mortar teams, bazookas, and the like. They both make progress to route the enemy from two different sides. The enemy, holding the high ground, realizes that there are two companies coming at them. As both platoons battle their way upward, the enemy takes retreating action down the north face of the hill. Air assault planes are making strafing runs on the mountaintop as both companies move upward. Timing is everything. That is why communications is so important.

"So, here we have planes flying several miles in a circle with their target set at the top of the hill. The two platoons are firing though brush and trees when they reach the top. You're in the preverbal din of war at this point. Many shots can be fired before they discover that they are actually shooting at each other. An attempt to put the enemy in a crossfire has failed because

the enemy responded with a well-timed retreat. Now both platoons are in the position once held by the enemy. The aircraft flying overhead are coming in for another run, but the hill has already been taken. Communications to the flight crew to call off the strike is not relayed in time. They're moving at a couple of hundred miles an hour and can't really tell who is on the hilltop, but they do see movement. This event could happen in broad daylight. It is even more complicated with a night mission. Everyone looks the same as they did when the aircraft first strafed the hill. You are locked into a perfect storm. Bombs are released, or machine gun fire from above is brought to bear. But by then, it is too late. Your men have been hit. I can't stress enough the value of being as exacting as possible in planning. Your missions have two objectives. Mission 1 is to complete the mission. Mission 1a, equal to mission 1, is to look out for your men. Events such as this happened during the Korean War. You have a duty to learn from these types of events. That is why a good commander studies his craft." [1]

It is in questioning such as this that Ray's talent really shines through. With experience and knowledge comes wisdom. He can make the transition from jungle to spit shines. He can also gain the respect of his men without demanding it. Working so closely with the higher brass has afforded him life lessons and techniques that he might not have otherwise been privy to. That is not to mention the contacts that would allow him to accomplish things that some men of his rank and caliber may not have been able to achieve. That is not to say that he can't be challenged. Every once in a while, a subject is presented to him that surprises him and requires him to reflect. As with any teacher-student relationship, the teacher is sometimes taken into subjects that have no great answer. But as an instructor, he is compelled to address the question nonetheless.

In a country under war, millions of people are trying to kill each other. They are relegated to move in areas that they are unaccustomed to. Ducking and dodging bullets and traps layed out to kill. The stress of these events can cause abnormal thinking under pressure. The issue of suicide is brought up. Ray addresses this issue in a broader sense. He explains, *"I think suicide of a soldier is one of the most courageous actions of a broken soldier may ever undertake. These men are put under enormous pressure. They see things that the majority of the world will only read about in the newspapers. Not everyone can keep things straight in their head. Because it is such an individual experience, there is basically no single answer that can be used to resolve all the different problems and variances for every soldier. It has been my experience that these men come home from war broken and beaten. They carry with them all these terrible memories of their times in combat. They may even feel guilt for being a survivor when all their friends were not so lucky. Some get entangled in issues that they thought, had they done something different, the outcome would have been more positive. It is, or can easily become, too much to bear. They realize their issues. They understand that they are broken and messed up. They don't want their families and friends to have to carry the brunt of their issues. They believe that they can only bring harm and problems to what they perceive as a normal life when they return. I believe this is the contributing factor to their choice. For me, it is great act of courage to step off and remove themselves. I am not condoning the action, but only trying to explain my take on the issue. Clearly we need more help within the military to help these men reclaim their lives when they return. For some, it is too little, and too late."* [1]

By 1968, with Vietnam in full gear, Ray finds himself in a troubling position. He had graduated many cadets by this point. The men of the training HQs had done a fine job of preparing these young officers for the positions of leadership for which they sought. These are not the times of precolonial Britain where officers held a safer position than that of the enlisted or draftee. There is no king of the United States, and officers do get targeted and killed in action. It is a somber day on base for these instructors. One of their cadets, who graduated as a second lieutenant under their tutelage, was killed in Vietnam. Lieutenant Rogers was sent back to Kentucky for burial. The officers and NCOs of his training brigade had cleared their daily rosters to attend the funeral fifteen miles north of Fort Knox. Bethany Cemetery is his final resting place. The graveyard sits on the corner of Interstate 265W and State Road 31W. Lieutenant Rogers was given a full military funeral. It is a truly sad day. Ray felt compelled to attend, but he knew this would not be the only funeral that he would be a part of. [1]

Out of the Mouths of Babes

Life at Fort Knox was curiously different for the Cottrell family than for their peers outside of the base. The home life is full of great social times with the family, but pitted and pocked with events that can never be forgotten. Brenda and Ray Jr. are at home with Lovey during the day in the summer months. Brenda has grown into a normal teenager with a gregarious personality, not so different from most girls her age. Ray Jr. is a very precocious young man that has taken to the outside like most kids his age. Communication between Lovey and Ray during his working hours is relegated to Ray making a phone call to his wife from the office when he is not busy with paperwork, educational processes, or educating in the field. Phone calls to Ray from Lovey during these working hours is virtually nonexistent. That tends to put the burden of childrearing squarely on Lovey's shoulders for the most part. Her chastisements to her kids on occasion would be backed up with a stern *"Wait till your father gets home!"* These words make most any young child freeze in his/her tracks. This process has been realized by many a mom in this age and time. Age and time has everything to do with it. The '60s are a far different world than the '30s and '40s that the young couple grew up in. Like the songs on the radio's top 100 list shows, things change. Sometimes slowly, sometimes more quickly than one would want to imagine.

Those Damn Phone Calls

Ray Jr. had found himself on the receiving end of one of Lovey's chastisements. At the age of five, he was being reprimanded in a teachable moment with his mother. Little Ray had let curiosity get the best of him, as most five-year-olds will do. Taking apart toasters, leaving bikes in the driveway for Mom to back over with her car, melting crayons on the heat register, and fixing their own breakfast as Mom is in the backyard hanging clothes out to dry are but a few of the events that can send a hardworking, well-meaning mother over the edge. It is the nature of things. And sometimes parents say something to their children that they wish they could take back. That is what occurs on this particular day.

Lovey's creative, self-sufficient young son has made a mess in the house. As if she didn't have a hundred other things to get done this day. She now has to stop and correct her son. In her frustration over the mess that he has made, she spouts to Ray Jr., *"I am going to kill you, son."* [2] This is a very innocuous statement as it comes out, but alas, the value of those words means something else to someone on the outside. As Lovey is in the process of cleaning up the mess, Ray Jr., in fear of the spanking that he is convinced is coming shortly, sneaks out the front door and heads off.

The Fort Knox base is littered with phones. These phones are put in locations that allow for communications to base authorities. It is a convenient system set out about the base to relay information quickly and easily. It is not unlike the phone boxes that are seen in New York in the '40s or the ones used by British constables in the UK. The exception to these phone boxes is that they don't need keys to access the receivers on the inside. The young boy is aware of this. In lieu of the stern teachable moment that awaits him, he has decided to call it in. He is just tall enough to get the door to the phone box open. On the other end is an operator. She has direct lines of communications to whatever department that might need to be called out for whatever emergency. The operator on the other end was not prepared for the words that she heard next.

Ray's child-sized voice responds to her, *"Hello, what is the emergency?"* with a very meek and cracking sound. "My mom is gonna kill me!" he says. Timing again plays a role in the matter. Lovey had finished cleaning up his mess and began the process of rounding up her son. She has searched the house to realize that Ray Jr. is not in it. She had made her way outside just in time to see him finish his statement. The phone is still in his hands. She yells for him to come to her immediately. Little Ray sheepishly hangs up the phone and sprints back to his mother. He knows by the sound of her voice that dawdling will do him no good. She grabs him by the wrist and escorts him back to the house as tears start to form. She is forced to grill him on what just happened. Fortunately, no one else on the street has seen what has just transpired. It takes a minute, but he confesses to her what he said to the operator. She now knows that both of them can be in trouble for the occurrence. The only thing to do is to do nothing. Word of this getting back to Ray Sr.'s superior officers will do him and the family no good whatsoever.

It takes no time at all before the entire neighborhood is swarmed with MP jeeps cruising the housing units in search of who made the phone call. Ray has been sent to his bedroom until further notice. Lovey, on the other hand, is now dealing with her decision and praying that it will all work out. In her fears, she sits near the window and looks out in the hope that the MPs will give up and just move along. After several minutes of nervous tension, that is exactly what the jeeps do. She has been a military wife for quite some time now. She understands certain protocols. Fortunately, her gamble has paid off. Adrenaline still coursing through her veins. It has all worked out. Ray Sr. is informed of the incident much later during one of his phone calls home. He is compelled not to speak of it while at the office but assures her that he will have his say with his son when he gets home. Ray Jr., on the other hand, is confined to quarters until further notice.

This will not be the first time that Ray Jr. is on the receiving end of innocent entanglements with the law. Life on the base is simple. It is not uncommon to see boys and girls riding their bikes in the streets unobserved by their parents. They could and would travel blocks away from their homes unattended. Safety for one's children is a foregone conclusion when living on a military base. But in and amongst this microcosm of security, children find a way to explore and, in so doing, create a much unexpected outcome. It is not unusual for Ray Jr. to take his wagon out in search of things to do. What could be more innocent than a young boy and his friend walking down the street, pulling his little red Radio Flyer? On this particular day, though, he is not pulling jugs of water or stuffed animals. He and his friend had managed to locate a tanker's unexploded ammunition round. Like some of his friends, his buddy and he were planning to place the shell in a vice, separate the gunpowder from the shell, and use it to make fireworks. He had seen this done with his friends, except his friends had used bullets.

For Ray Jr., he thought he had hit the jackpot. In his mind, "Oh what a firework this amount of gunpowder was going to produce!"

The intent was to put the shell in a vice grip to separate the ballistic from the sparkly gunpowder of its casing. It had worked with so many bullets before. Even at his age, he was aware that ignited gunpowder would burn out much in the way a sparkler would do on the Fourth of July. It is only when the fine powder is ignited in an enclosed environment like a casing that it generates a truly violent reaction. While the basics of making fireworks is a relatively simple process, what he is not aware of is the fact that these types of munitions can be set off easily and kill savagely. Ray had been toting this piece for several blocks and through many acres of terrain from which they found it. It had fallen out many times in the tumbling of the wheels that ran roughshod over the fields and through the streets. He had turned the wagon over more than once as his friend and he attempted to get it back to the house.

As the two boys approach the house, everything seems to be in order. It is at that moment that his mother sees the wagon turn over and his newly found toy comes rolling out. A very large tank round hits the ground. She sees the two boys grabbing the shell from both ends and quickly realizes what it actually is. Immediately she is thrust into a life-and-death moment. She yells at the boys "**STOP!** *Don't touch that! Don't move!*" She moves closer to the boys. "Step away from there and don't touch it again!" [2] The boys are a bit startled, but they are quick to follow her directions. She is flush with adrenaline as she moves in to collect the kids. The wagon and the shell are in a field a short distance away from the house. Somehow and from somewhere, these two had acquired their piece somewhere near the gun ranges on base, but for his parents, Ray Jr. was just emerging from the fields out front from one of his many explorations.

This event will require immediate and unavoidable attention. After securing the kids, she gets on the phone and calls the base operator. The operator is quick to take charge and urges Lovey to stay away from the fully intact shell. It was a request that was a foregone conclusion, but it is required to say. The operator gets off the phone after Lovey gives out her house address and all the particulars of the situation. Lovey hangs up the phone and puts a call into Ray's office, one of very few times that she would actually call him first. She is in luck. He is at his desk. She explains to Ray what is happening as she glares out the backdoor keeping an eye on the device. Ray is compelled to inform his superior and gets clearance to go home early. The emergency response teams are all buzzing now. Ray heads to his vehicle and makes the quick journey back home as fast as he dare.

Lovey is in the yard monitoring things to ensure no one goes near. She could have never have planned in a million years that she would be in this position. The first to arrive are the MPs. Two jeeps show up, and the four men that manned them are walking toward Lovey and the wagon. The first thing to do is to quarantine the immediate area. With their radios packed on their hips, Lovey hears the chatter as the base comes alive with action. Ray Sr. has arrived on the scene and is coming to Lovey's side. He consoles her as best he can and relays that everything will be okay now. The first firetruck arrives, and then another. A few more jeeps arrive. One of them has an officer of considerable rank on board. He immediately looks over the situation and begins the task of organizing everyone. Ray is focused on the matter at hand but also on the repercussions that play a role down the line.

Because Ray had conferred to his general the situation, the general himself had gone into action. He is motivated by the safety issue as well. "How can an unexploded shell fall into the hands of a minor on his base?" More importantly, "Who are the responsible parties? What are the protocols to resolve the current issue, and what is it that can be done to ensure that it never happens again." The information, first and foremost, needs to be directed to the base commander. Ray was quick to notify him. Specifically, there is no standard operational procedure for such an occurrence. While there are protocols for handling live shells, there is nothing in the manual on what to do when a child hauls one home in a wagon. These procedures are put into action. Fort Knox is not in short supply of explosive ordinance disposal (EOD) personnel. The U.S. Army EOD school is in Ray's home state of Virginia, but their graduates are spread amongst many major bases throughout the states and abroad. These few men are quickly brought into play at Ray's home.

More than a few hours have transpired before the EOD team make their final preparations to remove the ordinance. There are now more than twenty vehicles on Ray's street. Darkness is about to set in. Ray Jr., who had been standing outside with his sister and parents, notices that there are four men standing at "parade rest" in full field dress. It is assumed that they are part of the tank command that had originally lost operational control of this specific shell. They could have been part of a team that is required to manage live ordinance before it is issued to the tankers. They could have been part of the team that manages all fire on the tank range. Ray Jr. can't tell, but he knows that someone other than himself is in more trouble than he is in. All that he has been asked so far is, *"Where did you find this?"*

A truck had been put fifty-plus yards away from his wagon that is still in the field. A grounding wire had been strung from the truck and attached to the shell. The EOD team wants to ensure that something as simple as static electricity doesn't set the ordinance off. That is just one of the ways that Ray Jr. could have accidentally lost his life. It is a thought that is squarely on his parents' minds. The two specialists, in full bomb disposal attire, have placed the shell in a cradle from which the two of them could easily manage to carry. They have loaded the piece and are now making their way to the truck. They are well within earshot of the young boy. Ray Jr. has still not realized the gravity of the situation but still wants to be helpful. He asks the men, *"If you want, I can put that in the truck for you."* Lovey reaches out and squeezes his hand to promote his silence. Ray Sr. knows he will giggle over this event, but it will take years before he shares that humor with his spouse and his children. Lovey and Ray Sr. are both just thankful that it has come to an end. [2]

Woman of the House

Their daughter Brenda has also had her memorable moments as well. She is a very concerned and intelligent child in her own right. As the firstborn child of the family, she is the apple of her parents' eye. Like the other members of her family, she has a strong commitment to duty and responsibility. She is never fearful to act as needs be. Like her father, she has an innate ability to stand up for what is right and against what is wrong. She is quick into action when that need arrives. She will help Lovey around the house. She keeps an eye on Ray Jr. when her mother needs it. She gets her homework done when she is told.

All the things that a young girl has expected of her are in play in her life and a few extra to boot. While attending school, one of her fellow female classmates was found being bullied by a larger, more aggressive female. Brenda flies into action in defense of the smaller child. While Brenda is petite in frame herself, she showed no concern for her personal safety as she put herself between the girl and the bully immediately. Even though she was outsized, Brenda calls the larger girl out and insists that she should fight her instead. Caught off guard, and perhaps a little fearful of the outcome, the larger girl decides that it is not in her best interest to take part in what could have been an ensuing melee. When the girl moves off, Brenda informs her classmate, *"If you ever have a problem with this girl again, just let me know."* It is a welcome relief to the young girl to know that someone is on her side. The bullying comes to an end.

Like most teenage girls of her time, she is attracted to music, dancing, skating, and having sleepovers. It is such a night as this that Brenda, once again, goes into action in defense of her friends and family. One of her friends from the base is spending the night. Two young teens hanging out in her bedroom, talking about boys, listening to the radio, and skimming magazines are the order of the night. Lovey had stepped out to make a run to the commissary. She takes Ray Jr. with her so that Brenda is not distracted with babysitting on her night.

The radio is blasting, and the girls are working on their dancing styles. As the music plays, Brenda's attention is called to the window. A dark figure could be seen just outside. Her friend becomes quite scared and is not sure what to do or how to react. Brenda, on the other hand, knows exactly what to do. Her father had taken the time to expressly explain the workings of guns and what to do in an emergency. She has but one option. She moves into her parents' bedroom and retrieves the loaded rifle from their room. Her window is on the back side of the house. There is no reason for anyone to be in her backyard at this hour of the night, and they sure as hell have no right to be peeking into young girls' windows. She takes the loaded rifle to the backdoor, ensuring that it is loaded and ready to fire when it opens. Brenda has her friend open the door for her and stands behind it as Brenda ventures out to the back porch. When she looks down the back side of the house, she sees a figure running into the tree line across the backfield. She fires a shot toward the assailant and yells, *"You better get your ass out of here!"* She fires another shot in the person's direction. Both girls are now standing on the porch like sentries in the Roman legionnaires. Secure in the thought that this person will not be returning now, both girls go back to her room and talk about the event. She knows that she will have to inform her mother and father about this. [3]

A short while later, Lovey returns home. After a sufficient amount of time has been allowed for her mother to settle in from her trip, Brenda approaches her mother. *"I had a bit of a problem while you were gone, but don't worry, I took care of it"* she says. Lovey looks around the room for a possible issue and returns to looking at Brenda and asks, *"What happened?"* Brenda tells her, *"I think we had a Peeping Tom."* Surprised by this, and anxious to hear what has transpired, Brenda continues, *"I took Dad's shotgun out and saw a man in the field out back. So I fired off a couple of shots at him. I do not know if I hit him. I don't think I did but I am not sure."* Lovey asks, *"Where is the gun now?"* Brenda tells here it is back in her room and quickly goes and retrieves it. Lovey says, *"You know I am going to have to tell your dad when he gets home? I don't know what he is going to say or do about this."* Brenda lowers her head in agreement and stands there. Lovey informs the two girls to go back to her room and lets them know that it will be addressed in the morning after she and Ray had a chance to talk about it.

Brenda is informed that her father will speak to her about it when he gets the chance. He and Lovey have decided that there is no punishment to be issued over the ordeal. Ray gives his daughter a more specific lesson on when and where to use a firearm as a reminder. Part of him is proud and wants to congratulate the child for her actions. Another part of

ROBERT BROOKS

him has to maintain a certain amount of control over his reactions and her actions. Lovey, on the other hand, is working to come to grips with another aspect of life as a military wife. It is not a common event by any measure, but coming to terms with this type of thing will have to be figured in. The unexpected is slowly becoming part of the norm. [3]

CHAPTER 10

TET

IN LATE SEPTEMBER 1967, the CIA and MACV had joined to draw up estimates regarding the size and scope of the enemy forces in Vietnam. The CIA, after making discoveries in Operations Cedar Falls and Junction City, had decided that the combined forces of NVA in the north and insurgents in the south stood at about 430,000. Staff and intelligence at MACV held that the total was about 300,000. It was the intent to come to an agreement so that the administration would have a good working number to draw from in this war of attrition. It was the combined belief of all in Washington that, if we can take out more enemy faster than they could recruit, the war was winnable. No one in the United States at that time believed that the war couldn't be won. The numbers, on the other hand, suggested that they may have underestimated the driving forces of the communists. Confusion over the overall estimates created a quandary for the administration as they made their decisions on how best to approach. Thinking by all groups up on the Hill believed that there was no way, regardless of either perceived number, that the communists could gather a significant counteroffensive to drive out the Western forces.

[2]

In January 1967, the public viewpoint against communist aggression on the subject of Vietnam held a 25 percent sway against the actions in the country. By late summer, that number would grow to 45 percent against the war. By January 1968, all the combined knowledge of the commanders in the West were proven wrong in their conventional thinking on the enemy's ability, however. On *Tổng tiến công và nổi dậy Tết Mậu Thân,* January 30, 1968, the Vietnamese New Year (Tet), communist forces launched the largest counteroffensive in the engagement yet. A well-coordinated strike with over eighty thousand communist combatants in the field took one hundred cities and towns, gaining control of 36 of the 44 provincial capitals. This marked the day of the Tet Offensive. The communists killed thousands of civilians and military alike over the next eight months with a new influx of Chinese and Russian support. When control was returned, the Mini-Tet was brought to bear. It was the last gasps of a failing military. Control returned to the Western forces and their allies in the country in short order, but that is not how it was being perceived in the court of public opinion back home.

Meanwhile, back in the states, the media is having a field day misreporting and kicking up dust and dirty laundry. There were reports of U.S. forces carpet bombing villages along with a host of other realities of war that the U.S. citizenry was being presented with. No civilian area was ever carpet-bombed, but that didn't stop the media from sensationalizing the amount of bombs or bullets being used in the war effort. The media's lack of understanding of the issues of Vietnam offered them the opportunity to sway the civilians to a false belief of an unwinnable war, all for the purpose of getting people to read their papers and watch their TV channels. The truth is far and a field away from their reports. Simple truths are being overlooked and ignored, giving way to more specific personal views of the engagement. Tet produced eighty thousand enemy combatants in their push to overtake the south. This was a small number compared to the hundreds of thousands that U.S. was up against in WWII or Korea. Their firepower and logistics could not match the forces they were facing by any stretch. While the Tet Offensive caught our forces by surprise, it was defeated. The Mini-Tet was repulsed as well. By 1969, the majority of actions in Vietnam were driven by much smaller guerilla-type warfare. We were winning. At least until the media and the country swayed in the other direction.

For the family back home, Lovey is once again asked to bear the brunt of parenting for yet another tour. It is in November of 1968 that Ray finds himself being asked to go back to the front. He is finishing up with the training of Co. G of the OCS Bde at Fort Knox. A fine group of young men are now preparing to move out to the war-torn country. Ray has been asked by members of the 26th Infantry of the 1st Division to travel back to Vietnam as an E9 CSM. He will take up his position in Lai Kai. Ben Cat and Lai Kai is the stomping grounds of the Twenty-Sixth Infantry in

AHBAAS-OC   1 August 1967

SUBJECT: Letter of Commendation

TO: First Sergeant Raymond H. Cottrell
             Company G, Officer Candidate Brigade
             US Army Armor School
             Fort Knox, Kentucky 40121

1. On my departure from the Officer Candidate Brigade, I want to make a matter of record the truly outstanding contribution you as a first sergeant have made to the successful operation of the Brigade.

2. It is readily recognized that your duties as first sergeant are complicated and highly diversified in this unique unit. It is further recognized that the burden of detailed administration is many times that of a normal TO&E line company, yet the requirements for leadership remain the same.

3. Through such dedicated professional and untiring efforts as you personally have given in this Brigade, the officer candidates who have received their training in Company G have started their careers as Army officers well prepared to attain any goal they may have established in the pursuit of their military careers.

4. I am deeply grateful to have had the opportunity of commanding this unit, and feel that the privilege of serving with so many outstanding soldiers has made it one of the finest assignments of my Army career. It is my sincere hope that I shall be fortunate enough as to again serve with you in any assignment within the military establishment.

BERNARD E. McKEEVER
Colonel, Armor
Commanding

[2]

Vietnam. Their area of operation borders Cambodia to the northwest and just outside of Saigon to the southeast. The operational area is dissected by the infamous highway, Thunder Road, just like the arrowhead that defines the Blue Spaders. Ray is about to find himself again at the tip of the spear. The family will have to get by for another tour. It is not a quick decision for Ray, but it is the decision that he chooses. Lovey always knew that Ray volunteered for these events. She took his military orders with no complaint. Like Ray, it was who she was.

While Lovey is back in the states holding down the fort, Ray has landed at the Ton Son Nhut airport. He is armed before he makes his way to a bus that will take him to Ben Cat and Camp Dobol. He is reminded of the heat and smells of Vietnam; the oppressive humidity that weighs a man down just walking from one point to another. He is reminded of his time in '63–'64 by all the colors of the local shops and traffic. It seems to him that the sheer volume of people has increased dramatically. People moving about on bicycles and Lambrettas with no definable sense of direction. Things have changed much since his last tour. The military bus he is traveling in has wire screens covering the windows to prevent grenades from coming into it. It is a small defense, but necessary. The further he travels away from Saigon, the more rural the area becomes. He notices the changes in the buildings around the airport and the massive number of citizens and personnel.

Upon his arrival at Dobol HQ, he sets his attention to the changed parameters of his environment. It takes no time to get adjusted. Within the week, he is well-organized and producing for the army. His talents are sought after and highly respected within his circle of operations. His organizational skills, along with intimate knowledge of both Vietnam and military engagements, makes him more than qualified for the position that he was asked to fill. The decision to go had more to do with going where he is needed than to add to his accolades. He is a front-line man. Ray wants to be where the action is. He is a warrior, not a résumé soldier. He is a seasoned warrior at that with a penchant for details and planning as well.

Dobol HQ was appropriately named after the first-ever CSM in the U.S. Army. Dobol was a friend and mentor or Ray's. Their paths had crossed many times in his career. Camp Dobol is the HQ for the 26th Infantry of Big Red 1.

Getting accustomed to his men takes no time. Some of the men in his command had served with him before. This makes the transition from spit shines to jungle a little easier. He is quick to make connections in regards to finding who has what and where to go to get what the battalion needs, all the proactive thinking that makes him one of the best supporting NCOs to his officers that he can be. It is in this vein that has garnered him the ability to be in this position in the first place. His promotions have always been well deserved. His commanders take no time in deploying his skills to the benefit of the command center.

Ranger Joe

Relationships sometimes develop from an off-chance meeting. Sometimes those relationships go further than expected at first glance. Within the Twenty-Sixth Infantry, Ray comes to know a fellow Kentuckian. Ray's family is located off base of Fort Knox. The sprawling base that is found in three counties of Kentucky: Bullitt, Meade, and Hardin. Ray's home is in Hardin County. His property fronts up to the base itself along a forested area at the edge.

Not so far from his home is another family, a large Catholic family with many kids. The Greenwell family has many successful children in their clan, including a doctor and two nurses. It is a close-knit family with a mind to service. Of their children, one has entered the army. Joe Greenwell is a young adventurous soul who entered the army at eighteen. He had graduated ranger school and OCS. He found himself in the First Division along with Ray. Joe, because of his ranger experience, was nicknamed Ranger Joe. Greenwell is a first lieutenant of November platoon in the Twenty-Sixth Infantry. Ray is with CP HQ of the 2nd Battalion of the 26th Infantry. Ray's CP oversees three platoons. November platoon is one of these three. There are more than a few times when the two men's paths would cross.

It is uncommon to have someone so close to home as well as so close to the family. Joe Greenwell's mother is a close friend of Lovey's back in the states. A bond had developed between the two ladies quite organically. Their paths crossed while working with the women of the Twenty-Sixth Infantry back on base. The two families' interconnection would grow as time passed. With Ray's phone calls back home, Lovey would oftentimes relay information to Mrs. Greenwell as well on the status of her son.

It had come to Mrs. Greenwell's attention that the letters coming home from her son had slowed to a stop. She shares this with Lovey in hopes that she can convince Ray to put a bug in Joe Greenwell's ear. Mothers are attached to their sons overseas, and it is not uncommon for them to use any means necessary to look out for them even if they are 6,000 miles away. Out of respect to Joe's mother, Lovey relays the information to Ray in the hope of urging Joe to begin writing again. Joe, on the other hand, is a highly motivated soldier. Much like Ray, he is striving to make a difference with his men and within the Twenty-Sixth. One should never overlook the connections between a husband and his wife or the bonds between a mother and her son.

When Ray learns of the lack of communication from Joe and his mother, he takes a moment to go and speak with the young lieutenant. He was not hard to find. Ray tells Joe, *"I have gotten word through my wife that your mother had spoken with her. She informed Lovey that you have not been writing any letters home."* Ray takes advantage of this event as a teachable moment for the twenty-one-year-old lieutenant. He continues, *"Joe, you are supposed to be setting an example for your men. It is a conflict to have you require your men to be writing home and you not doing the same. They look to you as thier leader, and as such, you should be doing the same things that you expect of them, and in fact even better. Here is what we need to do. We are going to take my jeep to Lai Khe. The Signal Corps have tied in communications with the states via ham radio. I am going up there to talk to my wife. It is a simple process. You put your name on a list, and when they call your name, they are ready to make contact with home."* [3]

Convinced by Ray's admonishment, the two men take the ride into Lai Khe. It is just weeks before the holidays start. The two men head to the communications building. Everything is as Ray discribed. The two sign the list and step outside to await their names to be called. Joe had never taken advantage of this process and in fact didn't know that the option even existed. As they sit outside, Ray takes advantage of a cigarette as the two men talk amongst themselves and the other soldiers there.

It takes about thirty minutes for Ray to have his name called. He enters the building and has a five-minute conversation with Lovey. He is quick to inform her that he has Joe with him and that he has done as he has promised. Relieved, Lovey is quick to give Ray an update of the other issues at home. It is a pleasant conversation, and both are relieved for a time to have contact with one another. The conversation ends with a reminder to each other of their love and that Ray will contact her again as soon as possible. He leaves the building feeling a little grounded and relaxed, but he is quick to catch back up with Joe. *"I am going to hitch a ride back to base, Joe. You can have my jeep. Just wait till they call your name, and then you can talk to home."* Joe nods in agreement and thanks Ray as he heads off.

It takes no time at all for Ray to make it back to base at Ben Cat. When he gets there, he drops some things off in his hooch and heads back outside. When he walks out the door, he sees the lieutenant pulling up in his jeep. He realizes that Joe had to have left almost immediately from Lai Khe for him to get back to the base so fast. With out showing too much frustration, he admonishes Joe again and says, *"You could not possibly have been done calling home and gotten back here so quick. We are going back to Lai Khe. Your mother is awaiting your call and I committed to ensure that you do. So let's get this done."* Joe had gotten impatient waiting and that is why he left so quickly. He tells Ray that he has a lot on his plate and wanted to get back to get things in order. When the two men park their jeep and walk up to the building, a young soldier pops his head out and calls out, *"Joe Greenwell? Lieutenant Joe Greenwell?"* They had gotten back just in time for his call. Ray waits for him to return. When Joe gets back in the jeep, he appologizes to Ray but thanks him for taking the time to work this out. He had decided that it was a good thing to relieve his mother of her concerns and wished that he had done it sooner. He commits to Ray that he will be more dilligent in his letter writing. Joe had not really appreciated his mother's issues until he talked to her. He was so focused on his duties that he believed that in the end, it was okay to have such long lapses with his family. This phone call changed all that. [3]

Days later, plans had been made to take out three platoons, along with the HQ platoon, on a recon and ambush mission. The ambushes were a routine event and to be set up before nightfall. They would hold their positions through the night. Each platoon had stopped prior to their final locations to eat. Having an MRE in the field can be detrimental to scouting and ambush missions. The smell of the enemy cooking rice could give up their positions just as easily as the sound of opening up a tin can give up a platoon. Leaving the trash behind as well could be an easy marker for recon groups looking to cross the opposing forces. The simple act of smoking a cigarette could give up a position. It had been decided to break for a meal away from the original objectives to prevent giving up the locations of the ambushes. The area was a known hotspot for VC activity.

Each platoon had their own assignments for the night. Shortly after eating, while the men were still preparing to move out into their location, Ranger Joe wants to recon the area ahead before they move the company out. Three squad leaders, the point man, and the radioman move out with Ranger Joe into the jungle while leaving the company behind to rest up and prepare to move out. Joe is insistent on reconning the area they have to travel to get into their position.

Ray is working with the CP group behind November Platoon. He hears gunfire from his position. Immediately, he is on the radio and tries to make contact with November Platoon to see what the action was. But November Platoon was not answering their radio. The joint operation was designed to work in unison with each other. It will not do to have one platoon out of contact. Something must be wrong. Ray takes a soldier with him and heads out to the last known area of November Platoon. When he reaches their area he doesn't see Joe, the radioman, or any of the leadership of the company. He asks a soldier, "*Where the hell is everyone?*" The private responds, "Lieutenant Greenwell took Sergeant Baker, his point man, the radio, and all of his squad leaders forward to recon ahead."

Ray immediately takes command of the men and musters them to head out in the direction that the ranger had taken. The choice that Greenwell made was against army protocol. Ray knows this. It must be addressed immediately. You don't take leadership out on such a venture without backup. In this case, Joe had taken all the command structure of his platoon away from their command.

They travel about five hundred yards ahead before he finds the problem. The small group of men had walked into a VC ambush. They had gotten pinned down by a machine gun bunker and sporadic cover fire. Their point man Baker is dead, and the radio had been hit and put out of commission. Lieutenant Joe Greenwell is alive but wounded

ROBERT BROOKS

in action. He has taken a bullet to the chest and is in desperate need of medical attention. He was laying in front of the machine gun nest. It was too hot a position to take head-on. Ray charges the radioman to work on the unit to get it working again. He calls back to the CP with his radio to inform them of the situation. The VC, knowing that the injured lieutenant would draw more soldiers to his aid, was using him as bait to draw more soldiers forward. It created a delicate situation. Joe was laying up at a point in front of the machine gun nest. The nest was built up with sandbag walls just fifty yards ahead. Ray could see it and Ranger Joe from his position. No one could go forward to get the injured man down with out getting shot themselves in the process, nor could they take out the bunker with Greenwell still up there.

Ray moves forward and knows that if he can see the bunker, the VC in the bunker could see him. He calls out for some rope and a grappling hook. The hook is made of aluminum, which made it light and easy to throw. The plan was to throw it up to Greenwell and use it to drag him back to the men. The platoon is hunkered down to give cover fire on the nest, while Ray moves forward with in range and throws the hook up at Joe. After several failed attempts, he manages to hook his ammo vest. Three men gang up on the rope with Ray, and they start to pull the lieutenant out of range of the bunker. As they start to pull, the grappling hook sets off a green smoke grenade and a tear gas grenade. It complicates the issue with a nightmare landscape as the men work to pull the man over to them. When he is finally in a position to be pulled to safety, the medic races to work on Joe. Ray calls back to the CP for a dust-off. The company takes on the bunker in earnest with hand grenades and gunfire to end the threat. Ray is at his side and tries to calm Joe, telling him to hang on. The holes in his chest gush blood as the medic rushes to pack it. Greenwell looks up at Ray and says in a gurgling voice, *"I don't want to die, don't let me die."* Ray tells him to stay with him, that he is going to be okay. Helicopters are called in for the wounded and the dead. Joe is immediately moved to a stretcher. [3]

The medic loses the heartbeat, and Ray starts mouth-to-mouth with the lieutenant. The two men work on him frantically to try to keep him alive. In the process, Joe pukes up as he has being resuscitated. Ray spits out the blood that just came up. Blood is filling the soldier's lungs. They get Joe back for a few minutes before he codes again. Ray is pumping the chest cavity to try to get his heartbeat back again, but the entire chest area has softened up. It feels like a cushion on a couch. The entire body has gone limp. The medic looks up at Ray and tells him, "He is gone!" The entire situation comes to a vicious and frantic end. The area is swept when the other platoons converge on the area. Ray stays with Greenwell's corpse as they fly back to the hospital at Lai Khe. He and the medic had been working on Joe most of the way back.

The triage area in front of the hospital building is run by a doctor outside. As the dead and wounded are brought up to the area, a doctor looks over everyone presented and points to one of two buildings. One building is for immediate care, the other is the morgue. As the doctor looks over Joe, Ray watches as the doctor points to the morgue. A numbness crawls up Ray's spine as he sees Joe carried off to the other building. He had a fondness for the twenty-one-year-old soldier and holds himself responsible for his loss. Unfortunately, only so much could be done. He knew it only takes one mistake for something to go horribly bad. There was scant more than he could do, but Ray is committed to the man and to his family back home.

Ray stays at the hospital as other wounded and dead are brought in. *This is wrong*, he thinks to himself. This was all wrong. Baker is dead. Greenwell is dead. The PFC working the platoon's radio was injured during the fight along with the others fighting to take out the VC's bunker. The evening is coming to a close. When he felt secure that the injured were being well taken care of, he decides to go to the morgue to check on the fallen. When he walks in, the first thing that he notices is Lieutenant Greenwell's body still on the stretcher, but the stretcher is laid out on the floor. Ray is the highest-ranking NCO in the Twenty-Sixth Infantry here in Vietnam. He felt offended that there was an open table while his man was lazily spotted to a floor position. He immediately demands the orderlies to place Greenwell's body on the table. None of his men should be treated so. Ray has very little contact with the dead once they went to the morgue, but this was different. He didn't know the morgue's protocol, but that didn't matter. Out

ROBERT BROOKS

of respect, his men should be treated as best as they could. He feels warranted for issuing that order. No one in the building would think of questioning him either.

The following morning, Ray cuts a letter to Lovey to inform her of the situation. It only takes four days for the letter to reach her. In it, he tells her that Joe Greenwell is dead, but under no circumstances is she to inform his mother. That is the army's job. This is privileged information. The stress of that knowledge becomes burdensom for Lovey back at home. Mrs. Greenwell had told Lovey two days before that she received a letter from the army stating that her son Joe was MIA. It was more than the lady could handle. She asked Lovey, "*If you don't mind, I would like to come by to see if you hear anything. I will come to you every day so that you won't be put out.*" This process was started by Mrs. Greenwell before Ray's letter arrives. Lovey is forced to withhold that information once it does. Every day, Mrs. Greenwell would show up, and every day Lovey would have to tell her that she had not received any letters either.

The pressure of this comes to a head for Lovey. She doesn't want to lie to Mrs. Greenwell, but she knows that she is bound by military code not to tell his mother what happened. She is moved to do something. She decides that it would be best to contact Joe's brother. He is a doctor that works in Hardin County. She calls his office and speaks with one of the receptionists. The receptionist is an obstinate lady, but after several urgings by Lovey, Dr. Greenwell is finally put on the line. She tries to prepare him as best she can before she tells him that Joe is dead, but of course, the news is not well received. Dr. Greenwell admonishes Lovey and tells her, "*Don't tell me that! You are not supposed to be telling me this! You are not allowed to tell me this!* Lovey assures him that she didn't want to be the one to tell him that, but his mother had been coming by every day to get news of Joe and she felt compelled to pass it on somehow. She believed, as many mothers believed, that it was his mother's right to know. The doctor hangs up on her.

Dr. Greenwell is compelled to react as well to the news. He finishes up as fast as he can in the office and rushes out to go to his mother's house. As he parks his car in the driveway and gets out, an army limousine pulls up to the front of the house. When the doctor approaches the front porch, an army chaplain and an officer are getting out of their vehicle. The timing of the situation was surreal. Now, Joe's brother would not be required to tell his mother himself, but he would at least be there to comfort her and his father when the news is broken. When she sees the chaplain, she knows what's coming next. It was a scene that played out daily around the country. Today was the Greenwell family's turn in the tragic process. Every mother, father, and wife on base knew what it meant when the chaplain came calling.

For Ray, the commitment to do more is playing out. He had gotten confirmation from his superiors to travel with the body back to the states. It was Ray's intention to ensure the proper processes would be met as the young ranger returned home for burial. He had no problem giving up his leave to make the journey. It is one of the last things that he would ever want to do as sergeant major, but the closeness of the two families will have to be respected.

No Good Deed Goes Unpunished

Ray will be traveling with the body back from Vietnam. The journey will take them to Hawaii. From there they will fly into California. The body will be transferred here to a commercial airliner for the final leg home. The trip from Vietnam to Hawaii is uneventful and somber. He stays with the bird as they refuel it. The trip to San Francisco is also without issue until they land. Ray is required to change planes along with the body for the trip to Louisville. The two are expected to take the same plane from here to Standiford Field. He is in his dress blues for the trip home.

Ray is carrying his duffel with him as he gets into customs in San Francisco. Speaking with the agent, he is informed that the airport has an issue at the moment but hopes that he will not be affected. Ray inquires of him, *"What is going on?"* The agent informs him, *"We have an issue with protestors. Antiwar protesters have taken up their signs and are working in the breezeways at the front of the concourses to the boarding gates."* Ray thanks him for the heads-up and tries to plan for any situation heading out to his concourse. It doesn't take long before he sees a group of people gathered ahead of him. Ray was wishing that he was in plain clothes for this event, but the situation just would not call for it.

The protestors have made a human chain across the concourse exit. He can read the signs "Baby Killer" and "Make Love Not War" in their hands. He has no available options to him. Spotting a police officer nearby, he approaches and asked the man, *"Sir, I am traveling with a fallen soldier. His body has been transferred to my next plane. I have to get through this line to make that flight. Would it be possible that you can escort me through the line to get to my gate?"* The officer informs him that he is only there to ensure that the protest is peaceful. He could not force the people to break their lines to let him through. Ray asks him, *"What are my options here? I have to make that plane."* The officer shrugs as Ray is tapped on his shoulder. He turns around and up to see a very imposing first lieutenant. The young man looks to be about 6'5" and 250 pounds.

"Excuse me, sergeant," the young man interrupts. He has Ray's full attention. The lieutenant continues, *"I am traveling home to see my wife. I will not let this kind of bullshit stop me from getting me home. If you stay on my six, I'm going to rush the line. I can tell you, I am ex-football player, we will get though."* Ray responds, *"I have to make that plane, lieutenant. I am escorting one of our fallen home. I will be right on your tail."* The lieutenant tells him, *"We will start out slow and build up speed. Just stay close."* Ray winks. *"Lead on, son."*

The two men are thirty yards out from the picket line. They see protestors pointing in their direction as they start to move forward. Ray is just off to the side of the lieutenant as the two start to pick up speed. The officer picks his gap between two long-haired, skinny twenty-something males just off the center of the line. Protesters see them coming as Ray drops back to just behind the lieutenant. The protesters' eyes get larger as the two approach. They know what is about to happen and try to look determined as the two gain speed. Everyone is holding hands like they were playing Red Rover. The protesters' voices rise in insults and jeers as they come into the line. It was a split-second game of chicken. The officer puts his duffle in front of him like a shield. Ray has done the same. The two burst through the line as the two young men release their grips to each other and brace themselves for the impact. The officer drops his shoulder and blasts through. Ray sees two protestors spinning to the ground as he passes. Other protestors are yelling and trying to spit on the two as they go by. One guy throws his drink at them but misses. The two men had a clear path ahead of them. None of the protesters would dare to chase them down and confront them now. The two soldiers can now move about the airport as needed. [3]

When the airplane arrives in Louisville, the airport is much more subdued. There are no protestors chanting and marching here. Ray finds Lovey and the kids waiting for him at the gate. In another part of the airport, the Greenwell family watch from the windows as the body is being unloaded from the aircraft. The U.S. flag is draped upon it as it is slid into a waiting hearse. The group looks on as tears begin to form in the eyes of Joe's family. Ray is keeping his emotions in check, torn between the happiness of seeing his family and sullen by the nature of his arrival. It will not do to have everyone caught up in emotions at this point. He is not one for showing too much emotion anyway. There may still be decisions to be made, and Ray wants to be focused so that he can make them.

The Greenwell family moves out to the front of the airport and sees the limo pull up in front of the family's awaiting vehicles. Funeral flags are attached to the growing convoy of cars as they load in for the one-hour ride to the funeral home. Joe's mother is anxious and upset but is fighting to keep her composure. His father is stoic and holds his mother's arm as they pass by the hearse to get into their vehicle. She wants to see her son but knows this is not the time. She will have to wait until they get to the funeral home before she could have that chance. Ray and his family will not be in this procession. They depart the airport, separate from the convoy.

It is a somber day as the couple drives back to Fort Knox. Lovey informs Ray of the funeral arrangements. All this had been prearranged before their arrival. Joe Greenwell's casket will be put in state tommorrow for viewing. It is now two weeks since the young man fell. It will be a closed-casket ceremony. The funeral will be held that following day. Ray's focus now is only on getting home. The only thing he is looking forward to is getting some rest and some quality time with his family before he is required to represent the division at the funeral.

It is a military funeral. Soldiers carry the casket from the limousine to the burial site. The services are short but emotional. The flag is removed from the casket and folded in tradition as "Taps" is being played. The flag is presented to Joe's mother by the officer of the proceedings. It is done. The casket is lowered into the ground. Ray and Lovey approach Joe's mother and offer their last condolences. The families again begin to move off to their vehicles. When Lovey and Ray get into their car, she informs him that they are expected to arrive at the Greenwell house directly. They are to have dinner with the family. Mrs. Greenwell had insisted on this for all that Ray had done.

Several cars are parked in the driveway and yard. The Greenwell family is big; Ray thinks they have ten children. The friends of the family are also in attendance. Some have come to offer condolences, but almost all bring prepared food for the family and flowers from the funeral. Several people have gathered. Lovey is standing with Ray as Joe's brother, the doctor, asks to speak with her. She steps over to him and his mother. Dr. Greenwell had spoken with his mother about the conversation that Lovey and he had while he was at his office a few days before. At his mother's urging, he asks Lovey directly to forgive him for his reaction to her over the phone. He offers a deep, heartfelt appology for his actions. Lovey is quick to accept the apology. It is a welcome relief to know that he understood her actions. She apologizes as well for her actions in the issue. She was well aware that she had overstepped her bounds, but the doctor was quick to dismiss the need. A great weight had been lifted from her mind by the conversation. The two share a quick hug, as Joe's mother asks them to come to the dining room. This short interaction spoke volumes to Ray with regard to his understanding of the closeness and respect that the Greenwell family held as their standards.

Several tables had been linked as the large group take their seats. In a surprise outcome, Mrs. Greenwell asked Ray to give the blessing over the meal. Ray is a mildly spiritual man, but his duties in life offer few opportunities for him to focus on such thoughts. Life as a NCO is wrought with issue after issue and project after project. His responsibities offer little time for contemplation. It is the nature of his position. Prayer has not been a part of his thinking for several months now. As luck would have it, if he was involved in a situation when a spoken prayer was called for, there was usually a chaplain or minister to do the job. He had never been put into such a situation before. He finds himself choked up and at a loss for words. For the first time in several years, he actually feels fear. The request sends a cold chill up his spine. His brain freezes in time for a second. Everyone clasps hands with one another as Ray works frantically to find the words to speak. All attention is now on him. He was not sure if the words he chose were the best, but they were the best that he could muster under the circumstances. It is not until he hears the family say in unison, *"Amen,"* that he actually can claim full consciousness again. It is as if he blacked out for the event.

The Rat Patrol Revisited

Ray has returned to Lai Khe following the funeral. With Christmas fast approaching, there are many actions being undertaken in the field. The aftermath of the Tet Offensive is now giving way to the pacification of Vietnam. Day after day, troops are being sent out to hotspots around the country. Oftentimes, the units are set up to protect the villages from infiltration of the Viet Cong, communist sympathizers, and the NVA. It is no easy task, but the intent is to win over the hearts and minds of the citizenry and attempt to gain commitment of them to a more democratic society. It had been well-known that the communists would often force villagers to participate in their actions. It is the regard of the Western forces to prevent these types of control from ever coming into play. The tide is turning for the South Vietnamese and the Western forces, but it is hard to believe with all the news and protests going on back in the states.

In late December of 1968, Ray is at his hooch. A Christmas tree was put up by one of his fellow soldiers. At first glance, one sees a relaxed sergeant major enjoying a beer, but there is more to the story. The tree did not belong to him. He didn't have it for the sake of the oncoming Christmas season. He didn't look at it as a sprucing for the yuletide events just days away. It was put in his charge to look after it. On the day that Ray is pictured with the tree, this soldier had spoken to him regarding an uneasiness that he felt. The man believed that things were just not right. He had a foreboding of his assignment that night and was becoming fearful of what may lay ahead on this next mission. The man looked at the tree like it was the last thing of home he would ever see and wanted Ray to keep it safe.

Ray Cottrell, December 1, 1968, at NDP "Holiday Inn" Vietnam from his personal collection. This photo was sent home to his wife Lovey, showing a very comfortable and settled-in soldier. NDP Holiday Inn is ten clicks southwest of Ben Cat and well within the Iron Triangle. It has a series of sandbag bunkers for protection. [1]

Ray had seen this before. On occasion, his men in Korea had spoken of such issues. It was the jitters of war taking effect. He tells his fellow soldier, *"It's okay to be scared, man. Hell I am scared. I am scared every time I go out. The trick is to use that fear. It allows you to stay more focused. It keeps you on your toes. The worst thing you can do is to go out into a combat zone thinking you are comfortable or confident. It is that confidence that can get you killed. You don't want to assume anything when you are in the field. Trust your instincts. Your uneasiness is a tool. Use it."* [3] The soldier takes heed of Ray's advice. He is a little more settled before he heads out. Ray assures him that the tree is in safekeeping and will be here when he gets back.

The following morning the soldier doesn't return to base with his men. The soldiers platoon had encountered the Viet Cong that night, and in the ensuing engagement, the man was killed. This picture would make its way back to Lovey in the states, a reminder that all is well for Ray so far from home. It would help to alleviate some of the fears that she may hold. To the casual observer, it is a photo of him enjoying a small break in the action, but for Ray, it holds a deeper meaning and value. It becomes an homage to one of his fallen brethren and the many friendships lost to the fatality and finality of war. It serves as a marker, a signpost of his time in Vietnam as well. It is also a reminder of a day in history that he will carry to the end, allowing him to revisit from time to time, to help him regain his perspective and memories.

Ray hits the ground hard. By January 1968, he has received his first Air Medal. As the first sergeant, he has been on several reconnaissance flights as well as insertions and combat scenarios. It is not unusual in this country for infantry soldiers to have helicopter flights to and from engagements. The heavy use of helicopters is ideal for the issues brought to bear because of terrain and time requirements. It is the new face of war even though helicopters were seeing action in Korea in 1949.

*During the Vietnam War, the US Army awarded the Air Medal to a warrant officer or commissioned pilots and enlisted aircrew for actual flight time. Awards were also given to infantry troops who flew on combat assault missions. This became a bureaucratic nightmare to correctly log because of the short flight time of typical helicopter flights. Later, an equivalent "flight hours" conversion was created and an award standard was set by individual commands. This eventually was standardized in theater to one award per every twenty-four flight hours logged. A simplified set time was awarded depending on the type of mission, regardless of the actual flight time. Administrative or VIP flights counted for 1/4 hour, regular duties, such as visual reconnaissance or resupply, counted for 1/2 hour, and hazardous duties, such as combat assaults or extractions, counted for 1 hour. Pilots and aircrew could log over 1,000 flight hours a year and earn a 40 or higher numeral on their Air Medal ribbon. The scorecard system was retained after the war. This was changed on 11 December 2006 to an award for every six months of meritorious service instead of the number of flight hours. [4]

He has become frustrated over the processes of the actions in his operational area, the loss of Joe Greenwell and other members of the Twenty-Sixth, and the overall logic being employed in the field. The sergeant major feels compelled to address the constant loss of men unnecessarily. It takes no time at all to come up with a plan to overcome these obstacles. Under the command of Colonel Radcliffe, Ray is in study mode. He is endeavoring to come up with a process that is more applicable to the conditions of Vietnam. The landscape of the war is much different than the realities of the war back in 1963. He still has the support of the South Vietnamese forces, but the United States is now in a lead role as opposed to a supporting role as in his first tour. He is convinced that jeep patrols will fare better in this landscape as opposed to just infantry or tank TFs moving in and around the enemy forces. He is reminded of the rat patrols of WWII.

On March 2, one of Ray's worst scenarios is realized. It is 1630, and he and his men have set up an ambush. It was thought that there was enough firepower to overtake insurgents that were moving in the area ten miles west of Ben Cat. Enemy soldiers moved into the kill zone of the ambush. At the best possible timing, Ray gives the order to fire. As the firefight develops, the enemy forces effectively use their automatic weapons and rocket-propelled grenades on the TF. A few of his men are injured and pinned down as the engagement starts to degrade. He is aware of the situation for these fallen men and flies into action. Showing no regard for his personal safety, he starts off at a run throwing grenades at the enemy positions. He effectively uses his rifle to lay down suppressing fire as he crawls to the injured soldiers' position. Improving the cover and now fighting from this position, he directs fire into the area of the enemy. The platoon rallies and overtakes the enemy forces. The injured are taken out. This selfless attitude offers no peace for his wife back home, but it is a life-saving event for his men. Time and time again, Ray appears to be a balls-to-the-wall combatant force, one to be reckoned with, but in his mind, it is just doing the right thing. The actions of the day delivered a Bronze Star. It is his third Oak Leaf Cluster with V device for valor in his career. This award would be delivered in October of 1969.

A few people have argued that some men join the military because they like the structure. They like being told what to do and to have everything that they have to do laid out before them. It requires no thinking. No need to be caught up in the "What do I do next" scenario that pains a man's mind as they look at the future. Some say it's just for the education. Some have argued that there are those who join the military because of a lack of other options. Others, still, would argue that there are those who join because they have a misguided sense of honor and duty. All these aspects and opinions hold some weight to them, but that represents only a small number of men and women. If they hold these opinions going in, they most assuredly are awakened to the reality of the world and the military immediately when they arrive.

To be in the military is to have will. One has to be willing. At its root, this is a fundamental fact of becoming military personnel. For the combatant military man, he is taught, from the onset, to clear his mind in basic training. From there, that freshly cleared mind is filled with how to fight, how to react properly, how to prepare for battle, and how to kill. The natural will of man is to be human, or in other words, to be social. This must be overcome with the will to kill, and on the opposite side of that coin is to be killed. For the front line fighter, no war can be won without the will to kill. There must be a belief in the cause for the fight. Both these things must be in play to be on the tip of the spearhead that these men and women find themselves. It has been said, "If you have the true will to win, victory is not only possible, but imminent."

A platoon of these likeminded men are a force acting as one, a force to be reckoned with, each member tied to the other with a bond as strong or stronger than family. Each member is driven to not only win but to also protect the lives of the others in the process. They aggress, remove the dangers, and win. What is surprising to see in these actions is their ability to stay focused and sometimes to even be comical in their composure under physical attack.

Since WWII, the army has been evolving into a scenario of getting more done with less. For example, platoon sizes have shrunk from WWII to Korea, and again from Korea to Vietnam. Original platoon sizes in the '40s have shrunk to about twenty-five men per platoon. They are better armed and better trained. It is in that vein that Ray's idea starts to take shape. He remembers in his studies that jeep patrols of the American and German forces of WWII were highly effective in that engagement. Jeeps got men to where they were needed quickly. Gun-mounted arsenals on the vehicles made them more deadly. The terrain in Vietnam was supportive of jeeps in most areas. He knew he would have to get men into places fast. They would have to act fast, move fast, and be effective. The growing discontent of being tied down to certain rules of engagement has hindered them from being as successful as those soldiers knew that they could be. He knew that he could incorporate air support, mortar teams, and cannon fire into his targets with the use of radio communications. Ray wants to put all this into play with only eight men and be as effective as a platoon or an entire company.

With all those things combined, he knew he could be effective, but it was missing a vital component: qualified, highly motivated, committed soldiers self-prepared to fill the ranks. He knew he didn't want anyone to be forced into this service. Because the actual man count was going to be so low, any weaknesses realized in the field could create a total loss to the whole task force. He wants to complete his missions, but he doesn't want to lose anyone in the process. These parameters drive him to his final solution. All participants must and will be volunteers only. With all these things considered, he now has what he believes is the best way to accomplish the daily task given to him by his commanders. The only things remaining are to pitch his idea to the brass and get it approved.

That approval comes in short order. The new age of the "Rat Patrol" is now underway. He works to get jeeps into his motor pool. The gun mounts for two M60 machine guns are welded into position. He figures that each jeep would hold two to five men. A driver, a jeep leader, a machine gunner, a rifle man, and a supporting member to handle other pieces of this moving arsenal on wheels. The tools include two M60 automatic machine guns, mortars, radios for each jeep and its leader, a starlight scope, automatic machine guns for each member, and a few Claymore mines for each member just for good measure. This provides enough ammunition to complete the tasks as they come up. In short, they are loaded for bear. Resupply will be done by helicopter or driven out by orders to the TOC. Each jeep leader must be qualified to call in the big guns when needed. A hierarchy is established in the case one of these jeep leaders is taken out. Preparation before heading out will be one of the biggest keys to success in the field. He knows motivated, solid soldiers will bring out the best of these scenarios. A highly specialized and qualified leader will bring all this together. He will be that man. But who will be the other men from his group?

It's Hard to Kill a Moose

When the draft for inductees went into effect, very few men became conscientious objectors (COs). That didn't prevent them from being conscripted, and some would even end up on the battlefields as medics and support. Starting in 1964, over half a million men had enlisted in the U.S. Armed Forces. Many believed by enlisting, they could avoid active battlefield scenarios for more preferential assignments. But almost half of these enlisted men ended up in the Asian theater anyway. Some took to officer training in the hopes of a preferred outcome. In the end, there were more people enlisting than were conscripted by draft. The COs were not necessarily put out of harm's way for their beliefs as well. While there were thousands of COs moving to Canada to avoid conscription, there were many Canadians leaving their home country to take part in the U.S.-led forces against the expansion of communism. These men were highly motivated, some for their own personal ideologies, with others from their family-instilled sense of responsibility. Others still were looking for a purpose and a career.

A young soldier who had taken the path from Canada to the United States made for an ideal candidate for Ray's newly forming Rat Patrol. He would replace a rotating soldier to fill the gap in Rat2. His name is Douglas Archibald. He was affectionately called "Moose" because of his heritage and size. To say it any other way than respectfully might start a fight. He is a large man of many talents. He came to the United States from Saskatoon, Saskatchewan. He enlisted in 1966 and did his basic at Fort Ord. He then traveled to Fort Sam Houston for medic training. From there, he took on infantry officer candidate schooling at Fort Benning. On December 1, 1968, he became a naturalized citizen, one month before landing in Vietnam. His path would cross Ray's when he is assigned to November Platoon of Bravo Company of the Twenty-Sixth Infantry. He was in a light infantry company, ideal for the situation in Vietnam, and more specifically for Ray's purposes. Moose was coming from Ranger Joe's November platoon, a unique coincidence. Commitment and follow-through are but a few of the talents that Ray is looking for. Moose stands out in a crowd. He has made quite a name for himself as being rugged, fearless, detailed, and direct. That is what captures Ray's attention. Ray sees in him the talents that he would need to fill out his team.

Their meeting is short and to the point. Rays spots Moose in the mess hall. He is taking his meal by himself when Ray slides up next to him on the bench. His questions are direct and to the point. *"I know all about you."* Moose looks over a little surprised by the statement and says, *"Yes, sir."* Ray states, *"I am told you like to hunt."* Moose puts down his fork and tilts his head in Ray's direction. His actions confirm to Ray that he has his undivided attention. *"I need to fill a spot of a specialized team of soldiers to go out on night patrols. It's volunteer only. I can get you cleared so that you join us if you like. We will be using jeeps as our mode of transportations. It is essentially a recreation of the Rat Patrols that were used in the past. But these patrols will have specific targets of opportunity. Not just some random driving around at night. Are you interested?"* [3]

The lieutenant was well aware of Ray's Rat Patrols. Ray had made quite a name for himself running them. The Rats had already completed over one hundred missions by this time. Moose was currently finishing up his actions in the field and was moved into a support position to the rear. It is a position Moose did not want. However, even though Moose outranked Ray as an officer, he had much respect for the NCOs of the army. He held that the NCO was the very backbone of the army. He had no problem signing on. He knew all about Ray as well.

Moose sees in Ray and the Rat Patrol an opportunity to do something more effective, a groundbreaking opportunity to make a difference in the war and a chance to stay in the front line. Moose is tough, rugged, willing, capable, and motivated. His talents are rounded off by his total commitment to his TF leader. Ray and Moose had many missions together. It took no time at all for Ray to earn his respect, and in so doing, a friendship would begin. That friendship would never cross the line of command in the field though. He would never question one of Ray's orders. The young lieutenant had every confidence is Ray's ability to plan and lead. Moose, on the other hand, was so good at his job that rumors around the camp suggested that he was a trained assassin. Ray trusted him, and he trusted Ray. [3]

Ray had high expectations of his volunteers. His volunteers would range from cooks and MPs to ranking officers. At one point, Ray's own colonel, Colonel Radcliffe, would even go out on missions. Ray was afforded the pick of the litter. Their missions, like in other platoons, was to recon, capture enemy insurgents, and protect villages from any solicited actions from the enemy. They would encircle a village of known sympathizers and/or forced participants of the enemy and remove the enemy. As an example: if it was discovered that the enemy was buying and or stealing food from a village, it was the Rat Patrol's job to bring it to an end. They would set up outside the village before dark. The positions of the Rat Patrol jeeps would be clearly defined to all participants to ensure that there were no crossfire issues. The object was to encircle, cut off, and entrap any enemy attempting to get into the village. Known paths of enemy movements were ideal locations for setting up an entrapment or ambush. Ray wanted to ensure that all the men stay committed to the task at hand. He would tell all the men going out that night, *"There is only one rule in the Rat Patrol. Once we engage the enemy, if you disobey an order, you will become KIA. Everyone fights. No one quits."* [3] The veiled threat of becoming a KIA, of course, was not supported by any commitment on Ray's behalf, and as luck would have it, he would never be forced or called upon it. A little humor, now and again, is a good thing. Commitment to the task at hand is of the highest order. There could be no weak links in the chain.

The reality of how well this battalion was run can be surmised by the actions and talents of others. Lieutenant Moose Archibald, while serving with November Platoon, was fortunate enough to have a forward scout that took to the Twenty-Sixth as if it were his own. Ron Harper was an intense and capable soldier. He had many opportunities to work his trade throughout the different battalions in the area. It was in his observations, over the several battalions that he worked with, that the Twenty-Sixth was the best of the bunch. They didn't suffer from mistakes like he saw in the other units. Something as simple as quietly opening an MRE (Meal, Ready-to-Eat) in the field could result in a disastrous outcome for the men he was working with. In Ron's mind, the Twenty-Sixth didn't suffer from such mishaps near as much as they did in the other battalions. This spoke volumes to Harper. While other battalions were plagued with misfortune, the Twenty-Sixth was running like a well-oiled machine. They were truly a magical unit. As a result, whenever he was working with the Twenty-Sixth, he sought out to serve with Moose and the others of the Twenty-Sixth and November Platoon and welcomed the idea of working with them as much as possible. Trust in fellow soldiers is highly prized in Vietnam.

CSM Ray Cottrell and 1st Lt., now Capt. Douglas "Moose" Archibald pictured here. (Archibald left, Cottrell on the right) Picture taken from Ray Cottrell's personal library. [5]

Playing Both Sides of the Fence

There are many villages in Ray's area of operation. With the Vietnamization Plan underway, the U.S. Army has the dual role of protecting the citizenry and keeping the Viet Cong and NVA away from them. The main goal was to win over the hearts and minds of the South Vietnamese in the struggle to keep the communists from taking over. It was working. On occasion, as with human nature, some are only concerned with themselves and what they can get out of it.

Where there is war, there are prostitutes. The tradition of whorehouses springing up wherever there are large groups of soldiers exists here as well. It is commonplace in a war-torn country. As Kennedy showed, where there is chaos, there is also opportunity. The entrepreneurial spirit of man has taken many forms in many places under many conditions. Vietnam is no different.

In the Twenty-Sixth Infantry area of operation, an older Vietnamese woman has grown into the role of madam. She had gathered to herself women who were in need of making a living and thusly entered the oldest occupation. She is a butt-ugly rag of a woman. Her looks were so disconcerting that the soldiers that knew her affectionately gave her the name of Claymore. It was said that her looks reminded them of a face that was hit by a Claymore mine. She is a very unscrupulous businesswoman. Her area of expertise is alcohol and prostitution. While she fancied herself a successful businessperson, she was nothing more than a pawn in the game of war.

For the men of the U.S. military, as with human nature around the world, the need for sex is high and a motivation that can be hard to overcome. Her business is to fulfill that need. Her support of that need extended not only to U.S. servicemen but to the enemy and citizenry alike. She was no respecter of person. If there was a buck to be made, she availed her girls and herself to make it.

The S5 officer of the Twenty-Sixth had the job of finding civil solutions and support of the citizenry. It was his job to build schools, aid stations, and water wells. Whatever was thought to be well-spent money to win over the locals, it was his job to try to procure it. As a result, water buffaloes were purchased and shipped in so that local farmers could start producing on their own land to support their families. It is a much-needed element to small autonomous families. Water buffaloes in Vietnam are akin to a John Deere tractor to a farmer in the states. It was a status symbol for the locals as well as a much-needed farm instrument. Procuring these types of things for the locals went a long way in gaining their support for the western forces. Lady Claymore's house of disrepute was conveniently located near these structures. As a more influential person in the area, she believed she could use this influence to her advantage.

It was a well-known fact that her ladies would serve both sides of the conflict equally. The Viet Cong had their share of her ladies, and the U.S. serviceman had access to them as well. Once the final deal had been struck, these couples would consummate their transactions in the tall elephant grasses near Claymore's structure. As long as there were no altercations between the two military forces, there was no problem. Business was allowed to continue under the suspected control of the Viet Cong.

It was also a known fact that monies generated from this establishment were being funneled to the Viet Cong to pay for their efforts in the war. From a certain perspective, the U.S. soldiers were financing their own enemy. Claymore, from her perspective, was receiving benefits from both sides of the proverbial fence. Though delusional, she saw herself as an integral and important person. She was not.

It only took one altercation for it all to come raining down around her. On one specific night, and for reasons unknown, perhaps jealousy or retaliation for another incident, the actions of a motivated combatant had laid a small mine field on the paths in the elephant grasses known to be transaction spots for servicemen. The resulting effect of this left two U.S. soldiers with their legs blown off. Looking over the situation as a whole, Ray is motivated to end the issue once and for all.

Ray had sent out his Rat Patrol to a facing position near the newly built schoolhouse and aid station. He had received Intel from one of the locals that the VC were coming in to the area in an attempt to rob the aid station. Ray quickly arranges an ambush scenario for the area. His informant identified the enemy's intent and the expected movements of the night. He has ordered the security of the aid station to be sent back to Lai Khe for the night. It will be his Rat Patrol to ensure security.

The expectation, as with all the other plans before, is to stop the infiltration into the area. No one operates in Ray's OPA but Ray. The plan was simple. Helicopters would be put on station. The eighty-one mortars and fire bases would be dialed in, and Ray's Rats would take care of the first engagements. Again, things do not always go as planned.

It was expected to be a simple operation. The infiltration was expected to be light.

Late afternoon arrives and the men head out to their destination. The five jeeps are separated and in hidden positions around the area. From Ray's position, there are two jeeps spread out one-fourth of a mile out to his left flank, and two jeeps spread out a one-fourth mile to his right flank. Their line makes a half-moon around the target area. Darkness falls, and the men take to their starlight scopes for observation. Ray is forward of the schoolhouse and aid station. He has a bird's-eye view of the situation. Hours pass and there is no engagement. The area is quiet, with only the sounds of the insects and the water buffaloes pasturing nearby. Ray is intent in his surveillance. The starlight scopes are a piece of technology that gives a major advantage to the U.S. militarily and equally a major setback for the VC. They allow our soldiers to see in the dark, albeit in a green speckled vision.

As he surveys the field, the animals start to speak. It is the language of disturbance. What was once a quiet pasture now shows signs of movement, slow and methodical. The buffaloes, almost in unison, start to move in the field. They seem to be moving with purpose, but they are not moving to the pond for water. They are moving closer to the buildings instead. It is a pitch-black night, cloud covered with no moon glow at all. The earlier rains of the day had moved out, leaving the steam of the day behind. Ray almost doesn't see it. He almost doesn't realize it. He takes a closer look at the animals. What he sees now stands out like an

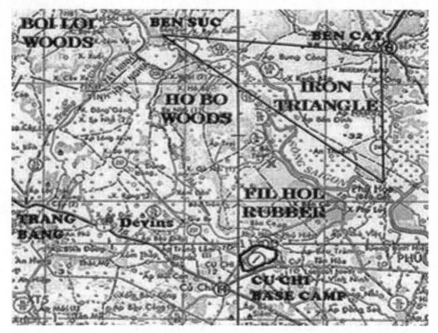

The map of operation 'Cedar Falls' two years earlier shows the Iron Triangle that Ray works in. Southwest of Lai Khe is Ben Cat, seen in the upper right of the map above. Both locations are well within the Rat Patrol's area of operation. NDP Holiday Inn is shown here just west of Ben Cat and marked as the only military camp inside the Iron Triangle. It is located to the north corner of the triangle. The events of the Claymore Engagement at Ben Me are not shown on this map. Ben Me is to the east near Di An (pronounced ZEE-on). [6]

eight-legged cow. In fact, that is what he sees: eight-legged cows moving in the pasture to the buildings. The VC are using the buffaloes for cover.

He radios over to the other jeeps and notifies them of the movement. The other teams are awaiting orders. He sees the cattle getting too close to the building. He orders his gunner to open fire. The other members of Rat1 are spread out to the sides of the jeep. When the firing starts, the VC are quick to respond. They make their way to the buildings for cover. Ray did not want to let the VC get entrenched into the buildings but he was not quick enough to realize their movement. The M60 is lacing the targets as two of the jeeps are making their way back. The other jeeps remain on station as secondary backups, covering Ray's flank. There are six enemy combatants acknowledged in this contest so far. Ray's team is four deep.

The firepower has scattered the VC and the sounds of AK47's and bullets whizzing into the trees continue as Ray takes to his radio once again. He signals his teammates to send mortars into the targets. The machine gun fire is coming and going in both directions. With the VC using the buildings now as cover, he takes to the radio once again. The howitzers are lined up and pushed into action. He knows that he has the enemy outgunned, and there is no reason not to use that advantage. The shells start to rain in on their target. He orders fire for effect (all batteries will fire on the coordinates given). The more the artillery comes in, the less they hear AKs firing back. As the other two jeeps come in, there are guns a-blazing in the direction of anything that moves. Ray calls in for a ceasefire on the mortars and the fire base. Dust is floating above the ground like a fog from the hits on the buildings. The return fire has stopped. The hard part now is to sweep it up. Ray calls in the remaining Rats and a walk off the area proceeds.

The men move out into the field and rubble in teams. Blood trails lead off into the woods behind the emptied buildings. The men move to track them. Ray will not risk his men for such a venture and calls them back. He cannot get confirmed kills in this engagement, save for a small herd of cattle. Heavy blood trails in the woods suggest that there are some that will not make it through the night without emergency medical care. In the end, there are losses in animals and buildings but no losses to his men.

A few days later, Ray is at his bunker in Dobol HQ. A soldier enters to announce that there is someone here to see him. Ray acknowledges the request and that person is led in. He doesn't get up from his seat. As if it was right on cue, he looks up to see Madam Claymore. She is in his office to complain. In broken English, she explains, *"No one comes to my bar. Where are the servicemen? I was told that they no longer come to me."* Ray acknowledges that fact. *"The men are barred from your place because of the injuries to my men."* He tells her, *"They are not safe there. I can't let my men go where they can be endangered. That is just common sense lady."* That part of her business had abruptly and officially come to an end. More than half of her clientele has just been taken away. Profits will not be the only things lost. [3]

She sits there humbly now. At a loss for words, she struggles to bring up another issue, the issue of the schoolhouse and the aid station. She argues that the people of the community needed the U.S. support and shyly asks why the Americans killed off their livestock. Again, Ray argues for the opposite in a stern voice. *"Why in hell would we purposely kill these animals? We purchased those animals for you. We are not in the business of wasting our efforts. If you want to find someone to blame, I suggest you ask the Viet Cong. They are the ones who killed these animals. You might want to take it up with them. They can't be trusted. You should be more careful in who you call friend."* Ray understands that she doesn't know what he knows, and he is not about to give up any hints to his plan as well. The conversation comes to an end shortly thereafter. There is nothing more that she can say or do but to rethink her position. [3]

A week goes by, and Lady Claymore is again in contact with Ray. She is motivated by the Viet Cong and her own self-interest this time. She wants and needs to get the servicemen's business back. Her revenue stream for the Viet Cong is also a requirement and a big reason why she is there today. Ray is well aware of this. He has been waiting for her return. The S5 officer has been scrambling to rebuild the aid station and the school. That action is well underway. Lady Claymore, on the other hand, motivated to get her business back, is in discussions with Ray on just how best to do it. She is informed again that Ray will not allow any of his men to frequent the business as long as there is a threat to their safety. If that could not be guaranteed, her business would be considered off-limits. Claymore suggests a meeting with the leaders of the Viet Cong in the area for a makeshift peace talk. Ray needed her to be the one to suggest this. He knew that, in the end, something of this nature would be brought up, and it was playing out just as he suspected. Things could not be working out any better.

She suggests that a small contingent from both sides could meet in a neutral spot, and the two forces could then come to some kind of agreement. Ray knows there is no neutral spot. Claymore informs Ray of the position and date. The Viet Cong were motivated to get their money flowing again. The Viet Cong insisted Claymore to get this done, and she too wanted to get her income up again. It was a simple issue of supply and demand. Ray agrees to this commitment. He tells her that he needed to be able to accomplish this in secret. Of course, she has taken the bait. Ray had no intentions of concealing this operation from his commanding officer though. In fact, his CO was brought up to speed shortly after the attacks at the aid station. This is what he was hoping was going to come about, and it has.

Through communications from Claymore, the Viet Cong command had decided on an open field. Behind this open field was a tree-covered jungle. The location was fairly remote to any villagers in the area. It was an ideal place for an ambush. They were the ones to set the place and time of the summit. The time that the VC negotiated allowed for him to prepare for the event. He had fears that an ambush as he had planned could easily turn into an ambush by the Viet Cong. But Claymore had no idea of what Ray had planned. Like the Viet Cong, she too believed the Americans to be basically inept. They also believed the Americans were on the up-and-up in their commitment to the meeting.

When Claymore leaves, he immediately gets out his maps and shows his plan to his CO. Looking over the terrain of the area, he shows that the plan accounts for all possible outcomes. His plan is well-conceived, allowing for the safety of his men and a proper outcome for the engagement. Looking over the map of the terrain, there is a creek bed, an open field, and tree lines to the east, west, and south of the field. It is the south tree line that will be used for an entry point for the Viet Cong. That was confirmed through Intel from a local scout. Ray's jeeps will be across the field from the Viet Cong on the other side of the creek. They will have a tree line to their back as well. There are no discernible roads to the south. Paths were discovered to the east and west of their respective cover as well. That meant that the enemy will have to enter into the field on foot. They would not dare show themselves on the roads or paths for such a secretive meeting.

Ray's plan is to cover the east and west sides of the field with gunship helicopters. They are on station and ready to go at a moment's notice. The fire base had sent practice rounds earlier that morning to ensure that they would be on target. The base will be instructed to aim their guns to the south of the field into the jungle area behind the field of engagement. With his jeeps in a blocking position to the north face of the field, all his flanks will be covered. Once the enemy is in the kill zone, the order to fire will be given. It will be an all-out blasting. There would be nowhere for the enemy to run, regardless of size of their entourage. He expects no loses on the side of the Rat Patrol. The event is to happen at night. That could prove to be a disadvantage, but the area was well-patrolled before the event actually takes place. With all his ducks in a row, Ray formalizes his plan and presents it to his commanding officer Colonel Radcliffe. The colonel quickly approves of the action and tells him to be about it. As an added bonus, Colonel Radcliffe wants to be a part of the event to oversee it. However, the division commander had other plans for the Rat Patrol that night. He expected a nighttime attack on the ARVN base one click away. It was an order that had to be followed.

That evening, all participants are in position as Ray had assigned them. Ray is in his jeep at the location that the division commander had prescribed, but he knew that the real action was going to be with Radcliffe at the original position. Three quarters of a mile away with his starlight scope, he has spotted 2 VC but rightly decides that these men are just a decoy. He is on the lookout for any large enemy elements in the area. Ray is positioned across a creek. He is fifty yards from these two guys. As the men get to knee-high water crossing the creek, he orders his gunner to take them out with the M60. Meanwhile, at the original location, Rat2, Moose's jeep sees movement in the tree line to the south from his position with Colonel Radcliffe nearby. Ray is immediately informed and is traveling in haste to the meeting.

It appears the Viet Cong are a bit naive and inept. Ray arrives from the rear of the other Rat units for the meeting and positions his jeep to the front. His jeep sits at the peak of a small mound looking over the field close to Colonel Radcliffe's patrol. His puts his starlight scope to his advantage. A small contingent of men has entered the field and are approaching the creek. Some of them have reached the waterline, waiting for Ray to get out of his jeep and come down. When a sufficient number of enemy are identified and settled into their positions, he gives his commander the sign to call in the strike. Colonel Radcliffe defers to Ray to call in the strike. Gunfire and explosions light up the area from all sides. It is over almost before it started. Like shooting ducks on a pond, the battle comes to a quick end after five minutes of machine gun fire and mortar shells. The Viet Cong managed to get off some shots but were capitulating and running for cover in short order. There are no injuries to the friendlies in the fight.

After any engagement, a sweep of the area is required. The United States requires a body count. When the all-clear is given, he sends his men down to the field to ascertain the damages. Ray's orders are to extend their sweep no deeper than fifty yards into the tree line. It was a safety issue for the men. Blood splatters and blood trails lead well into the woods behind the field. The body count is high, but the reports only reflect the actual dead that can be accounted for. Injured enemy forces are not added in. More dead could have been accounted for had they gone deeper, but the safety of his men overrule that thought. The reason for determining a body count is simple. An injured enemy soldier today could still be a combatant tomorrow. Vietnam at this time was considered a war of attrition.

Colonel Radcliffe is taking part in the sweep as well. It is a sign of his commitment to his men and a validation of his personal ideology as a commander. The site is still an active combat zone. The men are required to stay on their toes. As luck would have it, Moose is sweeping the area close to Radcliffe's position. He spots an injured enemy combatant in the bushes nearby. He starts to raise his AK-47 to take aim at the officer. Moose reacts quickly and shoots the man dead before he can fire. He makes no mention of this to Radcliffe or any other in the TF. He sees it as just another event in a long list of events. He neither wants nor needs a pat on the back for it. For him, it is just what needs to be done.

In this engagement, the Rat Patrol had taken out seventeen men of the enemy, some of which are high-value targets. The body count this night would be higher than the combined body count of the battalion within that month's service. Command and control of the Viet Cong in the area are now in disarray. Without leaders to lead, and with so many being removed from the field in one fell swoop, this creates much difficulty for the VC to regroup. Efforts to keep them out will be increased, and as a result, the area will be more secured overall. It will be quite some time before they can gain a foothold on the civilians again if they ever get it at all. Bounties on the Rat Patrol members are issued to the VC. Ray has a price tag around his neck.

For Lady Claymore, her brothel is all but closed. With no U.S. servicemen, and now no Viet Cong to keep her in business, she will have to lock the door. She will pack her bags and peddle her wares somewhere else. She has been a useful idiot, one of many in Vietnam. She leaves with the perception that the VC are not truly her friends and the westerners are more effective than she ever could have guessed. The area is now secured for the civilians to prosper more effectively and unabated. The water buffaloes are replaced, and the farmers' lives continue on. Ray's ability to think ahead, to play chess, has brought all this about. Staying at least one move ahead of the enemy is the true test of a good command sergeant major.

Accuracy Is Everything

When things don't go as planned during another engagement, Ray is in the lead role of Rat1. Approximately 150 yards away is Rat2. Moose is the leader on Rat2. The assignment was similar to many others. Because Ray had successfully received qualified info on the enemy's actions in the area, the Rat Patrol is on station again. A detailed examination of the area and the expected movements of the VC were brought to bear before the men headed out that night.

By this time, the Rat Patrol units have grown with an average of five jeeps going out on every mission. The missions are happening almost every day now. The Rat5 jeep is being led by a sergeant in the Sixteenth Infantry. Special approval had to be cleared with the CO of the Sixteenth for his men to participate in the autonomous actions of the Twenty-Sixth's Rat Patrols. That approval came easily and, as a result, was the only time that multiple battalions ever collaborate on such a venture. It was expected that this tactic, while shared with other battalions, would soon be put into use throughout Vietnam.

There are many actions performed by the volunteers in the Rats in which officers are actually answering to the commands of an NCO. A rare event in and of itself, this speaks volumes with regard to the value of the NCOs and their role in the U.S. military. In the Claymore ambush, for example, Colonel Radcliffe relinquishes control of calling in the fire mission to Ray because of his accuracy in the field.

The Rat units are covering the pathways leading into a village nearby. The paths are used by insurgents to and from a specific village. Keeping the enemy out of civilian areas is still at the forefront of their engagements. Twilight is setting in and the Rats have taken up their predefined positions. All is quiet in the jungle outside of the village.

It was expected that the VC would attempt to contact the village from one of four different paths. The men were well-versed in what to do when shit hits the fan. Sticking to the plan more often than not was enough to get the job done. On occasion, though, the best-laid plans need to be adjusted. This would be one of those days. While in his position on Rat1, a small group of enemy insurgents are making their way down the path. Ray and his unit quickly engage the small force. The attacking forces soon grow, and Ray is required to call in a strike from the fire base nearby. The coordinates are quickly dialed in, and the shells begin to rain down on his target.

Rat2 almost simultaneously finds itself under fire as well. Their engagement quickly escalates to what could be considered an untenable situation. Rat2 is receiving heavy fire, and reactions to save the unit must happen quickly. There were unexpected run-ins with two forces at that same time. There is no time to lose.

Military protocol requires that all firing requirements be done under field of site. In other words, a forward observer is always used. No fire missions coming from a fire base are to be done without seeing where the shells are landing. This is done to adjust accuracy to minimize collateral damage and friendly fire incidents. This creates a problem for Ray. It is also against military protocol to walk shelling over the top of known friendlies in such close quarters. For Ray, he has no specific location for his men of Rat2. They are at least one-fourth of a mile out from his location. The only things that he can confirm are the predefined position before they set out that night and that Rat2 is in desperate need of fire support.

Ray's unit is currently engaged so backing out to support Rat2 is not a plausible solution. Radio communications from Rat2 suggest that the situation is about to become dire. He is forced to make a decision. He can call in a strike from the fire base, causing the shells to travel not only over his head to a blind spot, but over the top of Rat2 to get to the expected targets somewhere downline. Or he can let Rat2 maintain as best they can until he gets there and risk losing his men. For Ray, the decision is simple. As his men apply their talents on Rat1, he calls in the strike for Rat2. The only thing he has going for him is the suspected location of Rat2 and the confirmed positions of the enemy forces attacking them. Moose's trust in Ray's talent does not go unwarranted. The shells are redirected and begin to hit the enemy insurgents nearby. Moose and his men were where they were supposed to be. Rays ability to call in support was both exacting and on target. In the end, the overall mission was a complete success. No losses were realized by the Rat patrol. That could not be said for the enemy forces attacking them. The body count increases.

There is no celebration among these men unless some requirements are met. First and foremost is that all men return to base unharmed. The men of the Rat Patrols were known to party, but none dare to drink a drop until then. Second, the Rat Patrols make a point to refuel and rearm before they call it a day. The reasoning behind this is largely based on preparation. The jeeps have to be reloaded and prepped in case there is an immediate need for the Rats to go back into action. Staying one step ahead is always required and considered before celebrations. It is an added element in what makes the Twenty-Sixth so efficient.

ROBERT BROOKS

Karma

Occasionally, circumstances lend themselves to coincidence. For Moose's part, there were no ill feelings toward Ray for walking the shells over his head. It was, after all, in the defense of his team, and more than warranted considering the situation of that night.

As happenstance would have it, Ray was equally protected by overhead fire on a separate event. The two Rat units, Rat1 and Rat2, were in very close to each other. On this event, Moose is manning the M60 of Rat2. The men of both units are near their jeeps and laying plans for the actions of the night. When in the field, it is wise to always be alert. It only takes a split second for a calm moment to turn in to something regrettable. Moose has always been of this mindset. It is fortunate for Ray and the other men that Moose is on the lookout.

Ray is taking advantage of this in-the-field meeting. He is busy laying out the plans for the night when Moose spots enemy insurgents in the area. His vehicle was in motion and pulling up as the M60 is wheeled onto his target and he opens fire. The bullets are firing directly over Ray's head, causing him to take cover. The ensuing gunfight comes to an end immediately, and the members of the Rat Patrol are victorious again.

Photograph of Ray Cottrell, 1SGT, OCS Bde. from his personal library. Photo taken during OLT at Fort Knox. [1]

Back on base, the men are celebrating with a much-deserved cold beer. Each member talks about what they saw, what they did, and what they were thinking. It is an opportunity for the men to hone their skills by using the knowledge of the others. It is also a venting process that allows the men to come down from an elevated mental status. These events are also called a spontaneous AAR. (After Action Review) Ray has little to add to the several conversations going on all at once. One of the men asked Ray what his take was of the engagement. His only offering is this: *"I don't have much to add, but all I know is some crazy son of bitch lit up that M60 right over the top of my head. Shit! He could have killed me because I was so close to them."* Moose butts in and tells him, *"Hell, Ray, that was me. I was working the M60!"* Ray knows that his actions could have saved his life. All he can do is raise his beer and offer a nod in Moose's direction.

The men of the Rat Patrols have had a great run of luck by this time. An estimated 200+ missions have been successfully completed by this time. Taking the time to wind down and enjoy a beer is somewhat commonplace for these guys. It goes a long way to keep morale.

NDP Holiday Inn

Night Defense Position Holiday Inn

There is a saying in the military: *"If you can find it, you can hit it. If you can hit it, you can kill it."* This saying is put into play with the U.S. Navy. It is in support of the logic of what a U.S. carrier brings to the table of war since it is always on the move. More often than not, the carriers have to be found before the carrier forces find you. It is an ideal situation for a military force. Land bases do not have this luxury of picking up and moving. That is what makes airports, supply depots, and military installations so regularly hit by their enemies. They are stationary. The base at Lai Khe was hit so frequently that it was called "Rocket City."

In the words of Napoleon Bonaparte, *"In the end, if your only offense is defense, the next option is to surrender. The most important qualification of a soldier is fortitude under fatigue and privation. Courage is only second; hardship, poverty and want are the best school for a soldier."* [7]

Within the first six months of the Rat Patrols actions, the successes of their engagements have garnered them much attention. The surrounding Army personnel are starting to hear more and more about them. On the night of the "Claymore Engagement," for example, they had taken out more enemies than the whole battalion had accomplished in any one month of his hitch in '68–'69. The attention was not all coming from his peers; it was also coming from the enemy. The VC had put out a bounty on the men of the Rat Patrols. Anyone verifying a kill or a capture against the Rats would receive a reward. Word of this has gotten around. Ray receives verification of this from some of the locals that he had befriended over his time. Smaller military bases are being hit with a low amount of regularity but still with a regularity. One of the greatest fears of a soldier on base is to be overrun by the enemy. No base is ever left unmanned without at least one company of men from the division being there. Ray is locked into a company of men with his Rats, but he is afforded time on base at Lai Khe and Di An. He is not always in the field. Today he is with his men at NDP Holiday Inn near Ben Cat.

It is on May 1, 1969, that his location, Ben Cat, is under attack from VC forces. As the map shows above, there are no direct offensive lines. The battle environment in Vietnam has few similarities as were found in Korea. No direct lines of battle are clearly drawn with the exception of the DMZ to the north. There are bases, camps, and military installations, and everywhere else are considered war zones for the most part. Oftentimes, barbed wire is the only exterior defense to separate the soldiers from the enemy. So it is with Ben Cat.

Di An is the divisional HQ for the 26th INF. On the IA road heading northeast is Long Binh. This was the base of operations for Ray Cottrell during his hitch in 1963. [8]

Ben Cat is a smaller base camp, but its location is with the "Iron Triangle." The Iron Triangle was a major operational area (OpA) for the VC. Operation Junction City in 1968 discovered many underground bases and stores for the enemy during the Tet Offensive. The results of Operation Junction City and Operation Cedar Falls yielded treasure troves of intel on the enemy, its force sizes, and their intentions. Ben Cat is squarely placed inside the Triangle, putting Ray in the heat of the action.

While on base, the observers are always on the lookout for enemy movements against these bases. Companies are continuously sent out to do recon and search/destroy missions from Ben Cat, much like they are at the many other military camps. Because these locations are locked in, it makes them a natural target for the VC.

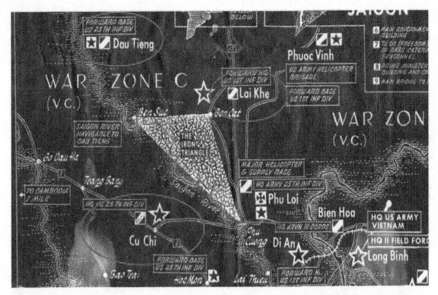

Ray is attached to the Lai Khe forward base of the U.S. 1st INF Div. there. But his hooch is at Ben Cat. Ten miles inside the Iron Triangle is the NDP Holiday Inn. He spends about 10 percent of his time at Lai Khe, preferring to be in the field with his men in the actions of the front lines. This is uncommon amongst CSMs as a rule. [8]

On the afternoon of May 1, 1969, observers see enemy troop movements as they approach the camp. A stealthy approach by the VC had successfully allowed for the enemy forces to break through and get into the wire. The base is under siege from multiple directions. It is a large contingent of VC, and the base is not prepared for the action this day. As the attack begins, Ray acts quickly and jumps to his jeep. He orders his driver to get in front of the enemy. Ray takes his position in the back and is manning the M60 machine gun on board. With his weapon loaded, the driver heads out of the wire into the face of the oncoming hostiles. His vehicle is moving in a zigzag pattern across the front of the VC. Machine gun and rifle fire is directed toward the jeep as it moves.

It is an all or nothing moment for the two men. His driver gets hit as the vehicle moves down toward the forces. Ray knows that there is some friendly fire coming from his rear as the vehicle rises and falls over the terrain. He has managed to put himself in a crossfire. The jeep's movements are causing his aim to falter as well. With his driver hurt, he orders him to stop the jeep. He needed a solid footing from which to return fire. With the vehicle at a stop, he could better unleash the hell of his weapon. From behind him, the NDP has now leveled their M134 miniguns (an electric Gatling gun that fires .762-caliber ammo) directly into the enemy. Ray and his man are safer standing still than they are moving. While reloading his weapon, and now receiving cover fire from within the wire, he signals to the camp to do a sweep off and get someone out to move his driver to safety. He continues shooting to break off the enemy engagement.

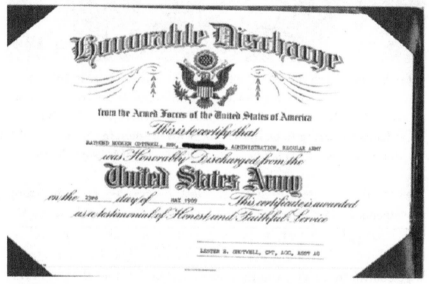

This document is the verification of last time that Ray Cottrell will re-up in the U.S. Army. He continues his career for another cycle. Taken from Ray Cottrell's personal library. [1]

Helicopter gunships were called in from a nearby base to assist in the defense of camp. From the bunkers in the base, the soldiers of the Twenty-Sixth have rallied in the onslaught. It is not without injuries and losses. It is because of Ray's actions that the men of the Twenty-Sixth were offered some time to react to the attack. His blocking position offered the opportunity for the bases defense to come to life.

Very few things will get a soldier to react faster than the "call to arms" when it has been identified that the enemy are "in the wire." Ray didn't have time to think about his personal safety, nor did his man when he got into the jeep to drive for him. It is not unfair to say that many a combat soldier is brave, but the word "heroism" should never be thrown around lightly. It is brave to look an enemy in the eye and pull the trigger, but it is heroism that goes above and beyond the call to duty in defense of his men with no regards for his own personal safety. Ray and his man are heroic this day.

Some commanders are noted for their aggressive actions against the enemy. The soldiers that are serving under these commanders can definitely be considered brave. To offer insight on the difference between heroism and bravery can be shown in the case of Sen. John McCain. McCain was shot down in his craft while bombing Hanoi. He had suffered two broken arms and a broken leg from his ejection of his aircraft, nearly drowning in the lake that he landed in. That part of his story is most definitely a brave event. To be culled out and put in the infamous Hanoi Hilton prison camp requires a certain amount of bravery. That is never argued. But it is his actions during the burning of the USS *Forrestal*, and his unselfish acts in the Hanoi Hilton, which would get him the Distinguished Flying Cross, the Silver Star, and the Bronze Star. One of the best way to judge a man's leadership ability is to ask his men. How they see and follow their commander speaks volumes to the ability of the man.

Ray's ability can be summed up in the actions of his men. During one engagement with VC forces, his Rat Patrol has overtaken several enemy combatants. A sweep of the area revealed that they had overtaken and killed a paymaster for the Viet Cong. Evidently this man was in the process of delivering the wages and or payments for their soldiers before they were ambushed. Because the Rats were an all-volunteer force, the money collected was shared equally among the men to support the morale of the Patrol.

In turn, the men took advantage of the opportunity and used the money to fly back to the states during their R&R. They were required to fly through Hawaii because it didn't require a passport to reenter the United States from there. They could get flights back to the mainland from the islands or meet their families in Hawaii. This afforded the men a rare opportunity to see their families. Under normal conditions, this could not be arranged through the military short of family emergencies. It is not the fact that they used the money to leave Vietnam and returned home; it is the fact that they returned to Vietnam when they could have easily just said, "I quit." They did not. Every one of these men returned to the action upon the end of their R&R. They are a group of committed soldiers, and they realize that they are making a difference. They know that they are valued by their commanders, but more importantly, they are committed to each other. The latter is their greatest motivation to return.

Bringing It on Home

In November 1969, after 305 night missions with only three minor injuries, the Rat Patrol is coming to an end. Ray had traveled to other divisions to explain their processes in order to share their working knowledge to others. It was hoped that other battalions would take up their ideas and use them. Some aspects of the war had changed and Ray was quick to adjust to it. During the first thirty days in on his second tour, he became frustrated with the process of sending out platoons in hopes of finding large groups of VC and then calling in air and gun support to take them out. He saw no great value in that process, and he knew his process would be more effective. The records would show that it was.

In his last thirty days, an IG inspection found some weak spots that would cause the Twenty-Sixth to fail. It was simple things that got them. There were not enough chalkboards relating the information of the division hanging on the walls. The jeeps were not sent out for maintenance in a timely manner. These were issues that had more to do with the bureaucracy of the military as opposed to the effectiveness of the units that served in it. Ray had no major direct link to these issues, but was asked by his CO to help with improving the situation. Ray had three weeks to get the platoons up to snuff. It was basic organizational skills to meet military SOPs. This extended his stay by another thirty days, a situation that would break the average soldier's heart, but in his mind, it is just another opportunity to look out for the ones he cares for. Another thirty days in the Vietnam didn't rattle him at all. It was a favor to the colonel, and for Ray, it was just another opportunity to take on the hard jobs to ensure that they are done right. There was nothing he wouldn't do for Colonel Radcliffe either. Upon the IG's return, the Twenty-Sixth was up to snuff. Even the jeeps had been replaced with new vehicles to ensure that the unit would pass with the highest level of satisfaction.

With the completion of all his tasks, and his paperwork caught up and ready for the rotation home, Ray contacts HQ in Lai Khe for his best opportunity to fly out. To his surprise, the sergeant major in Lai Khe tells him that there is a plane on the tarmac in Tan Son Nhut preparing for departure. If he can hurry, he can board that bird and head out today.

He gets his driver into Rat1 and throws his sole remaining duffle bag in the back. They make their way through Di An and onto the airport with a fully loaded Rat jeep. His driver takes him straight to the airplane on the tarmac. He approaches the plane with full gear on and two M60 machine guns attached to his jeep. He asks the boarding officer if there is room, and the young airman immediately adds his name to the flight manifest. Ray is quick to remove the ammo from his web vest. He drops his old holster, cap, and loose articles into his duffle. He asks his driver to return his rifle to the store clerks back on base. It is now official. His time in Vietnam has come to an end. There is no fanfare. No bands playing. No banners flying. Only a quick, firm handshake to his driver. He heads up the steps and finds a seat. He secures himself and settles in for the long flight back to the United States.

The flight home is not a direct endeavor. He will have to stop off at least once on his journey home. It would require him to take a two-hour layover in Hawaii for refueling. When they reach the islands, the plane is emptied for refueling, but it gives him the chance to get a sandwich and something to drink from the bar. It is dark out, and the bar is mostly empty. It is his first meal back in the country in over a year. A good warm sandwich is as good as a Thanksgiving dinner at this point. No more MREs.

U.S. Army map. The town of Lai Khe is in the circled area. (center left) Approximately ten miles to the southwest is Ben Cat. The map shows a military camp just southwest of Ben Cat. That is the location of NDP Holiday Inn. The Iron Triangle starts at Ben Cat and covers the west and southwest through the rubber plantations to its farthest westward perimeter. Holiday Inn is inside the northeast corner of the Iron Triangle marked only as a military base. [9]

DEPARTMENT OF THE ARMY
Headquarters, 1st Infantry Division
APO San Francisco 96345

GENERAL ORDERS   31 August 1969
NUMBER   9563

AWARD OF THE ARMY COMMENDATION MEDAL
(Fifth Oak Leaf Cluster)

1. TC 320. The following AWARD is announced.

COTTRELL, RAYMOND H ████████ STAFF SERGEANT MAJOR United States Army
Company C 1st Battalion 26th Infantry

Awarded:	Army Commendation Medal (Fifth Oak Leaf Cluster) with "V" device
Date of action:	1 May 1969
Theater:	Republic of Vietnam
Reason:	For heroism in connection with military operations against a hostile force in the Republic of Vietnam: On this date, Sergeant Cottrell was serving with his unit at Fire Support Base Holiday Inn when the friendly encampment was suddenly alerted for possible enemy activity. Observing several insurgents moving towards his position, Sergeant Cottrell unhesitatingly ordered the driver of his light vehicle to position the vehicle and its heavy machinegun to the front of the aggressors. While proceeding to their tactical position, the friendly element was suddenly subjected to an intense automatic weapons and small arms fusillade which seriously wounded the driver. With complete disregard for his personal safety, Sergeant Cottrell personally led the small unit on an assault of the aggressor emplacements. Placing a devastating barrage of suppressive fire on the insurgents, Sergeant Cottrell led his men in a rout of the enemy forces. His courageous initiative and exemplary professionalism significantly contributed to the successful outcome of the encounter. Staff Sergeant Major Cottrell's actions are in keeping with the finest traditions of the military service and reflect great credit upon himself, the 1st Infantry Division, and the United States Army.
Authority:	By direction of the Secretary of the Army, under the provisions of AR 672-5-1.

[1]

Upon arriving in the states, Ray's plane lands in California. Again, there are no bands playing or banners waving in the winds. There is no one there to greet him when he touches the U.S. mainland. That doesn't bother him. As long as there is no one there to protest his arrival like they did back in January, he is good to go. The only thing that exceeds his expectation is that the customs inspector offers him a quick pass through to get him home. The young man notices his stripes and offers a salute. A quick transfer from one plane to another and he is off again. On the plane trip back to Louisville, it dawns on him that his duffle bag is not locked. He had picked up a few things for Colonel Radcliffe's wife, and he is a little concerned about someone rummaging through it.

It was just a few Asian items that would have cost substantially more in the United States, but, more importantly, it was a task that he wanted to complete for the colonel. While on the ground in California, he calls Lovey and lets her know just how soon he will be home.

When he lands in Louisville, things are a little different. Again, there is no fanfare. No one is holding a sign with his name on it. As he exits the plane, he finds Lovey, Brenda, and Ray Jr. there to meet him. This was the type of homecoming that he wanted. All is right with the world for today.

Back in his home off base, Ray is sitting on his porch relaxing. But that won't do for Ray. Sitting idly is not part of his makeup. It goes against his grain to just be sitting there with no specific purpose. It dawns on him that he has been home for three days now, and he still hasn't emptied his duffle bag. Today is as good a day as any, and he thinks to himself that he should have done this already.

He brings his bag out and sets it in front of him. As he opens it, he discovers that in the changeover from the jeep to the airplane, he had brought back a couple unwanted items with him. When he put his ammo vest into his duffle bag, he didn't clear all the ammo that he was carrying on him. In the excitement and rush of meeting the plane and getting on the plane, he overlooked some small explosives attached to the back of his webbed ammo vest. He doesn't tremble. He doesn't get emotional. He just acknowledges to himself how careless he was to bring back grenades on the 6,000-mile journey from Indochina.

The danger was higher than most would normally think. In the field, soldiers found that the steel pin that secured the grenade would sometimes stick because of rust. In the hot, humid air of Vietnam, this process had become more and more of a common occurrence. It was not uncommon for soldiers to come up with working ways to overcome such issues on their own. It had become commonplace to have the pins removed from the grenades before going into the field. Rubber bands would be doubled up tightly over the firing mechanism. The pins would be discarded and the clip itself would remain in place. When the grenade is thrown, the rubber bands would release or break, and the three-second count would begin. It had proven to be a very effective process, but not without its dangers. These two grenades of Ray's had been secured in his duffle for the entirety of his flights back home. His guardian angel had brought him luck from killing everyone on the plane, including himself.

The issue now is what to do with them. Ray has never failed to be cool under pressure or duress. That has been his trademark throughout his life. It is an attribute that had managed to get him out of situations that would have been more than detrimental to his men or himself. This would be no different. His front yard meets the street as most homes do along his road. On the other side of his road is the Fort Knox reservation, a large piece of property that Ray is intimately familiar with. He takes the two grenades with him a few hundred yards into the reservation. He takes the time to ensure that there is no one working on the edge of the base. After sweeping the area, he throws the grenades into a safe area and they explode. Vietnam is officially behind him. It is an odd thing to have to deal with at the very least, but then again, his life up until now has been anything but normal.

Back to Spit and Polish

When one door closes, another one opens. By the end of his tour in Vietnam, his accolades had grown considerably. He was as well-regarded as a soldier as he was an NCO and leader. An opening at Fort Knox would come into play for the final leg of his military career.

Ray leaves Vietnam as an E9 CSM in December as an NCO. The only elevation from here is SMA. He has no aspirations of being in DC and serving with the Joint Chiefs, so the logic of aspiring to such a position is off the table. His has responsibilities on a board. He is there to help the review board for promotions of other NCOs and officers. He has accumulated many medals, awards and accolades by this time. That is not to say that he doesn't have a job to do. He has refilled his position with the Fourth Brigade OCS as well.

It takes no time at all for Ray to yet again distinguish himself within his position. From quality management to organizing a wives' organization, he is exerting his expertise and value to the Fort Knox military community. One of the strongest additions to his credit is the recycle welcome program for returning soldiers. Its value significantly decreased the AWOL numbers on base. Again, it is a situation where he sees a problem and comes up with a logical and supportive, positive answer to it.

In 1970, Ray is approached by the movie industry of Hollywood, California. An acclaimed screenwriter has been looking for a project to do. He has come across Ray's story in his search. Ray comes to understand that this man was the screenwriter for the Academy Award–winning film *Butch Cassidy and the Sundance Kid*. It is his intention to take part of Ray's life and create a film based on that history. They conduct a few interviews, and Ray gives the gentleman a brief history of his life. A short outline had been put together and he moves to put it into production. The issue then becomes if Hollywood be willing to produce a movie that involves the Vietnam War during its height. Of course that answer is no. Ray is informed that the project is being put on the shelf as are many films. It is now intended to bring the story out later when it would be better received. For Ray, it would have been a conflict of interest to be in the military and also working on a public film project. He is sure that the army brass would not green-light such a venture.

THE COMMANDING GENERAL FIRST UNITED STATES ARMY
AWARDS THE MERITORIOUS SERVICE MEDAL TO

COMMAND SERGEANT MAJOR RAYMOND H. COTTRELL ██████████

UNITED STATES ARMY

While serving as Command Sergeant Major, 13th Battalion, 4th Training Brigade, US Army Armor Center, Fort Knox, Kentucky, from January 1971 to June 1972, Command Sergeant Major Cottrell distinguished himself by rendering outstanding meritorious service. He distinguished himself through his superior administrative knowledge, outstanding leadership, keen insight, demonstrated professionalism, attention to detail, and high standards of conduct. He developed a Recycle Welcome Program for incoming recycles to include a personal interview and welcome by himself as well as company and platoon welcome. This program significantly reduced AWOLs. He arranged for briefings on various subjects including CHAMPUS, VOLAR, NCO education, MOS testing, EERs and Quality Management. In conjunction with this, he was instrumental in organizing an NCO wives organization with the objective of getting the young soldier and his family actively involved in life. His efforts resulted in boosting membership in the Noncommissioned Officers Association to the best percentage on post. In conjunction with the VOLAR Program, he organized and set up a centralized mail drop and pickup to expedite mail delivery for trainees and eliminated the requirement to have a drivers license to operate a push lawn mower. Command Sergeant Major Cottrell's outstanding achievements and devotion to duty are in keeping with the highest traditions of the military service and reflect great credit upon himself and the United States Army.

[1]

THE UNITED STATES OF AMERICA

TO ALL WHO SHALL SEE THESE PRESENTS, GREETING:
THIS IS TO CERTIFY THAT
THE PRESIDENT OF THE UNITED STATES OF AMERICA
AUTHORIZED BY ACT OF CONGRESS JULY 9, 1918
HAS AWARDED

THE SILVER STAR

TO

SERGEANT MAJOR RAYMOND H. COTTRELL, ██████████, UNITED STATES ARMY

FOR
GALLANTRY IN ACTION

IN THE REPUBLIC OF VIETNAM ON 14 JULY 1969
GIVEN UNDER MY HAND IN THE CITY OF WASHINGTON
THIS   THIRD   DAY OF   NOVEMBER   1969

A. B. Milloy   Stanley R. Resor
A. B. MILLOY   SECRETARY OF THE ARMY
Major General, USA
Commanding

[1]

THE UNITED STATES OF AMERICA

TO ALL WHO SHALL SEE THESE PRESENTS, GREETING:

THIS IS TO CERTIFY THAT
THE PRESIDENT OF THE UNITED STATES OF AMERICA
AUTHORIZED BY EXECUTIVE ORDER, 24 AUGUST 1962
HAS AWARDED

THE BRONZE STAR MEDAL

SEVENTH OAK LEAF CLUSTER

TO

STAFF SERGEANT MAJOR RAYMOND COTTRELL, ████████, UNITED STATES ARMY

FOR
MERITORIOUS ACHIEVEMENT
IN GROUND OPERATIONS AGAINST HOSTILE FORCES

IN THE REPUBLIC OF VIETNAM DURING THE PERIOD 17 OCTOBER 1969 TO 17 NOVEMBER 1969

GIVEN UNDER MY HAND IN THE CITY OF WASHINGTON
THIS   FIFTH   DAY OF   DECEMBER   19 69

A.E. MILLOY
Major General, USA
Commanding

[1]

CHAPTER 11

From Rat Patrol to Rat Race

B Y 1972, RAY is back on base at Fort Knox. The Twenty-Sixth Infantry's involvement in Vietnam has also come to an end. They have been sent to Fort Riley. The Twenty-Sixth is decommissioned and will have their colors boxed up and put into storage. Its men and command are reinstated and scattered under different divisions and battalions within the army. For Ray, it is the end of an era. From his first enlistment in 1950, he has re-upped six times, each time taking advantage of the extra pay by basically selling back part of his leave time. Members of the high command approach Ray one more time. They want him to take a position as the CSM to a two-star general in Germany. He will be assigned to the management of a nuclear missile site in the country. It is not the front lines that he is generally motivated to be a part of, but the offer is tempting. It will have to be discussed with Lovey before he takes this appointment.

Lovey has followed Ray around the world and back again. By this time in her life, she has started a career with Sears and Roebuck. She had been at it for several years by this point. Ray is not quick to agree to the position without talking to her. It is not how he operates. If Ray takes the job, Lovey will have to give up her career to go back to Europe. They speak together on the subject in short order. It is quickly determined that Lovey does not want to go back out of the country. She had made friends. The kids have become settled in their schools. They have friends and stability here in Kentucky as well. Ray understands that Lovey has followed him for twenty-two years. He wants her to be able to follow up on her now-blossoming career. It is time for Lovey to come first. The decision is simple. He will officially retire.

He has accomplished much in his career. He has supported his family by his choices, and with Lovey's help and commitment, successfully brought him to the end of a full and rewarding career. He has amassed several friendships and contacts both here and abroad. He has an intimate knowledge of the U.S. military that few would ever come to understand. At this time in his life, he has few regrets looking forward. Only the bleak question of what to do next is on his mind. A quick phone call to the army is all it takes to start the wheels of retirement in motion. He respectfully declines the position and moves to get his business in order to cycle out.

By the end of Vietnam, Ray has accumulated many medals, awards, and commendations. His first Silver Star was received in the field just outside of Pusan in South Korea in 1951. His second and third Silver Stars were received in Vietnam in 1969. A smattering of seven Bronze Stars were awarded to him as well along his career. He received a Purple Heart for his injury protecting a pinned-down soldier outside his NDP. A Vietnam Gallantry Cross, Air Medals for his work with helicopters, an Army of Occupation Medal with German Clasp, along with several army commendation medals make up the fruit salad on his uniform. His six Overseas Bars, Combat Infantryman Pin, Meritorious Service Award, and the Rockers of his rank fill out his uniform as he puts his dress blues on for the last time as an active soldier.

At the end of his army career, he has earned more medals than Audie Murphy. Missing from this accolade is the Distinguished Service Cross and the Congressional Medal of Honor, the two medals that Ray does not hold. For Ray, that is okay with him. He didn't do the things he has done to get praise anyway. All his actions were purposeful to the point of being the best that he could be, to help others be safe and become the best that they could be. His innate unselfishness in the field is what sets him apart from the pack. Nothing he did was ever done with the expectation of having a piece of cloth pinned to his chest. No good soldier thinks that way. He sees his life based in chance with a large amount of measured risk. Six times he could have gotten out of the military, and six times, the issue of family or country took precedence. As he looks forward to his life, one of his biggest concerns is whether or not he will have to pawn his shotgun to make ends meet again.

ROBERT BROOKS

Gen Adoms Visits 505th Inf

8th Inf Div Assault Gun School Ends Final Phase of Training

Outstanding US Choral Group To Begin Three-Week Tour

Die Safety Officials Caution All Swimmers

8th Inf Div's Pilots Become Instrument Trained

United States Army paper clipping taken from Ray Cottrell's personal library. Then- Platoon Sgt. Ray Cottrell is showing the M56 to Brig. Gen. John Keating, ADC, who is along for the ride. Center column, with picture to the right. [1]

DAZED ACCIDENT VICTIM AFTER ROUTE 1 WRECK—Master Sergeant Raymond Cottrell, of 2515 Hargrove Ave., was returning to Fort Meade, Md., after a 30-day rest leave when he fell asleep at the wheel. His car struck the guard railing on U. S. Route 1 near the South Anna River Bridge at about 1 A. M. today. News Leader Photographer John Wood happened along just after the crash and snapped this picture of Cottrell leaving his car with a warning flare. Cottrell, a Korean veteran was not injured, but a companion received slight injuries.

M.Sgt. Ray Cottrell making his way back to Fort Meade
before his marriage in December 1951, above. [1]

Left: dead Korean soldier being removed from the
battlefield at Suwon. Bottom left: Three men of Company
E near the Suwon Airport, southeast of Inchon. A young
Ray Cottrell is on the right (bottom left photo). [2]

Learning Normal

In June 1972, Ray's military career is officially ended. He receives his last documents to add to his white pages. The first is the certificate for his honorable discharge. The second document is a certification of his official retirement. It was time. It had been twenty-two years since he arrived at Fort Knox. At age seventeen, he was amongst the youngest men to ever enter the army. He had a great run. More importantly, he was home safe and physically whole, an attribute highly prized by his wife and family. He had been injured. He had his scars. No one leaves the battlefields of the world without taking something back with him. But physically, he was whole and complete.

As with many armed combatants before him, Ray would have his own monsters to bury. It would not be until 1978 that the government would accept the science of post–traumatic stress disorder (PTSD). Ray had gone through his twenty-two years with the weight of shell shock, the original term for PTSD. It would not be addressed with the help of psychologists or therapists. That was just not an option for him. Ray could hardly see himself taking advantage of such things even though there was such an offering. For him, it was just bad dreams that he will have to come to terms with.

For Lovey, with Ray being home, the weight of his career would bring a new challenge for her. She would be front and center as the one to help Ray through the night terrors that PTSD brought with it. It was very scary time for her. Ray would toss and turn in his sleep from time to time, and it would be Lovey on the receiving end as well of his sleepless nights. This issue would come to a head on one occasion, when Lovey was awakened from her sleep with Ray's hands firmly gripped around her neck. Adjustments had to be made. For the most part, the events were sporadic and uncommon. The two would have to work this out. After much trial and error, it was determined that there were certain triggers that created Ray's sleepless nights. Lovey had noticed that, more often than not, the events occurred whenever Ray watched a war movie on television. It would be nights like this that Ray would take his sleep on the recliner in the living room. It afforded him a chance to get some hard sleep in, and when he woke up, he would then join Lovey in the bedroom. It was a tough road to plow, but the two managed to work this out. Lovey's commitment under this type of collateral damage cannot be understated. It is her love and concern that kept the two together. The two's commitment to each other prevented the couple from becoming divorced as was happening to so many other couples throughout the country. In 1968, the divorce rate in the United States was starting to climb. It speaks volumes on the family's makeup and character. Many a military wife suffered through this changeover, and many families were broken because of it. That is not the case in the Cottrell house.

On the Road Again

With Lovey working at Sears on her career, Ray is now challenged with finding a new career of his own. The country, with all its issues, is in growth mode. Qualified, well-educated employees are highly sought-after at this time. The R.E. Gatti Company out of Bowling Green had won a state contract for work on Dixie Highway in Muldraugh to Radcliffe. A concrete separation barrier was needed in sections of the highway heading to Elizabethtown. Ray had many connections from his time in the army, and a good friend, Lon Field, had put him on to this job opening while he was still on the base. When Field left the military, he had come up through the union and became the steward over the worksite.

Muldraugh is a unique town. It is the only city entirely located within the confines of an army base. It also holds some small acclaim for being the only city built entirely one side of a highway. Ray had gotten the job through some contacts back at Fort Knox. It was hard work, but he was accustomed to that. The physicality of the army made him well suited for the job. It also suited his routine of getting up early in the morning before the sun rose and staying at it to nightfall.

As winter sets in, work on the highway begins to dry up. He will be laid off from late December through March of 1973, but fortunately the company was nice enough to inform him of the impending layoffs. He could sit back and collect unemployment through the state, but Ray is not built for sitting around. As with most men at this time, being on unemployment is considered an embarrassment. The family needs the second income as well. His pension money, along with Lovey's paycheck, could make the ends meet, but there could be no gaps in the money coming in. A drop in income for a month or two would create an instant hardship for the family.

Not unaccustomed to work and eager to stay employed, Ray starts asking around for other opportunities. He is trying to stay ahead of the layoff. Ray spoke with Lon Field again. Field worked for a dealership previously and suggested that he contact Jim Moore, a friend of Lon's from Fort Knox. Lon had sold cars before and suggested that Ray go down to Knox Ford to get some work. Ray was only intending on working at the dealership as part of the labor force. He expected to wash cars, fill gas tanks, and clean floors. But Jim Moore had another idea for him. Moore wanted him to try his hand at selling cars.

Ray had never sold cars before and had no expectation of ever being able to. After much urging from Jim, he gets persuaded to give it a try. Ray would be paid for his training time as well as a commission based on sales. Uncomfortable in a street suit these days, he reports to work as part of the new sales staff. He still misses putting on the uniform, but this is not the same thing. Then he was in charge. Ray has never been afraid of taking on a challenge though. It is more accurately stated that challenges are Ray's bread and butter. Every challenge for him was an opportunity. Every opportunity was a learning experience. It would take no time at all for Ray to get into the groove of things.

Along with his longstanding military career came many contacts and friendships. Word got out quickly that there was a retired CSM selling cars just outside of base. If nothing else, the army takes care of its own. That motto would bode well for Ray. As his notoriety was high back while he was in, he was starting to enjoy his notoriety out of the army. Soldiers started to flock to the dealership. The buyers trusted Ray, and Ray was always prepared to make the best deal possible for those that came to him. He became so well-known that records were being set. In his first month, Ray managed to sell forty-four cars to soldiers and their families, an unheard-of number for a break-in salesman. Flushed with customers, he was forced to pass off some of his sales to the other salesmen to keep up with the demand. Ray was succeeding exponentially and again is making a name for himself. He never turned down a possible sale, and he never tried to get more than what was expected from any of his customers.

During the evening on one of his shifts, a young soldier comes up to the dealership. The sales staff is working in rotations. The next customer would be attended by the next available sales staff. It is a process that is very common in the industry. If a salesman was not currently working on a deal, he would take turns with the next customer on the lot. It is the way of things. This young soldier was actually to be addressed by another salesman. The young man was walking around outside looking at car window after car window. The salesman who should be going out to greet the young soldier looked at Ray and told him, *"Why don't you take this one, Ray?"* He believed that the young man had no money and basically didn't believe that he would have gotten a sale out of him anyway. Ray, on the other hand, believes that everyone should be treated equally and as such was more than happy to go out and speak with the guy.

The soldier tells him that he has just gotten out of basic training. Soldiers were not allowed personal cars while in basic, but now that he is out, he wants to buy one. He was looking for a car to drive back to the northeast. Ray asks him all the normal questions. Do you have credit? Can you make a down payment? Do you have any references? The young soldier is quick to interrupt him. He asks Ray, *"Can you take cash?"* Ray tells him, *"Sure, we just need some ID to get the paperwork going. You do have an ID, don't you?"* Of course Ray knew he did but politely asked the question anyway. All good soldiers carried their IDs. The young man answers in the affirmative, and hands his driver's license and military ID card to Ray. He looks it over and checks to make sure it is all legitimate.

A curious thing catches Ray's eye. The young man's last name is Rockefeller. Ray questions him a little further. Ray's inquisition is more out of curiosity than need at this point. If everything checked out, he felt strongly that he could find a car worthy of the young man's need. As it turns out, Private Rockefeller is the grandson of J. D. Rockefeller of New York. A New

A result of his first month as a car salesman for Jim Moore at Knox Motors. [1]

York driver's license and the Rockefeller name on it gave little fear to Ray that this car deal was not going to happen. The other salesmen's eyes are wide open when the soldier starts counting out his payment. In a remarkable side note, Rockefeller turns to Ray and asks him, *"Are you sure that is enough? I can give you a few hundred more if you are not making any money on this."* Ray assures him that the $3,500 was enough. Ray takes the car over to fill up the gas tank at a nearby gas station. When he returns, he hands the keys to Rockefeller and bids him a safe journey home. All the other salesmen are watching in envy from inside as the young man drives off. Ray heads back in with a smile on his face and starts the nightly routine of closing shop. Perhaps, had the man treated the soldier with the same mindset that Ray did in treating everyone equally, he might have found his paycheck a little bigger that week. [3]

Off to the Races

In 1973, Richard Nixon is the sitting president of the United States. The American involvement in Vietnam is drawing down. Exchanges of POWs had been agreed upon. In that group is an air force pilot named John McCain.

Nixon is a beleaguered president. While having success with the Chinese government, culminating in a trip to the country, the Cold War now finds the United States with a new ally against Russia. Back in the states, protestors against the war are starting to wane, but a new issue has come to light. It is called Watergate.

Watergate is a building that houses the Democrat National Committee offices in Washington. A plan to break into the building in hopes of bugging it for gaining a political edge over the Democrats was hatched. Investigative reporters working in DC discovered the crime through an informant called Deep Throat. Carl Bernstein and Bob Woodward were the two reporters breaking the news at the *Washington Post*. The story was gaining traction and suggested that the misdeed had connections that led all the way to the Oval Office. The story comes to a head by 1974. Nixon officially resigns from the presidency, and control is given over to Vice President Gerald Ford.

Gen. Alexander Haig, advisor to the president and a former colonel in the Twenty-Sixth Infantry Division, receives a phone call from a friend. Ray was on the phone to him to urge the president to not resign. General Haig informed him that it was too late. Nixon had already made up his mind. General Haig was formerly the deputy security advisor and was now the fifth White House chief of staff. Ray's paths crossed with Haig all the way back to Chosin when the then-colonel flew by helicopter with Maj. Gen. Ed Almond to meet with Colonel Faith. Haig was there when Colonel Faith was pinned with the Silver Star. Ray's efforts held no sway over the decision, but General Haig thanked him for the call nonetheless. [3]

Even though Ray is officially out of the army, he still has a connection to it. Old habits are hard to break. He will always have his eye on what is happening to his country and his army. But that doesn't mean that he can't have a normal life as well. After spending nine months on the road crew, and producing well in his new career as a salesman, Ray can now take a little time for himself.

A favorite pastime for him is going to Churchill Downs, Turfway Park, and Keeneland racetracks. After a long week of sales, he finds time to head to Louisville and Lexington for a day of fun. Gambling has been a part of his makeup since his early days in Korea. Playing cards on board the ship to Korea was his first introduction, and the bug has bit him. His analytical skills has served him well on his jaunts to the track. It took a couple meets to figure it all out, but he is slowly getting into the mastery of horse betting. By the end of the fall meet at Churchill in 1973, he has managed to net himself a nice bit of profit, an unlikely outcome to the average horse better.

By the spring of 1974, he is well engaged at the track. A close friend, Dave Rideour, had spoken with him in regards to going even deeper in to track life. The opportunity to buy a horse in a claiming race is brought to his attention. He is regularly at the track and, with the knowledge and influence of Dave, works hard to convince him to take the chance. His children were all but grown up and needed little at this time. Lovey is well engaged in her career, and Ray is experiencing free time. He had never had much of it, and he always felt compelled to fill it wherever possible. Because he was flushed with cash from his successes at the dealership, the expansion into this world is a fairly easy jump to make. Besides, it was a sideline venture working with expendable cash. If luck would be on his side, he could even turn a small profit.

It is not but a few months in when Rideour decides that he is done. He asks Ray if he would consider buying him out. The claimed horse was $5,000 for the each of them. This did not include stabling, feeding, hot walking, and training. Part of his decision in getting into this was relegated to the concept that the financial end of it would be a shared commitment, a 50/50 split that made the idea plausible in the first place. He now has to consider whether or not to sell out as well or buy out his partner and continue. It is not a quick decision. [3]

John Churchman is his trainer. The horse's name is Mobile Express. Ray's partner is wanting to get out because he doesn't want to lose any money on the deal. Ray, at Churchman's urging, convinces him that Mobile Express has some talent and that if he sticks with it, he can turn a profit that way. Originally, Mobile Express was owned by a well-known veterinarian by the name of Dr. Hardeal. The doctor originally bought it for his daughter, but she had changed her mind on what she was wanting to do as a hobby thus leaving the vet on the hook with a horse he didn't want or need. Mobile Express was originally purchased by Dr. Hardeal as an obstacle and jumping horse. His daughter was heavily interested in being in the ring at that time, but perhaps a fall or two was more than she bargained for.

Churchman is no slouch. He is a very accomplished trainer who had made a name for himself at Keeneland, Turfway, and Churchill Downs. Ray's trust in him is not unfounded. He buys out his partner, and by the fall meet at Churchill Downs, Mobile Express is in his first allowance race. Ray's excitement at watching his horse coming out of the gate and pushing to take the lead is the linchpin. He is officially a horseman hobbyist. He couldn't have been happier even if the horse had come in dead last. The thrill of the race, and his love for these work horses, has now locked a place in his heart that will never be removed.

Making the changeover from better to buyer is no small matter. He had done his research. He had many conversations with other owners and trainers. Ray has never been one to get into anything blindly. So getting into the race industry was no small matter or quick judgment. Like most things in his life, it is a calculated risk with minimum damage if failed. Fortunately for Ray, Mobile Express earned his keep.

In the gambling world, more specifically the casino world, an old saying has always been that *"the worst thing that can happen to you is to walk in for the first time, put in your coin, and win big on your first try. The gambler will walk away from that event thinking, 'Wow, that is easy. I can do this all the time!'"* This is never the way to approach professional gambling. The house always wins in the long run. For anyone that thinks it is easy, or that they have a way to beat the house, he can rest assured that there is racetrack expansion or a new casino opening up in his honor.

Ray's venture with Mobile Express was not that kind of event. He knew that racing was only a sidebar venture, not his sole means or career. He had a family to protect and support. Racing will never be more than a gentleman's hobby. He knows that profitability in such ventures is rot with losses. He holds to himself, as long as the losses don't interfere with first responsibilities, he can stay with it. And stay with it he does.

John Churchman and Ray form a bond with each other. Under John's tutelage, Ray becomes better educated. There is a trust that gets built up higher every time he runs his horses. This trust must be maintained, and it is easily done with the successes on and off the track. Churchman becomes the buyer, and Ray becomes the financier. Ray handles where the horses will run and what stables they will be housed at, while Churchman handles the buying of the animals and the training. It is a good unwritten partnership. By 1977, the two men are now running four horses in Ray's stables, with others being bought and sold to keep the ledger balanced and controlled. With Churchman's keen eye for horseflesh and breeding, and Ray's meticulous eye for financing and bookkeeping, the two begin to amass success after success. As long as the hobby pays for itself, Ray is willing to stay the course. Thus far, it has been a good choice.

Venturing Out On His Own

It is a good year for the Cottrell family. With a racing career holding a modicum amount of success, tied with a very successful sales career, Ray finds himself flushed with cash, enough at least to allow an attempt to break out on his own. He had found a lot that was available for purchase. Out of his own cash, he buys a six-acre lot. Locking that down gave him a sense of security. Even if the company should fail, he would at least have the land as an asset. After a quick trip to the bank, he secures a $100,000 note for the business. Compliments of being on the G.I. Bill, Ray is running lean and mean here. He rents a trailer for his offices and has it placed on the lot. Ray's Motors opens the doors in Muldraugh. It is not a big place, but he figured he had made quite a name for himself at the dealership, and as such, had enough of a following to take the venture on. A trailer was moved onto the lot to use as an office. It has a couple rooms in it and was purposed just for the business. He purchased eight good used cars with clear titles and has them moved onto the lot to get things going.

Ray is built for the challenge. The argument had been made several times that Ray likes to be in challenging positions. It gives him purpose. It keeps his drive and motivations up. Doing the hardest thing is actually fun for him. That logic explained why he had been in so many situations in his life that most angels would fear to tread. He had been a calculating individual even when he was a child and showed no fear in taking this new challenge on as well. Several years in the army had convinced him that he could do anything as long as he put his mind to it and the work to get it done. Preparation and planning, tied with commitment and the will to work, had not failed him yet and, in his mind, would not fail him now. At this point in his life, Ray had been on a successful roll since that mistake back in high school.

He is by the nature of his experiences an intimidating individual when he wanted to be. Being an instructor at Fort Knox ensured that, but as a salesman, he has improved his skills as a personable sales representative. This bodes well for the new business as well. He could be required to be tactful in some situations and aggressive in others. It was the army that played the biggest role in forming the man he has become. Learned tricks of the trade balanced all that out now that he is the top guy in the company. There is still some honing to be done, but he has always left room at the end of the day for self-improvement. There are some things that he will not compromise on though.

As a summer job while on break from the University of Kentucky, his daughter Brenda was brought in to help with the office duties. She was asked to be in charge of title searches and other office-related duties. Brenda is well equipped to do the job and is all too happy to help her father whenever possible. There is nothing she wouldn't do for her father or family. Ray once told her that if shit really ever hit the fan, he would want her by his side because he believed, like him, she would do whatever it takes to get the job done. As she is working with him, she held the opinion that the office needed some adjustments.

On the walls of Ray's office, Brenda is put off a bit by all the war pictures on the walls. Some of the pictures are rather graphic, and she took a moment to address that issue with her father. At this time in his life, Ray doesn't like to be told what to do. He answers to no one now that he is out of the army. He rides a motorcycle, has long hair and a beard, and completes his look with a gold chain and a leather jacket. It is a transitional period for him, and he is just keeping up with the times in his mind.

Brenda tells her father, *"You can't have these pictures in your office like that. They can be detrimental to selling cars. Some little old lady could walk in here and get grossed out or pissed off by seeing these things."* Her father says in a stern intimidating voice, *"It is my business, and my office, and I'll run it the way I want to run it. Customers don't come into my office much. These pictures aren't hurting anyone. I will hang up whatever I want in here."* Brenda responds, *"That is fine. Keep them up if you want to run business off. It is not professional. But if you're wanting to make money, you need to bring them down."* Ray says, *"It's not going to happen!"* With that, she storms out of the room. He can be really stubborn when he wants to be. [4]

Brenda can be stubborn too. She has learned to be manipulative as well. And why not? She has learned from the master. Ray's grit has more than rubbed off on his daughter. He has made many a calculated decision in his life, and Brenda knew that if she was going to affect a change in her father, she will have to get one step ahead of her dad. That is no easy task. He has always been one step ahead of most everything he played a role in, and it was no different with her. As a father, he managed to stay one step ahead of Brenda her whole life. She takes a minute to work out how to handle it.

The following Monday, Ray comes into Brenda's office. He has brought in some title searches for her to resolve. As he lays them on her desk he spies a very disconcerting picture behind her. She has taken a picture from _Time Magazine_ of a Vietnamese mother holding her bleeding baby in her arms. It is now framed and hanging behind her chair. It is very graphic. The picture depicts the collateral damage that the child must have suffered from the fighting in the war. This of course puts Ray on his heels. He immediately tells her, _"What do you think you doing? You need to take that picture down. No one wants to see that."_

Brenda is quick to respond in a mocking tone, _"The last time I looked, this is my office, and I can hang whatever I want in it. If you don't want to look at it, all you have to do is call me. I will come to your office if you need me, but you don't have to come in here! You won't have to see it."_ Ray responds, _"I don't give a shit. You need to take that down!"_ Brenda retorts, _"I will take it down when you take your pictures down!"_ Frustrated and annoyed, he exits her office mumbling under his breath. He feels like he has just been had.

By the end of the week, Ray's pictures are down and his office takes on a more professional look about it. Ray had always associated himself with the army even though he appears to be rebelling. It was no easy thing for him to cut back on memorabilia and reminders, but he also knew that Brenda was right. He needed to bring a more professional look to the business if he really wanted to get ahead. No words are spoken with his daughter, but he noticed that her picture came down the same day as well. [4]

The business is growing. The successes far outweigh the losses. Ray knew how to balance the books and what it took to keep things going. It took only a couple of years at the dealership to figure out all the ins and outs of selling cars. It was in his nature to consume all that could be consumed in the ways of knowledge whenever it was available to learn. This business kept him running full steam and under control. The added challenge of maintaining his fledgling horse career filled his days completely. This is what Ray likes: a full day's worth of challenges and decision-making. It is as if he is still that NCO back at Fort Knox, handling this and handling that for his superiors, except now it was all on his shoulders and for his benefit. When he leaves the house in the morning, he even informs Lovey that he is "heading to camp." Working all day, and going home at night, leaves him with the sense of a job well done. That is his way. By 1979, his lot has grown to forty vehicles.

Before his second year in business comes to a close, the success of Ray's Motors had caught the attention of people who could bolster his career. A Ford representative had come forward and asked Ray if he would be willing to take his talents to the next level. The Ford Motor Company was interested in having a dealership in Meade County. Only twelve miles away from his current location, the proposition has captured his attention. Meade County was devoid of any main dealerships at the time. The research revealed that the growth within the county was suitable and sustainable for a Ford dealership. He would be in a position between Corydon, Indiana, and Fort Knox, Kentucky. In fact, it would be the only dealership from Corydon heading south, all the way to Dixie Highway. Anywhere on a main road in Brandenburg would suit the needs of the business just fine.

When a business decides to invest in such a venture, many calculations are considered. Things such as: what is the growth potential of the surrounding 5-/10-/25-/50-mile radius of the business? What is the population within that prescribed area? What is the average income of the residents within the area the dealership will operate in? Can a suitable sales force be brought to bear at the new site? What would the expected sales rate in units within the community and outlying area be? What are sustainable sales goals to be to make the business and the investment logical and profitable? The sales representatives at Ford knew all these answers. Ray and his small sales force fit the bill completely. In fact, Ray himself believed he could pull it off. After all he was not only pulling phenomenal numbers from the base at Fort Knox, but he was also pulling business from the surrounding counties as well. Not all his business was relegated to Fort Knox. Ray is a little nervous about the venture, but it is, yet again, another challenge that he must be successful at. Challenges are his thing.

Ray sees in the dealership more than just a challenge or a test. It is an opportunity not only for him but for the entire family. Lovey was learning the ins and outs of the horse racing industry. She is getting more and more involved in his hobby and is understanding the management side of it. Ray Jr. would be given the opportunity to learn several skills that he could use throughout his life as well. Ray realized as well that, with the dealership, he could get the family in a better home. Lovey could start to enjoy many of the things that, as a military wife, she had gotten used to doing without. The mere chance to expand the family budget is a welcome thing. Ray's successes are becoming family successes. It is an opportunity for the entire family to get a secure foothold that would offer many opportunities going forward. The days of pawning the old shotgun have seen their last days. Contracts are drawn up, and again, Ray is off on a new challenge.

Opening day at the new lot is a nervous but exciting time. Friends of the family come to show their support. Ray has a few cars that will be sold before the doors are even opened. Several people were awaiting this opening day. These buyers were putting off their purchases just to get the business off to a good start. Banners are hanging, balloons are floating on every car in the lot, and the entire business is abuzz.

The building sits on the bypass of Brandenburg. It is the busiest road in the county. Across the street is a large shopping center with a Kroger store as its anchor. Ray owns several acres and a large road frontage. The Brandenburg bypass is the link between Corydon and Brandenburg. Just a few miles away is the main thoroughfare that leads to Dixie Highway and Fort Knox. It is the only direct route to Louisville. A better site could not have been chosen for the business. In six short years, he has gone from rookie salesman to a major business owner. His tenacity cannot be overlooked. Ray is built for success. He doesn't like to lose. His talents minimize that action.

Author's note: I offer this note at this point because the actions Ray is taking this day is happening in real time. At the time of this writing, on March 24, 2016, Ray Cottrell is suffering from a major hernia. According to his doctors, the need to correct the problem could no longer be put off. The risk of internal infection was becoming too great. The pain from the issue is becoming too much as well. Ray has other medical issues complicating the surgery. He suffers from diabetes and heart problems. He is now eighty-three years old, and the surgery has put his family and many of his friends into an anxious state. His outlying issues could result in a very unwanted outcome as a result so late in life. The surgery was scheduled at 1600 hours in Louisville. He was kept in the hospital for observation. In true Ray Cottrell style, by 1441 on March 25 Ray personally takes my phone call. NOT to my surprise, he was sitting in his desk at the dealership conducting business. I asked him if he was doing anything for the pain. He responded, "The doctor offered me some medication that he said would remove all the pain that I have. I told him to just prescribe something that was a little stronger than a Tylenol." I reminded him of what I told him before the surgery, "I am not worried for you Ray. You can't hurt gristle." We both enjoyed the laugh. It is in the tradition of the man that I have come to know. He has a warrior's heart, and that beat cannot be easily extinguished. This is not the first time that Ray has made such a choice. When he was told that he had to have his pacemaker replaced, he did so only using a local anesthetic. The event is a shining example of his fortitude and commitment. Some would argue that he borders on the insane, but when looking at his full body of work, it is just another Thursday. Lovey was once asked if she thought that Ray should retire and take life easy. She responded, "He can't do that. That will kill him." [6]

CHAPTER 12

There are several grazing paddocks for his retired racers.
The fillies are separated from the geldings and studs. One
of three fillies is pictured here still bearing its winter coat
as the Keeneland spring meet gets underway. [2]

BY THE MIDDLE of the 1980s, Ray's Ford is very well-established. The business is flourishing, and so is the family. A new house had been purchased in Meade County. It is a large parcel of land that is sided by a hill to the west. The original property has been partially broken up by piece and parcel, but the bulk of it was left intact. Because of the tireless work of his son Ray Jr., who has developed part of the land, a sprawling neighborhood now surrounds the family home. Upon coming onto the property, the first things seen are a painted pony and a soldier standing guard at the entrance. While there are several animals on the property, including two guard dogs, it is a stray Canadian goose named Goo Bird that is the true sentinel of the land. To cross him is to take the flogging of a lifetime. Even the dogs know better than to mess with this beast.

The income of the company and Ray's diversifications in the market have helped in the building of stalls for some of his most prized possessions—his horses. Lovey has become more involved in racing, and that takes up a lot of the family's free time. She has even been known to travel to

Pictured here is Goo Bird in all his glory, a stray Canadian goose that has decided to take over the land by force. [2]

One of two horses bought by the Cottrell family. It is a promotional item with proceeds going to charity. The second painted pony is located in the dealership as an automotive theme. This one stands to the left of the main entrance to the property. [2]

The guard at the gate. Posted on the right side of the main entrance. In the background is one of the gelding pastures. [2]

the tracks without him. They travel to Keeneland, Churchill Downs, and Turfway Park pretty regularly. It is a great way to spend the weekends when he chooses to take a day off from the dealership. His stables are growing in size as well as the herd of horses that he is working. He has come a long way from the early days of Knox Motors and the kick-start that Jim Moore had offered him. By the end of 1989, Ray has accumulated over twenty horses. Some are in stakes races, while others are in claiming and maiden races.

With so many horses in the mix, his need for more help also increases. Other trainers had to be brought in to keep up with the need. Paul McGee and Kenny McPeek are now part of his work group. Marsha Lee Butler and Helen Pitts are also added to the group as trainers. This speaks to Ray's belief in treating everyone equally. It is a major enterprise now. Horses are stabled in all three of the race tracks in Kentucky as well as his private stable at home, but it is not until 1990 that Ray gets to step into the world of royalty.

John Churchman and Ray had decided that they had a horse that was worthy of the highest honor in the racing industry, having one of their horses in the starting gate of the first leg of the Triple Crown. The Kentucky Derby is without a doubt the most prestigious horse race in the world. Over 128,000 people show up in person to watch this race take place at the southern center of Louisville. This number is consistently growing year over year since its inception 114 years earlier. It will be watched by millions of people worldwide from Australia to Dubai. The breeding value of a Derby winner could yield a $35,000-per-stud fee, and the purse of $2 million is what makes it one of the most wanted trophies in the business. The only thing greater would be to win all three races in the Triple Crown, which also includes the Preakness Stakes and the Belmont Stakes. Only twelve horses since its inception has made that goal so far. Ray is reaching high at this point, but it isn't just the love of the competition or the race itself. It is his love of the animals themselves.

The biggest motivation for going after the Derby in 1990 was set at the behest of one his granddaughters. Ashley is Brenda's daughter and is now six years old. She is suffering from the healing process of a brain tumor operation. She is rehabbing in the hospital in Louisville. Ray and John originally wanted to run his horse Fighting Fantasy in a shorter race in the Illinois Derby. It was a race where the horse would have been one of the favorites and stood a great chance at winning the $200,000+ purse. Ray decided earlier on that Ashley wouldn't be able to watch that race and wanted to ensure that she saw Fighting Fantasy run. He knew that the horse was a long shot for the Run for the Roses, but he has always favored beating the odds when a logical chance availed itself. Besides, he had never experienced the Kentucky Derby from an owner's point of view.

Over one hundred horses have been in and out of his barns, but this one is special. It is named after his granddaughter Ashley Tyree. A winner! [1]

Fighting Fantasy has five wins and three shows at this point, enough to qualify him as a Derby hopeful. The $30,000 entry fee is put up. John Churchman worked with this horse extensively to prep him for the

Illinois Derby. The horse came from good breeding lines and was made for speed. Fighting Fantasy shares a lineage with the great Man O' War through War Relic. He is adorned with Ray's colors, which are based in a vibrant pink silk. It was one of only two horses that Churchman ever offered up to Ray as a possible Derby contender. The majority of Churchman's selections for Ray would run claiming and stakes races up to this point. None were higher than Grade II races until now.

When the gates open, Fighting Fantasy moves up with four other horses jockeying for the lead. By the 1/4 mile pole, the lead group is well formed and starting to separate from the field. At the 1/2 mile pole, Fighting Fantasy is running hard with the leaders who are four wide at the turn. By the 3/4 mile pole, he is still hanging with the lead pack, but as he makes the final turn to the finish line, the two leaders have broken from the lead pack and the distance had proven to be just a little too much. Fighting Fantasy is out of gas by the finish line and was laying off. By the time the other fourteen horses cross the line, Ray's horse is at the very back. The race finishes in 2:02 flat, three seconds over the track record. For a moment he is a shining star, and by the end, like all comets, he is falling out. He had burned too brightly and too fast. The Kentucky Derby is regarded as the fastest two minutes in sports for a good reason. Shane Sellers, the jockey on board, just couldn't get the production out of his horse. Today's race would fall to the winner, Unbridled.

Ray is not diminished by the results of the race. The opposite is the actual effect. He is more than content to just be a part of the pinnacle of racing history in and of its own right. Lovey has also there with him in all the excitement. He is just grateful that the horse and rider crossed the line unharmed, and he is now considering his options in recreating the day's events for next year's race. Like every other committed owner, he wants to start work immediately to find the combination to pull off one of the toughest titles to hold. It takes a strong man to deal with such a financial loss, but Ray takes the positive approach. A lot of time and money had been spent to get Fighting Fantasy into the race, but the horse had proven himself prior to that by winning enough money and races to qualify. It was not a total wash. He is reminded of his first time in battle and how sometimes he just had to go through it and worry about the lessons to be learned after it is done.

In the following year, the 1991 Kentucky Derby is firmly in his sights. Wilder Than Ever is the hopeful for him this day. The country is under its third year with a Republican president and had been enjoying a rather peaceful existence up until 1989. That peace had been severed by the actions of a little-known ruler in the Middle East.

Gen. Norman Schwarzkopf is the commander overseeing the Gulf War for a thirty-eight-country coalition. This war is the largest coalition of nations since WWII, known in the United States as Operation Desert Shield. Two years earlier, Iraq had invaded the gulf country of Kuwait, a major oil distribution hub and refinery country in the region. It is a small country on the Mediterranean with no standing army. Saddam Hussein and his Ba'athist Iraqi forces had marched into the sovereign country under royal rule to plunder it and hopes to hold it for their own uses. Desert Shield is the operation for the buildup of U.N. forces in protection of Saudi Arabia and other Middle East countries and will be the launching point for the counteroffensive Operation Desert Storm. The objective is to dislodge Iraqi forces from Kuwait and send them packing. When Desert Storm is launched, the Iraqi forces are quickly depleted and sent running back to Baghdad. In a surprising turn of events, President George Bush holds the forces back from the nation's capital and taking Saddam Hussein out of power thereby initiating a free and democratic Iraq. General Schwarzkopf's notoriety on the national level is what prompted Derby coordinators to invite him to the event.

Louisville is all consumed for the two weeks leading up to the race. It is kicked off with North America's largest fireworks show, Thunder over Louisville. A mini-marathon, a balloon race, and "The Great Steamboat Race" round out just some of the other events leading up to the fastest two minutes in sports. The Derby Parade shares equal billing with these other events as precursors to the derby. General Schwarzkopf was invited as the marshal for the parade this year.

Picking winners. From the Cottrell library. [1]

John Churchman had been working Wilder Than Ever up for the Derby specifically. He is hands above the rest in the Cottrell stables. Instead of being a long shot, he goes off at race time as a 14-1 shot in the race of sixteen. The track is slow this day under partly cloudy skies, but the temperature is warm and just right for racing. When the gates open and the race is off, Wilder Than Ever is biding his time in the back with Strike the Gold. With many Derby winners, it is common to stay off the lead horses to the rear and then make their run for the Roses coming off the final turn to take the lead. The pace is slow at the half mile and seconds off the race's record pace. The horses are running as a pack with only four links of separation. At the half mile, and in 46.5 seconds, Strike the Gold had moved up to twelfth as Wilder Than Ever is still behind him. Strike the Gold has started to make his move, but Ray's horse is still behind. At the wire, Strike the Gold takes the trophy in 2:03.08 seconds, as Wilder Than Ever starts his final kick too late and comes up short of the money. Ray will have to accept another loss, but at least his horse was not last. It is disappointing, but all the buildup to this day and the family's chance to once again share in a part of his love and racing history is all Ray needed to make the entire few minutes worthwhile. It is another moment in time which he or his family will never forget and look back upon in fondness.

In the mid-'90s, Ray's stables had grown to forty horses in various levels of the racing industry. Most are in the claiming and stakes levels. He is searching, along with his four trainers, for that winning combination that might put him in the winner's circle. While his sights are high, the overall majority of his horses are at the lower levels of competition. His experience has taught him what it takes to make the commitment to a Grade I race like the Kentucky Derby, but those opportunities are rare and fleeting. On the other hand, he was enjoying great successes at the other levels. Wilder Than Ever would take third in the Jim Beam Cup as a five-year-old just two years later, thus solidifying the horse's ability to be a good earner.

Not all of Ray's successes would be on the dirt track. He has linked into a proven turf horse in the early 2000s. Under the training of Kenny McPeek, Prince Arch would win against other proven horses from great trainers such as Bob Baffert and D. Wayne Lukas and notable owners such as Toby Keith. His wins put Ray and his family in such circles as never realized before. After all, it is the sport of kings.

Working with McPeek, Prince Arch would prove to be one of Ray's best horses and was offered a spot in the Dubai Classic overseas. He is to take part in the $2 million purse of the Sheema Classic. To race there is an honor in its own right. It is by invitation only and is achieved by catching the eyes of their sponsors. In 2005, Prince Arch set a new course record for 1 3/16 miles while winning the Grade I Gulfstream Park Breeders' Cup Handicap over the lawn. While Prince Arch was a proven winner, and Ray was looking at an all-expense-paid trip for the chance to run there, the offer is officially taken up by Brenda and her husband Mike. It was too far to go for Ray and Lovey, and he had no interest in being in a plane for that long. The trip would prove to be exciting, but unfortunately Brenda was not lucky enough to bring home a trophy in her father's stead. Prince Arch would finish fourth in a tight race with other champions. Perhaps the journey was just a little too much for the Prince to take as well. Perhaps he needed Ray there to psych him up before the race.

The family that plays together stays together. Florida, 2005. [1]

While he would not put another horse in the Kentucky Derby, he would hold more horses that made his hobby worthwhile. The successes still outweigh the losses. Ray's favorite horse in his stable is Birdbird Is The Word. The horse was bought in the fall sale at Keeneland for $40,000. Douglas Archibald, his friend and fellow combat veteran, is in attendance with him. Moose and Ray are in the stable area of the track following the purchase. They were discussing the value of the horse and what to name it as they stand in front of his stall. As they talk, a starling flies in and lands on the horse. Moose tells him, *"There is your answer, man. That bird just swooped in like we used to do in Vietnam with our helicopters."* Ray asks, *"Are you saying we should call him Bird? Is bird the word?"* Moose retorts, *"There you go. It is just that easy."*

The helicopter pilots were called into battles and rescues a thousand times in Vietnam. Oftentimes, the only words the soldiers want to hear are "The bird is coming in" or "We will have birds on the ground any moment!" For many a warrior on the ground, the word "bird" is all they needed to give them hope in such desperate situations. The timing of the conversation with the timing of the starling landing is the light-bulb blinking on. Ray's affinity for the army and those who served in it will always hold a special place in his heart. It is decided that the horse would be named in the honor of all the chopper pilots that served so valiantly during the war. The name is registered shortly thereafter.

Like many of his horses, Ray holds a special place for Birdbird as he is called by his handlers and owner. He is their third Kentucky Derby hopeful. With Kenny McPeek at the helm for training and several years of racing experience behind both him and Ray, they think they finally have a combination that is worthy of the task. For McPeek, Ray is one of the first owners to take a chance on him as a new trainer. After years of teaming together, the relationship is more than just business. A strong friendship had formed. For Birdbird to get to the garland of roses, criteria had to be met. Ray and McPeek made sure all the others lines crossed and I's dotted, but it would all be for naught if the horse couldn't produce.

However, producing is what Birdbird does best. On August 18, 2006, the horse is entered into his first stakes race. The win follows eight furlongs later on turf. The two are literally off to the races. Owner and trainer couldn't be more pleased. Plans are immediately made for his next race. One month later, Birdbird hits the starting gates again, but this time on dirt. He is shooting for the $100,000 purse in the Harrah's Juvenile in Louisiana. Again, Birdbird steps up for the win. The horse is now carrying some of his weight. Ray hasn't broken even yet on the horse financially, but the second win got him closer. The two men are sharing in the excitement of a 2–0 start, and McPeek says that he will be ready to race again in two weeks. He holds that the horse has spunk and drive, and his owner readily believes that he has the heart of a fighter.

By October 7, Birdbird is slated for the Breeder's Futurity and had been shipped up from Louisiana to Kentucky. He is stabled at one of

Ray's favorite tracks, Keeneland. This was the land of D. Wayne Lukas. As a trainer, Lukas has more wins in this race than any other trainer in the field. Lukas started winning this race in 1991, but his last win came in 2004. This race has a $500,000 purse, and the competition for two-year-olds was high. It stands until this day as a great training ground for horses gearing up for other Grade I races like the Kentucky Derby. With a few issues coming out of the gate, and just a few seconds of the win, Birdbird comes in the lead group in fourth place. Other trainers such as Bob Baffert and Dale L. Romans also had the hope to bring their horses through the finish line at the Breeder's Futurity as well. It just wasn't Birdbird's day. He was coming on and driving as the horses cross the line that day. Ray believes if this race had just a few more lengths to it, Birdbird could have taken the win. Had he not been pinned on the rail early in the race and had started his kick a little sooner, the results would have been different. Ray sees heart in this horse and is easily convinced to stay with him. He goes back to Louisiana for another chance to bring home a win.

Ken McPeek believes that Birdbird needed a little more training. He was a good strong horse that liked to run, but if he is going to become as productive as the two men wanted, he would need more time off between races to be at his best. Birdbird had great results in Louisiana with two previous wins. Perhaps the familiarity with the track there offered a good opportunity to get something going as well. With hat in hand, McPeek and Ray move the horse south for warmer climates for the oncoming winter racing schedule.

Delta Downs in Louisiana is one of four racetracks in the state. Its location is closer to Houston than it is to New Orleans and over one hundred miles south of Shreveport, where Birdbird knocked off his first two wins. The Delta Downs jackpot is the second highest purse in North America behind the Breeder Cup Juvenile for two-year-olds with $1 million in purse money at stake. It is safe to say that had Birdbird won in Keeneland two months earlier, the trip to Louisiana would be unnecessary. Delta Downs was struck hard by Hurricane Rita in 2005, so the restorations have finally been completed for the 2006 racing season. All the preparations for the race that could be made had been made. The track record to beat at this 1 1/16–mile course is 1:45.34, and Ken McPeek feels that Birdbird is in a good position to beat it. The seasoned jockey Robby Albarado gets the nod to mount up. Robby is a native of Louisiana and started his racing career at age twelve in 1985. He got his first win at Evangeline Downs, 100+ miles to the east in the heart of Louisiana racing in 1990. He was a great choice for this race now that Albarado had almost twenty years of experience in his home state along with Ray and Ken's trust.

Night racing is all the rage these days, and this race is set to be under the lights as well. Ray is in full traditional mode. He makes the walk from the stables to the paddock area with his horse and handler. Birdbird is regaled in the Cottrell hot pink silks and will be set in the eighth gate, and Ray himself is donning a hot pink tie with a light pink oxford shirt under his suit. He had racing colors to fly as well, and this was his tradition. It is a ten-horse field on this cool December 1 night. If Birdbird can do well here, the plans going forward had already been laid out. Ray's ability to plan ahead was still in the forefront of his thinking as he approaches his late seventies. It is what CSMs have always done, and it is something he will continue to do. As the horses are moved to the track, Ray takes his seat with his family. His bets had been laid hours before.

Once the last horse is locked in from behind in the starting gate, it is only seconds before the front gate is opened and tons of electric energy is unleashed on to the dirt and into the air for another mad dash to the wire. The horses haven't traveled a hundred yards and Birdbird is bumped four times from both the horses to the sides of him. The first one-sixth mile takes the horses past the last turn and in front of the grandstands. Seven of the ten horses immediately jockey for a place near or on the front. Albarado comes out of the gate a little slower than the rest and is running ninth as they pass Ray's first head-on look at this beast of power and torque. At the 1/4 pole, Birdbird is at approximately 25.00 seconds, while the leader is clocking off at 21.92. He is holding ninth as they go into the first turn, five lengths off the leader. When they come out of the first turn, Albarado is waiting for his moment.

On the backstretch, Birdbird is starting his move. At the 1/2 mile pole, the leaders are slowing up and timing in at 44.96 seconds while Birdbird was surging faster and coming in at 46.00 and change. He loves to run straight, but more importantly, he just loves to run. Robby had held him back and was riding high to what they knew would be a fast pace. He didn't want to burn the horse's power out too early, and Albarado is feeling the power under him. At the 3/4 mile pole, the leader is holding but coming in slower at 1:10.78 and 1:38.29, respectively. Birdbird had closed the gap running in the middle of the track on the backside and put himself on the outside of the final turn as he starts taking horses out like so many scalps in the wild west. He is four horses wide going into the final turn and has passed seven horses with a one-length lead coming out of it. It was like watching Secretariat in the 1973 Kentucky Derby. The overall favorite had been holding second the entire race until the end of the backstretch where he takes the lead. In this race, it was Malt Magic and not Sham, the second-place horse in all three of Secretariat's Triple Crown wins. But like Secretariat's race, out of the corner of the viewers' eye, there was this disturbance off to the left of the others. It was Birdbird stomping past seven horses in the final turn like a light switch had been turned on or like nitrous oxide was poured into the carburetor of an engine. In the last twelve seconds of the final turn, Birdbird thundered past like the others were just trotting along. By the time Birdbird goes into the final stretch, Malt Magic is one-and-a-half lengths behind. The 9–2 favorite was gassing out after a short lead in the final turn.

Just like Secretariat in 1973, Birdbird had successfully ran every 1/4 mile faster than he ran the one before. In the last four hundred yards, Albarado offers a couple light taps with the crop to ensure Birdbird doesn't lay off now that he is firmly in the lead. As they cross the line, Malt Magic has dropped off to fourth, but that doesn't matter. Birdbird crosses the finish at 1:45.42 and misses the track record by 0.09 second. Pirate's Deputy was challenging at the end and places one-half length off the lead, followed by Exchanger to show. Exchanger is three lengths back at the finish. Birdbird had successfully held both these horses off as they surged past the favorite as well after the final turn. After a quick cooldown deep into the track, horse and jockey make their way to the winner's circle one more time to meet with the owner. It is Birdbird's fourth win in five outings. Tonight's win puts Birdbird's winnings at over $700,000. Great production for a year's worth of work.

In March of the following year, Birdbird is trained up for the Louisiana and Florida Derbies, respectively. He finishes fifth in the Louisiana on March 10. By March 31, at the Florida Derby, he accomplishes seventh place in the $3 million purse out of the #7 gate. The loss to Liquidity and Scat Daddy was enough to convince Ray that this will not be another derby horse. That doesn't mean that he is done with racing, but he is done traveling. A horse only has one chance as a three-year-old to win the Kentucky Derby's garland of roses, and it has to be at peak performance to win the Triple Crown in the five grueling weeks over the three states of traveling that make it up.

Working out his prerace jitters and putting on their war face. Left to right, Prince Arch, Ray Cottrell, Larry Green. Horse and owner share the same mindset. [3]

Over the next few years, Ray is starting to back down on horse racing. It was a hobby in the beginning, and it was now time to be just a hobby again. Birdbird runs his last race in 2009 as a five-year-old and comes in fifth at the Kee Allowance.

When asked about the possibility of returning to the track, he tells his friends, "I am only in a holding position now." With all the racing enthusiasm now on the shelves of his trophy cases, Ray takes the time to visit with his retired workers of the track. Ray stables eleven horses at his barns back on the farm in Kentucky. His grandson, Ryan Tyree, tends to their needs daily now as well as handles most of the physical requirements on the farm. Ryan is Ray's number one go-to guy on the weekend too. Oftentimes, he can be seen as Ray's personal assistant on the weekends when the bulk of the staff are otherwise engaged. Sunday is the day that he gets to spend with his grandfather the most. It is Ryan's and Ray's day together.

Ray is content in knowing that his team of running warriors can now retire in peace under his oversight and care. They have all brought great joy to both the family and himself for many years, and he finds it only fitting that they be well taken care of because of it. It had been four decades since he bought his first horse, and ten of them are still with him today.

Ray has more than made his mark in racing. He was a two-time "owner of the meet" at Churchill Downs. This same title was afforded him also at Turfway and Keeneland as well. These titles were unintentional consequences in a good way and lent themselves to his love of the horses and the people that helped him get there. One does not shoot for titles such as these in his mind. It is just a welcome sign of respect to owners whose horses had consistently been at the winner's circle during the sessions. Only the top winners get this award. He accepts these titles in the same humility that he has taken all his other compliments.

Photo of one of Ray Cottrell's trophy cases. [2]

In the Meantime

There is much more going on in the house of Cottrell other than horse racing and selling cars. Ray Jr. is the general manager and is the number two man at Ray's Ford. He has been working with his father for over thirty years now. He travels to auto auctions and handles the inventory moving in and out of the dealership. His oversight, like his father's before him, moves the company

Photo of one of Ray Cottrell's trophy cases. [2]

Photo of one of Ray Cottrell's trophy cases. [2]

There are six trophy cases held in state at Ray's Ford. This does not include trophies that are held at home and other locations. A reflection of his horse's accomplishments over forty-two years of racing. [2]

Author's note: In a personal phone interview with Ken McPeek on April 11, 2016, Ken revealed that he was only twenty-seven when Ray Cottrell offered his full trust in Ken's decision-making, buying, training, and handling of any of the horses that Ray approved money for him to buy. Ken holds that Ray, while not the first owner whose horses he has trained, is actually the first owner who catapulted him into the upper levels of the industry. Ken went on to say, *"Horseracing is like climbing a ladder. You start out with maiden races, and if the horse does well, you go up to claiming races. The next step is stakes races. From there to Grade III, Grade II, and Grade I races."* The Louisiana and Florida Derby are GII and GI races, respectively. While Birdbird is a great horse, he didn't produce well in the climb up the final rungs. When I spoke to Ken during the spring meet at Keeneland, he held nothing but great regard for Ray saying, *"He has been a father for me, and our relationship is over twenty-five years and still going. He doesn't get off the phone with me without him telling me that he loves me."* [4]

Turfway Park 1999. The signage in the upper left corner reads "Congratulations Leading Owner Raymond Cottrell". Ray is pictured here on the right receiving the award for the meet. [1]

forward in these changing times. Holding three college degrees, one in automotive technology and two in business, not to mention being an accomplished builder and contractor, he has become somewhat a jack of all trades. One could try to make the argument that it is tough to live under the shadow of his father, but Ray Jr. holds no such ideas. He is happy being so close to his father for so long. It is a blessing that most men don't get to enjoy or experience. The two men have been a traveling pair for decades now, from going out on motorcycle rides as a young man with his father, to army reunions and a trip to the racetracks, there are times they are inseparable. Ray Jr. holds the same work ethic as his father. A week's vacation would still yield a daily visit to the dealership to ensure that everything was going along as needed in his absence. [10]

As a respected and prominent family in Brandenburg, it is not uncommon for organizations to seek the Cottrell family out for help and support of the activities of the town. The degree of philanthropy that the family takes part in is no small matter. Ray Jr. enjoys being a part of it and another driving force in the community. He is a little more low-key than his father, but has the same big heart.

Photo taken from the meeting room at Ray's Ford. Just a small snapshot of the type of support the family helps with. [2]

Sickened by the loss of lives of the military men and women serving in Iraq, Ray's Ford holds a benefit concert on the property in 2005. In honor of the fallen, an American flag was bought and placed in the grass to the front of the property. One flag for everyone lost in the war was brought in. By the war's end, over two thousand flags adorned the grass medium along the bypass that is the front of the dealership. Proceeds from the benefit went completely to the KIAs' families. The daylong event included music, food, and refreshments. The turnout was in the hundreds and considered to be very successful.

Ray's Ford was also a major contributor to the "One Tucker at a Time" crusade whose intent is to help prevent child abuse of minors in domestic disputes. Tucker Wimpee is the grandson of a Cottrell family friend. He was murdered by his mother's live-in boyfriend. The intent is to not only bring awareness to minors and their plights but also to get legislation passed in the Kentucky legislature to help prevent such things from happening again.

Letter of appreciation from the Fort Knox Veteran Service. [2]

Dancing with Demons

In the era of conflicts with Afghanistan, and two conflicts with Iraq, the issue of working with our military as they come home rises to the forefront yet again. The focus of the citizenry is driven by media, and the distractions of everyday business in the United States leaves little room for the care and maintenance of our veterans. While there are plenty of programs to support our military, the general population's vigor for national pride and commitment to our armed forces has waned tremendously since 9/11 and the falling of the World Trade Center buildings. We no longer spit on our returning soldiers like we did in the '60s, but we fall way short in the support of our returning soldiers to the level that befits their needs.

The discovery of misappropriations, poor management, and a breakdown of services in the Veterans Administration and their hospitals has garnered a surprising amount of focus by not just the ones that rely on their help and support but also by the citizens and those currently in office. The two sides of the coin of our political parties continue to use the issue of veteran support to keep getting votes for their own political gains while the soldiers themselves are ultimately paying the price for the lack of true help.

It was discovered that many patients were listed as being seen by their doctors and making their visits but the reality showed that these documents were being shuffled in such a way as to pad the numbers to make the VA look better and generate more monies, but in the end, the work was not being accomplished. Also, the need for good psychiatric help and practitioners was high while qualified doctors in the field were in very short supply. This led to long wait times to get into the offices to get help and in some cases resulted in the loss of soldiers that could have easily been saved had they got the treatments that they needed. The suicide rate of returning soldiers had elevated to twenty-two soldiers a day. While the VA is built on good intentions, bureaucracy and other issues still plague the government ran organization.

Some doctors were over burdened with patients, while some patients were being misdiagnosed with issues that they didn't have or given prescriptions that they didn't want or need. There seems to be a push to label as many of these veterans as having PTSD, while some patients were working as hard as they can to not be labeled with it. To be assigned the detriment of having PTSD while still on the line was just as dangerous as having frostbite damage back in the '50s. It would be sufficient cause to have the soldier honorably discharged. This issue would lend itself to a conflict with the soldier who was approaching his retirement.

One such marine was in his nineteenth year and approaching retirement while his doctors where trying to prescribe him antipsychotics during a time that he was still required to be in the field manning his tank command. The need to have all his faculties while manning multimillion-dollar weapons of war are in direct conflict with leading your men in wartime America while under prescription medications. The lack of support offered through the VA generated the movement of new organizations to help close the gap between what was needed and those needs fulfilled. To this day, the VA is still in turmoil, but some of the issues are being addressed. While the VA is the biggest organization to help the soldier, it still falls short of supplying the needs of the veteran returning home. It is still far from being effective to the level of need.

Coming home is only the start of reintegration for our returning soldiers. Some of these men have been on the front lines for years while others were injured almost directly upon arrival to the war front. Their physical rehabilitations can take years and multiple surgeries only to bring the individual back to a level short of who they were before they left home. Never reaching a full rehabilitation. And that is just the physical part of their equation. We still have veterans with families fighting the ravages of Napalm from Vietnam and physical issues from the Korean and WWII engagements.

While the country is working on helping the new influx of soldiers coming home from their engagements some soldiers of our past are still fighting to overcome their issues from older engagements of war. For many of these men and women, their ailments and the way the government sees their issues have left them short of what would be considered fair and just in support for putting their lives on the line. The metrics that are used are still considered short minded and ill advised by many in the bureaucracy and citizenry. "Are we doing enough?" will always be the issue.

The mental aspects of our returning combatants are another story altogether. Soldiers of WWII, Korea, and Vietnam are still battling their issues. And for most of them, their rehab takes on a more personal note and oftentimes requires a more personal approach to healing. Oftentimes that help can come from family and friends or maybe a chance encounter with a stranger. It is the small steps that the soldier must take to endure the ravages of the mind. Time and support are two of the biggest components of their healing process. Each brings with them their own personal walls to break down along with their own personal memories that have to be reconciled. That in and of itself is only a part of the healing process. For some of these people, the healing process is never complete. And they take their issues to the grave without ever fully realizing peace.

For Ray, the opportunity to take a leading role in support of veterans takes on many aspects. He is not just relegated to putting up signs, posters, and sending money to charitable organizations. Like Moose, who spends his available time visiting VA hospitals, Ray is called to take an active role on a personal level to help his fellow soldier.

While working at the dealership, late in his life, he receives a phone call from a very distraught wife of a Korean veteran. The lady explains that her husband has become all but catatonic. He will not speak to anyone but his wife. His depression has elevated to the level of stating that he is ready to commit suicide and wants to end it all. She is calling in hopes that Ray may be able to help. After she explained her husband's condition, Ray asks her to bring him in to see him.

The situation is highly critical, and Ray immediately goes into command and control as he sees fit for the situation. When the couple arrives, he offers them a seat in his office and shuts the door. They sit in the two chairs in front of his desk. He immediately speaks to the man, who is insistent on remaining silent. His wife speaks for him. Ray attempts to coax a verbal response but again fails. He speaks to him directly. *"You are a fellow survivor like me. You are home safe with your family. What is it that you can't overcome now?"* The man blankly stares at the desk in front of him and never makes eye contact with Ray.

His wife reports that her husband has needed a doctor's attention for weeks now, and this ongoing problem is just getting worse. She is required to monitor him 24/7 to keep him going. She can no longer keep up this pace. She urges Ray to do something to relieve both of their stresses. Ray grabs the phone and calls the VA hospital in Louisville. He immediately asks to speak with the main desk of the psychiatric unit. He is careful to ensure that he gets names of all the ones he speaks to along the way. Having been a patient at the VA many times before, he is well aware of the operational structure of the hospital. He is direct in his assertions and quickly explains the situation noting that the man is suicidal. When a doctor gets to the phone, he again explains the situation. The doctor tells him that he will have to make an appointment, to which Ray immediately lightly chastises the young woman and states his rank and the situation again. He notes that having the man wait a week or two after waiting so long already is completely unacceptable. *"He needs help today!"*

Now with a greater since of urgency the doctor commits to seeing the couple that day, and with that, they leave and drive off to Louisville. Ray is left sitting at his desk mildly secured in the outcome but still a little uneasy in not knowing the result. He tells the man's wife to contact him again if there are any other issues going forward and that he will do what he can to assist. The unsettling feeling for Ray lingers for weeks before any responses come back over the ordeal.

Three weeks after his chance encounter, he is notified by his secretary that there is a couple here to speak with him. He finishes his phone call and messages back to the front desk and says. *"See them in."* When the office door opens, there before him is the couple from a few weeks earlier. The Korean War veteran before him is full of life and very responsive as if nothing had ever happened. A jubilant wife full of smiles and with a glow upon her face is quick to thank the sergeant major for his small kindness and restoring her spouse back to her. She tells him that her husband had received the much-needed medications that centered him to a working normality. The veteran himself adds his thankfulness as well and expresses that he was about to totally lose his mind and probably would have had Ray not intervened. Ray tells the couple that he is grateful that all things worked out but adds that even if there is no issue, they both are welcome to come visit him at work anytime. His door will always be open for them.

A Man's Work Is Never Done

Ray is still working hard and keeping his plate full. By 2016, he is still at the top of his game in certain aspects of his life. He was part of the Automobile Commission of Kentucky, having received his first appointment by Governor Wallace Wilkerson in 1987. These are three-year appointments. Most get one appointment, maybe two. It's a twelve-person committee. They have five inspectors and the entire department is funded through licensing. No taxpayer money is used to get their finances. Ray only bills for the hours that he works. If he puts in five hours, he bills for five hours. Licensure is $100 a year, and all car sales staff pay $20 a year. Even the manufacturers pay for a license to do business in the state.

The Kentucky Motor Vehicle Commission has been longstanding and is there in protection of the consumers. Ray has been the chairman for that commission for all his time there except the first six months of his original assignment in '87. The law states that an individual gets paid for every day of work on the commission. One hour or ten hours of work are considered a day's worth of work under the guidelines, and Ray is expected to bill accordingly. He chooses to come in much lower than that, though. He only has so much authority as the commissioner, so when he has to, he goes to the committee for a resolution.

The placards seen here were set up during the war in Afghanistan. Like the Vietnam Memorial, the names placed here are the names of U.S. military that were KIA. [1]

Approaching his thirtieth year on the commission, Ray has set two new records. He is the longest-standing committee man in the state's history, and he is also the longest sitting chairman of any committee in Kentucky's history. As such, Ray has shaken hands with five of the last six governors of Kentucky, and it is entirely likely that he will be receiving yet another appointment from the new governor Matt Bevin in the weeks that lay ahead. Within his time under Governor Wilkerson, he was appointed to the subcommittee to determine the viability of adding the lottery to the state of Kentucky's gambling ordinances. Ray was strongly supportive of the measure. When the bill hit the house and senate, it was passed in short order. Kentucky is now part of the national Powerball lottery as well. Funds from the program help pay college tuition throughout the state as well as offering significant revenue for the state. [9]

The life of an NCO CSM is always full when in uniform. The work ethic that he developed as a result of his time in the army has seen to that. Not being in the army has never stopped that level of work and commitment that weaves its way through all that he does. He keeps close ties with his family back home. A day never goes by that he doesn't speak with one of his brothers, Clyde or Billy. To stay prepared and ahead, he always keeps his desk calendar set one day ahead. If it is set on October 4, rest assured that the actual day is October 3. He will glance at it as one of his last things to do when he leaves work so that he knows what to expect the next day. It is always good to have something to look forward to. Always.

Approaching his eighty-fourth year, Ray says, *"I am mellowed out a bit in the last few years. I am a little more forgiving of the smaller things than I used to be."* His grandson Ryan, who just overheard the statement, chimes in and says, *"A little? More like a lot. He used to have his kids police the yard for cigarette butts. But to make sure that they did a good job, he would go out and hide some in the grass just to make sure that they did it."* Ryan then reminds him of the times he would go and visit his grandparents as a child and would have to get up when Ray got up so that Ryan could get his chores done. Ryan tells us that getting them done and getting off the property was always a high priority for him as a kid. It gets a small giggle from his grandfather and a warm smile. Ray knew the value of it. Ryan did too.

Don't Run When You Can Walk

Even this late in life, Ray still holds a keen eye for trouble and a commander's mind for how to handle it. On a road trip back from his job in Frankfurt, he stopped at a convenience store to get something to drink. As he exits the car, he sees two young men in their late teens or early twenties, one white and one black. Both are rather large and could easily overtake him if he wasn't prepared. One is sitting on a bench just in front of his parked vehicle as the other stands next to him. Ray is still a good judge of when something bad is about to happen. As he passes the two on his way into the store, he spies them looking him over as he goes by. Ray is careful to not make eye contact with them.

While at the register, he casually looks outside and sees that the two are still watching him intently. In short order, he notches out his plan on how to handle it. These guys really have no idea whom they are messing with. Ray exits the store and opens his door fully to put some space between him and the two in the front of the vehicle. The door is making a three-sided barrier with the car he is parked next to. His first order of business is to lower his window all the way. When he gets this done and starts to sit down, he puts his key in the ignition and starts the car before he gets settled. He also ensures that he only pulls his car door but doesn't let it latch. He doesn't bother with a seat belt. At this point, the black man of this daring duo is approaching him. His buddy is still sitting on the bench only a couple of feet in front of his bumper. The car is running and in drive, but the man doesn't seem to notice this as he leans toward Ray's window.

The usual line is uttered. *"Could you give me some money so that I can get something to eat?"* Ray is in position to set his trap but looks the guy over and says, *"You look like you could afford to miss a few meals."* This undoubtedly was true as the man looked to weigh over 300 pounds. The guy goes for a more confident approach and asks again, *"I am really hungry. Could you give me $20?" "I don't think you need it, son. You might want to skip a meal."* The thug takes it to the next level and is now leaning into the car window as Ray leans back a bit to keep him out of his space. Ray now has him where he wants him. He tells Ray, *"Listen, old man. I am not fucking with you. GIVE ME $20!"* Ray couldn't resist messing with him a little more and asks the dumbass, *"Twenty dollars, is that all you want? Why don't you want all of my money?"* The kid retorts, *"GIVE ME SOME MONEY!"*

Ray continues long-playing the situation and calmly says, *"Okay, let me get my wallet out."* With his right hand, he opens up the console and retrieves his wallet. He quickly flips it open to reveal his deputy's badge that Sheriff Joe Greer had issued to him years ago. The now-retired sheriff was with the army in Vietnam in 1968. He was attached to the command HQ of MAAGV in Saigon when Ray was at Camp Holiday Inn. They have been close friends for over forty years. Ray had been sworn in as a deputy sheriff of Brandenburg as a result of this friendship.

Very few reasons had ever arisen for Ray to have to use his badge these days, but today is one of those days. He shows his badge to the idiot as he grabs him by the wrist and quickly tells him, *"Now don't run away. Whatever you do, don't run!"*

The man, now turned boy, is frozen in his tracks. He doesn't know what to think. Ray extends his story. *"This store is currently under surveillance. There are several unmarked officers with a sniper squad in play. So the worst thing you can do right now is take off running. We are looking for a murder suspect and while you don't look like our guy, if you take off running, that might make the officers a little jumpy. You follow me?"* He pauses for a second to ensure that the idiot understands what he is selling to him. He continues, *"So do yourself a favor and walk away all normal like. Don't run!"* Ray puts his wallet in the seat beside him and releases his grip on the now-very-nervous aggressor. The boy now walks over to whisper in his white friend's ear. His buddy slowly gets up, and the two walk over to the end of the building. As they turn the corner, Ray can see them running straight away from the parking lot. He enjoys a small giggle as he fastens his seat belt and closes his door. His plan, should it have gone south, was to pull the big guy into the window and floor the gas pedal. He would have driven all the way past the bench, hitting his buddy and throwing the other to the ground as he drove forward. The door would have ensured that the first guy was thrown forward and put down as he slams into the building. Ray figured in all the commotion that he might get slightly injured, but the action would have ensured that the incident would not escalate beyond that. Cars can be repaired, and the two wannabe gangsters would at worst hobble away. More likely, though, they would have been rendered out of commission until the police got there. The two idiots had no idea just how lucky they truly were. Ray has never lost when it comes to combat. Today would be no different. He never underestimates his opponent, but he prays that they underestimate him. More often than not, awareness, a cool head, and confidence is all that is needed. [8]

Another Unexpected Accolade

Ray Cottrell has amassed many friends and admirers. One such person is fellow infantryman Joshua Ruth of the current U.S. Army. Joshua is a family friend and fellow military man. When Joshua became aware of Ray's full body of work within the military, he took it upon himself to take his appreciation to the next level. In his opinion, Ray Cottrell was worthy of being in the Order of St. Maurice. The award is issued to inductees by suggestion only. It is given by the National Infantry Association (NIA). Joshua had received the award himself months earlier but believed that if anyone deserved the award, Ray Cottrell was it.

The NIA has five levels for this award. Nominees are chosen and awarded based on their contributions to the infantry of the armed forces of both foreign and domestic armies. The Peregrinus Award is given to foreign military personnel who have served in or supported the U.S. Infantry. The next level is called the Civis for civilian personnel who have supported the infantry. The third level is the Legionnaire Award of St. Maurice. It is for outstanding or conspicuous contribution to the infantry. Infantrymen and soldiers of other branches and other U.S. Armed Services are eligible for this level. Active and RC infantrymen who are nominees must be members of the NIA. The fourth level is called the Centurion Award. It is for midlevel brigade and battalion officers or NCOs. It stands for an outstanding contribution to the infantry and the recipient must have been in an infantry branch. Active and RC nominees must be members of the NIA as well. [6]

Ray has been nominated, unbeknownst to him, for the highest level attainable of the Order of St. Maurice. It is called the Primicerius. This award is for those who have made a significant and lasting contribution to the entire infantry with a special version of the award going to the Infantry Doughboy Award winners each year. Recipients of this highest level must be or have been in an infantry branch. Being a member of the NIA is also a requirement as well. Like the two men at the convenience store, Ray has no idea what is coming.

On the day of the ceremony, he was prepped for the day's events by misinformation. He was told that they were giving away free food as an incentive to get people on the lot and that they were celebrating a current Fort Knox soldier. The expectation was to use the front lot as the staging ground. Ray was kept out of sight of the podium and microphone, which had been set up earlier in the morning. Everything was going along as planned.

Ray is none the wiser of all this. It was common to have special events at the dealership. His curiosity is only modestly raised over the issue, but when he realized that it wasn't April Fool's Day, he becomes more settled into the idea. On April Fool's Day several years prior, he was returning to the lot and sees an ambulance, a fire truck, and Sheriff Joe Greer's car holding a position on the far end of his property. Police tape was employed as well to set up a mock shooting. All his employees are standing around at what looked like a body completely covered with a blanket on a stretcher. Even the county coroner was in attendance. Ray knows all these people personally. All this was laid out as a really intense April Fool's joke that nearly got the sheriff punched in the mouth. Ray had sworn off doing any April Fool's jokes after that day. But it wasn't April. To sell him on a lie is not relatively easy. They got him where he lives. He has always been eager to help out a fellow military man. This is what made it all come together.

By early afternoon, attendees are starting to arrive. Everyone invited was held to secrecy on the intent. The news channel was setting up for the broadcast as his employees endeavor to ensure that Ray has no reason to leave the property until the ceremony begins. He just believes that everyone is there for the free food, so it struck him as a little strange to have TV cameras. But in the end, he dismisses it all. When everything is in order, all his employees are asked to stop what they are doing and head outside to take part in the ceremony. Joshua Ruth takes the podium and starts to explain the medal and its history. They were informed that there many great recipients of St. Maurice Medals, but the Primicerius Medal was a little more rare. The audience was also informed that Gen. Collin Powell had been a recipient of the Primicerius. After a short speech, Joshua announces the true intent of the event. Ray can do little more than blush at the surprise. He is really taken aback. This award put Ray in some really strong company.

Ray Cottrell pictured here receiving the Primicerius award from fellow Legionnaire recipient Joshua Ruth. [5]

It is extremely hard to shock Ray these days, but this does it. He understood the value of the award, but he hasn't thought much about military awards for forty years. It goes without saying that he had no expectation of receiving one himself. When he is asked to come forward for the presentation, he finds himself struggling a bit for what to say. In true Ray Cottrell style, he offers a simple and humble "thank you." He tells the audience that his military career had more to do with doing his best over anything else. He explains why it is important to do so, even when no one is watching.

All those involved offer their congratulations as he leaves the podium. The news channel reporter allows a few minutes for him to shake hands with friends and to hug family before they put him on camera. Again, Ray has little more to add than sincere and humble gratitude as his acceptance. He does make note with the reporter that he had no idea it was coming.

Of all the awards and medals that Ray has received, this one has become his favorite. St. Maurice is the patron saint of the infantry.

Maurice was a Christian, but he was also the leader of the legendary Theban Legion of the Roman Army in the third century. The legion was 6,600 men strong at the time of his leadership. Born in Thebes, Egypt, and raised up through the Roman Army, he and his men are in Italy. Maurice is a professed Christian along with his men at a time when Christianity was considered a threat to Rome. The Theban Legion was called into service to Maximian to wipe out peasants who rose against the ever-pressing Roman taxation in the far reaches of the Western territories. [6]

The legion comes upon a town that is Christian based. Maximian gave orders to harass the Christian peasants. Maurice convinces his legion to disregard the order because it is unlawful. In rebuke of the legion's disregard, Maximian orders one of every ten legionnaires to be executed in a process called decimation. More orders are given again, and again Maurice convinces his men to not follow them. A second decimation is ordered and more men are killed off by the lottery. When Maximian orders the killing of the Christians and the men again refuse, the entire legion is put to death. The event takes place in Switzerland where now stands the Abbey of Saint Maurice-en-Valais. Saint Maurice became a patron saint of the Holy Roman emperors. In 926, Henry I even ceded the present Swiss canton of Aargau to the abbey in return for Maurice's lance, sword, and spurs. The sword and spurs of Saint Maurice were part of the regalia used at coronations of the Austro-Hungarian Emperors until 1916. At the same time, the Mauritius Kloster in honor of Maurice was founded in 961. It is easy to see why Maurice is the patron saint of the infantry. [6]

In the seventeen years that I have come to know him and his family, I have struggled to find a good short list of words that I think exemplify all that he is. He has touched so many lives. Oftentimes, he is unaware of the impact of his actions and words and how that has played out upon all who know him. All that you have read thus far is but a short glimpse of who and what Ray Cottrell is. It is my sincerest hope that all that he stands for and has stood for is remembered and mimicked. He has made his mistakes like all of us but has worked to atone for them. He has survived through eight decades of life and almost two and half decades of war on the front lines. His life spans through two centuries. His eyes have seen the worst and the best in man, but in his way, he has laid out a path that is worthy of respect and honor. To follow in these footsteps might seem hard, but for him, it boils down to just a few simple rules. *"Treat everyone the same."* Like the Golden Rule, which teaches us to be unto others as we would have them be to us, so goes Ray. *"Even if they don't treat you well, treat them the same."* The second one is *"do the right thing even if no one is watching."*

Most human beings complain about the meanness of nature, because we are born for a brief span of life, and because this spell of time that has been given to us rushes by so swiftly and rapidly that with very few exceptions life ceases for the rest of us just when we are getting ready for it. Nor is it just the man in the street and the unthinking mass of people who groan over this-as they see it-universal evil: the same feeling lies behind complaints from even distinguished men. Hence the dictum of the greatest of doctors: "Life is short, Art is long." Hence to the grievance, most and proper to a wise man, which Aristotle expressed when he was taking nature to task for indulging animals with such long existences that they can live through five or ten human life times, while a far shorter limit is set for men who are born to a great and extensive destiny. It is not that we have a short life to live, but that we waste a lot of it. Life is long enough, and a sufficiently generous amount has been given to us for the highest achievements if it were all well invested. But when it is wasted in heedless luxury and spent on no good activity, we are forced at last by death's final constraint to realize that it has passed away before we knew it was passing. So it is: we are not given a short life but we make it short, and we are not ill supplied but wasteful of it. Just as when ample and princely wealth falls to a bad owner it is squandered in a moment, but wealth however modest, if entrusted to a good custodian, increases with use, so our life time extends amply if you manage it properly.

Taken from the words of Seneca the Younger, Roman stoic philosopher, "On the Shortness of Life." [7]

ROBERT BROOKS

Ray's Credentials

Ray's Awards from Chosin to Churchill

U.S. Army Silver Star   **CSM Stripes**

U.S. Army Bronze Star

The Purple Heart

Army Commendation Medals   **U.S. Air Medal**   **Meritorious Service**

Vietnam War Medal   **Vietnam Service Medal**   **Overseas Service Bars**   **Combat Inf. Pin with Star**

U.N. Korean War Medal, 1950–51   **Army German Occupation Medal**   **St. Maurice Primicerius Medal**

Of his Silver and Bronze Stars, seven of them are for valor.

"Here are my Credentials" This display case holds all of Ray Cottrell's military medals and a smattering of memorabilia that had been gifted or collected over his years. It is located at the far end of his show room past the Willy's jeep.

[11]

Below is a snippet of the Korean War. It clearly shows the confusion and drama that played out as the rush to control the country went fast. The example below is what leads the author to believe that Ray Cottrell's 2E/31 was diminished by frostbite and created the opportunity for him and his men to end up walking on the ice of the Yalu in late November 1950.

SOUTH TO THE NAKTONG, NORTH TO THE YALU, page 632: The movement to Pusan was not without incident. On two occasions enemy forces ambushed convoys in the mountains near Mun'gyong. The first ambush caught the head of the 2d Battalion, 31st Infantry, at 0200, 6 October, and inflicted nine casualties; the second ambush at 0230, 9 October, caught the division headquarters convoy in the pass three miles northwest of Mun'gyong. Enemy machine gun fire killed six men and destroyed several vehicles. Elements of the 1st Battalion, 17th Infantry, succeeded in clearing the pass area that afternoon. This battalion thereafter patrolled the pass above Mun'gyong until it was relieved on 11 October by the 27th Infantry Regiment of the 25th Division. [19] **SOUTH TO THE NAKTONG, NORTH TO THE YALU**

ROBERT BROOKS

EIGHTH ARMY AND X CORPS ENTER NORTH KOREA, page 635: An unusual incident growing out of this work occurred the night of 16 October. At the north end of the Wonsan Harbor ROK troops had stacked about 1,000 20-pound box mines they had just lifted from the beaches. A ROK lieutenant and five enlisted men decided to have a private celebration, and, moving off about 200 yards, the lieutenant fired into the stacked mines. The mines exploded, shattering panes of glass in the provincial capital building two miles away. Unfortunately, they also killed the six ROK's.

THE CAPTURE OF P'YONGYANG, page 645: North Korean soldiers. The leading soldiers fired at him but missed. Nielson shouted to his driver, "Put your foot on it!" The driver did, and raced four miles through the marching North Koreans. Clearing the last of them, Nielson and his driver took to the hills and stayed there until morning. This enemy force, fleeing in front of the 18th Infantry, 24th Division, and approaching Sariwon from the south, did not know the town had already fallen to U.N. units.

There were many times during that wild night in Sariwon when U.N. soldiers thought the North Koreans were South Koreans coming up from the south with the 24th Division, and the North Koreans thought the British were Russians. There were several instances of mutual congratulations and passing around of cigarettes. One group of North Koreans greeted a platoon of Argylls with shouts of "Comrade!" and, rushing forward in the dim light, slapped the Scots on the back, offered cigarettes, and gave them the red stars from their caps as souvenirs. The ensuing fight was at very close quarters.

Lt. Robin D. Fairrey, the Argylls' mortar officer, walked around a corner into a group of North Koreans. Maintaining his composure, he said to them, "Rusky, Rusky," and after receiving several pats on the back, turned another corner and got away.

During this scrambled night at Sariwon about 150 North Koreans were killed; strangely enough, the British lost only one soldier. Most of the North Koreans passed through the town. North of it the Australian 3d Battalion reaped a harvest, capturing 1,982 North Korean soldiers at its roadblock. Maj. I. B. Ferguson played a leading role in capturing this large number of enemy troops. When the first of them came up to the Australian outpost a night battle seemed imminent. Ferguson mounted a tank and called out in the gloom for the North Koreans to surrender, telling them they were surrounded. After some hesitation, the leading enemy unit dropped its arms and surrendered, and most of the others followed its example. [12]

During the day, while the 27th British Commonwealth Brigade advanced on Sariwon along the main highway, the 7th Cavalry Regiment, with Colonel Clainos' 1st Battalion in the lead, hurried along the poor secondary roads through the hills north of it. This column was about three miles from Hwangju and the main highway above Sariwon when at 1600 in the afternoon it received a message General Gay dropped from a light plane. The message said that the roads out of Sariwon were crowded with hundreds of North Korean soldiers, and it directed Colonel Clainos to have one battalion of the 7th Cavalry turn south at Hwangju on the main highway to meet the British and help trap the large numbers of enemy soldiers in the Sariwon area, while another battalion turned right and held the town of Hwangju. Clinos and the two battalion commanders agreed that the 1st Battalion would turn to meet the British and the 2d Battalion would hold Hwangju. [13]

Soon after turning south on the Sariwon-P'yongyang highway the leading . . .

SOUTH TO THE NAKTONG, NORTH TO THE YALU, page 738: ON THE BANKS OF THE YALU, *two soldiers look across the valley into the mountains of Manchuria.*

ROBERT BROOKS

. . . action that occupied the 17th Infantry during the next week, as long as it was in that part of Korea-daily fights with small but stubborn enemy forces that blew bridges, cratered roads, all but immobilized the regiment, and kept it from making any appreciable gains. At the same time, in front of the 32d Infantry, enemy forces fought effective delaying actions north of Samsu so that not until 28 November did Task Force Kingston, reinforced, reach Sin'galp'ajin. [19]

The intense cold of northeast Korea in late November took its toll in frost-bite casualties in the 7th Division. The worst to suffer was the 31st Infantry which operated in the remote mountain regions east of the Pujon Reservoir. A total of 142 men in the division were treated for frostbite up to 23 November; 83 of them were from the 31st Regiment. Of the 58 men evacuated because of frostbite, 33 were from that regiment. [20]

[12]

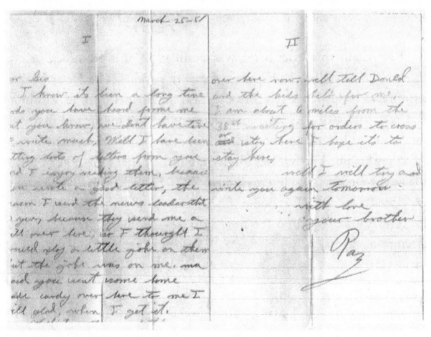

A letter sent home from Ray Cottrell to his sister. The letter starts,

Page I "Dear Sis,

I know it's been a long time since you have heard from me. But you know we don't have time to write much. Well I have been getting lots of letters from you and I enjoy reading them. ????? you write a good letter. I sent the News Leader that 100 yen knowing that they would send me a bill over here, so I thought I would play a little joke on them but the joke was on me. Mom and you sent some homemade candy over here to me. I will glad when I get it." ??????????

Page II "...over here now. Well tell Donald and the kids I said hi for me. I am about 6 miles from the 38th awaiting orders to cross or stay here. I hope it is to stay here. Well I will try and write you again tomorrow.

With love, your brother

Ray.

Ray recalls this letter being written in 1950. It is presumed before the UN Forces follow ROK across the 38th parallel. The News Leader mentioned in his letter refers to the local newspaper back in Virginia. Ray was attempting to pay for an outstanding bill for an add that was taken out for his missing dog. It turns out that 100 yen was not enough to cover the bill. The bill was forgiven, but the paper took note of Ray's inability to understand international monetary exchanges. Their article explained all that back at home. The article was a slight embarrassment for Ray. A One Hundred Yen note amounts to about 45 cents. He was attempting to pay a bill of 5.42$. The newspaper made light of the issue. [11]

ACKNOWLEDGMENTS

TO CSM RAY Hooker Cottrell for his weekly commitments to me week in and week out for fifteen months. The countless phone calls, video interviews, and relentless questions you have taken by me cannot be understated. Your candor and extreme honesty should also be noted to be of the highest order and in keeping with the U.S. military standards. The amount of trust and respect that you have shown me is far and beyond anything I have experienced before. I have a new understanding of what it is to outperform expectations. It is your example that kept me from falling into a state of slack throughout this entire writing. It is your example that has elevated both my thinking and actions in most all that I do now. I have been able to elevate my understanding of the world through a new and better lens for having known you and for taking this project on. May God bless you every day, plus one.

To Lovey Cottrell, thank you so much for your trust in me with regard to the interviewing process and for taking an active role in the research of the book. Seeing the interactions between you and your husband over the past years has motivated me to be a better person and to work harder at it.

To Ray Vallowe, U.S. Army 57th FA and author, whose total knowledge of the Chosin Reservoir experience provided the avenues and data needed to complete the early chapters. From the countless e-mails and phone conversations, I would not have been able to complete almost half of this project without your help and guidance. As a military novice going into this project, I believe your unyielding support in helping me find the critical evidence needed to provide an accurate account of the movements and command structure of the 31RCT and other issues with the Chosin Reservoir account is priceless. Your findings helped in verifying all of Ray

Cottrell's experiences via the validations of Lieutenant Coke of Company E 2/31st INF and Macca Peter Hansen of the 57th FA. Words cannot express my gratitude for your efforts both with the Korean War Project and myself.

To Col. George Rasula, U.S. Army Ret. 31st Polar Bears, whose constant questioning and providing of information allowed me to ask better questions and kept me motivated to press on to the completion of the project.

To Capt. Douglas (Moose) Archibald, whose telephone conversations provided more detailed information and venues of which to research Ray Cottrell's story. It is duly noted that the friendship and landmarks that both Ray and you shared together should not be overlooked. Thank you so much for your trust and support as we got into the Vietnam era of his story. Your support could not be replaced.

To Bob Rowen of the _Changjin Journal_, who was my first contact at the beginning of the project. Your conversations were the first to get me started and pointed me in the right direction. Had the letter by Corporal Dill not been found on your website, the story of Ray Cottrell would have had an extreme gap that might have been impossible to uncover. Thank you for allowing me to take part in your ongoing projects within your website. I am truly honored and blessed by the respect that you have shown me. May God bless you for the work that you do.

To Robert McQuillan, whose dedication to both me and my work provided all the genealogical data and verifications that added a new life and prospect to the final result. Your friendship throughout the decades of both your family and yourself will always be cherished.

To Ryan Tyree, grandson of Ray Cottrell Sr. and son of Brenda Cottrell Tyree, for the companionship and favors that helped in my management of the work. Knowing you throughout this work helped solidify my insights to the strength and love that your family shares with one another. Your insights were extremely valuable.

To Karen Cottrell, whose urgings to me got this project going in the first place.

To Kenny McPeek for helping me understand the horse racing industry and for taking the time in a busy racing season to take an interview from me. Thank you for your input.

To James Zobel, archivist at the MacArthur library and museum, for your guidance and information.

To Mandy Moss, for filling in the gaps so many times as secretary, friend, and confidant. For helping me understand the nature of things when I got confused. For your tireless commitment to me. For the many times you patently sat and listened to me and acted as my sounding board. Words cannot begin to express my gratitude throughout all this. Your support of me through this decade has no measure. All my love. You know why! You know!

To all the Cottrell family members who took time out of their busy lives to take interviews, phone calls, and offer insights that gave this project the color and depth that makes it so rich. I hope you are all well pleased by the outcome.

To Gunnery Sgt. Dominic Dillon, U.S. Marine Corps Ret., for proofreading and offering insights on a firsthand basis of what it is like to be a part of this group called brothers-in-arms. For giving me a fuller understanding of what it like to be both a marine and to be in the U.S. Armed Services. Your friendship throughout the years played a pivotal role in me taking on this project. Your understanding helped tremendously in giving this project the respect that this project and the U.S. military so richly deserves. It is an honor to call you friend.

To all the others who have been there for me both at work and at home who listened and asked questions and showed me the support to finish. May God bless you all. Thank you.

BIBLIOGRAPHY

Chapter 1
[1] Videotaped interviews with Raymond Hooker Cottrell from December 2014 to May 2016.
[2] Conversation with Bill Kuster, close friends with Ray Cottrell.
[3] Photo taken from Ray Cottrell's personal library.

Chapter 2
[1] Compliments of the Truman Presidential Library.
[2] Videotaped interviews with Raymond Hooker Cottrell from December 2014 to May 2016.
[3] Compliments of the Koreanwar.org website dedicated to the Korean War.
[4] U.S. Army insignia for delineation of the Thirty-First Infantry. Compliments of the Center for Military History.
[5] U.S. Army photo, Japan, 1949.
[6] Photo taken from Ray Cottrell's personal library.
[7] https://en.wikipedia.org/wiki/USS_Herbert_J._Thomas_(DD-833)
[8] https://en.wikipedia.org/wiki/1950_Pacific_typhoon_season#Typhoon_Kezia

Chapter 3
[1] Photo compliments of U.S. Army historian Ret. Bevin Alexander from bevinalexander.com.
[2] Inchon Landing photo. Compliments of Britannica.com.
[3] Compliments of the Koreanwar.org website dedicated to the Korean War.
[4] Compliments of the Truman Presidential Library.
[5] Video of these strikes can be seen in the documentary *The Korean War in Color* by RGM Entertainment.
[6] http://www.history.army.mil

[7] http://www.koreanwar.org/html/maps_navy.html

[8] http://www.freeforumzone.com/d/10557720/sotto-tiro-francia-1944/discussione.aspx/5

[9] Videotaped interviews with Raymond Hooker Cottrell from December 2014 to May 2016.

Chapter 4

[1] "South to the Naktong, North to the Yalu," history.army.mil.

[2] Photo compliments of U.S. Army historian Ret. Bevin Alexander from bevinalexander.com.

[3] Photo taken from Ray Cottrell's personal library.

[4] West Point Atlas. Courtesy of westpoint.edu.

[5] Map from Koreanwar.org.

[6] Report comes from the Center for Military History titled "Winter of the Yalu." Reprinted in whole at the *American Heritage Magazine*, December 1982, vol. 34.

[7] Videotaped interviews with Raymond Hooker Cottrell from December 2014 to May 2016.

[8] Map is from *Ebb and Flow* by Billy C. Mossman. Printed by the Government Printing Office and available at the Center for Military History.

Chapter 5

[1] From *Ebb and Flow* by Billy C. Mossman. Printed by the Government Printing Office and available at the Center for Military History.

[2] Photo compliments of U.S. Army historian Ret. Bevin Alexander from bevinalexander.com.

[3] The data is available at https://armyhistory.org/nightmare-at-the-chosin-reservoir/, United States Army National Museum by Mathew J. Seelinger, chief historian.

[4] *To the Last Man* by Maj. Franklin D.R. Kestner Sr. This book offers us the details of his events while at Hagaru base and airstrip. It also speaks to the organizational issue that the U.N. forces are working with at that time of the war. Major Kestner would later attend officers training at Fort Knox in 1968 in Armor. A training

program of which SGM Ray Hooker Cottrell would be heavily overseeing for his commanders there.

[5] http://www.Koreanwaronline.com/arms/31RCT.htm

[6] Excerpt from information at Koreanwaronline.com.

[7] Videotaped interviews with Raymond Hooker Cottrell from December 2014 to May 2016.

[8] Photo available at the bevinalexander.com and the Center for Military History (CMH).

[9] *The Chosin Chronology* by Col. George Rasula. PDF file available online at http://www.benning.army.mil/library/content/Virtual/ Donovanpapers/korea/TheChosinChronology.pdf. Photos of 2Bn/31st INF are also available on this document.

[10] *Task Force Faith*: *A Documentary*. http://www.taskforcefaith.com/ by Julie Precious.

[11] *What History Forgot to Record: Chosin Reservoir: A Phantom Force - Lost to History,* ISBN 978-1-63068-144-9, by Ray Vallowe, www.koreanwar-educator.org/topics/chosin/vallowe_research/ index.htm.

Chapter 6

[1] From *Ebb and Flow* by Billy C. Mossman. Printed by the Government Printing Office and available at the Center for Military History.

[2] **Author's note: a full description of the makeup of TF Drysdale and their actions can be seen at http://www.koreanwaronline. com/arms/41RMCpub.htm.**

[3] Photo available at the bevinalexander.com and the Center for Military History (CMH).

[4] Photo courtesy of the Center for Military History.

[5] Videotaped interviews with Raymond Hooker Cottrell from December 2014 to May 2016.

[6] Photo taken from Ray Cottrell's personal library.

[7] Map courtesy of West Point Atlas from westpoint.edu.

Chapter 7

[1] Certificate discovered through public records. Courtesy of Robert McQuillan.

[2] Photo taken from Ray Cottrell's personal library.

[3] Photo courtesy of the Center for Military History.

[4] Videotaped interviews with Raymond Hooker Cottrell from December 2014 to May 2016.

[5] https://en.wikipedia.org/wiki/Buddhist_crisis

[6] https://en.wikipedia.org/wiki/Viet_Cong

Chapter 8

[1] http://www.history.army.mil/books/Vietnam/Comm-Control/ch01.htm, p. 23.

[2] http://www.panoramio.com/photo/6593326

[3] http://www.history.army.mil/books/Vietnam/Comm-Control/ch01.htm, p. 19.

[4] Personal interview with Gunnery Sgt. Dominic Dillon, U.S. Marines, retired.

[5] http://www.jeep-cj.com/forums/f92/barrett-jackson-2009-1951-willys-jeep-412/, dated May 6, 2016.

[6] Photo from Ray Cottrell's personal library.

[7] http://phovui.vietbao.com/yaf_postst32321_Lambro---Mot-thoi-de-nho.aspx#post518188

[8] Photo taken by Mandy Moss

Chapter 9

[1] Information from personal interviews with Ray Cottrell from January 2015 to March 2016.

[2] Information from verbal conversation with Ray Cottrell Jr., 2015.

[3] Information from video interview with Brenda Tyree, Ray Cottrell's daughter, March 2015.

Chapter 10

[1] From Ray Cottrell's personal library.

[2] Document from Ray Cottrell's personal library.

[3] Information from personal interviews with Ray Cottrell from January 2015 to March 2016.

[4] https://en.wikipedia.org/wiki/Air_Medal

[5] Photo from Ray Cottrell's personal library and taken by Douglas "Moose" Archibald.

[6] Map courtesy of West Point College, westpoint.edu.

[7] Military quote from http://www.military-quotes.com/Napoleon.htm.

[8] U.S. Army map of Vietnam, https://katzenmeier.wordpress.com/2011/11/03/katzenmeiers-vietnam-diary-1968-1969.

[9] https://facultystaff.richmond.edu/~ebolt/history398/WarInTheVillagesAndTunnels.html

Chapter 11

[1] Article taken from Ray Cottrell's personal library.

[2] Photos from Ray Cottrell's personal library.

[3] Story taken from video interviews with Ray Cottrell.

[4] Story taken from video interview with Brenda Tyree, February 2015.

[5] Record of events between the author and Ray Cottrell over a twenty-eight-hour period March 24, 2016.

[6] Personal phone conversation with Ray Cottrell, March 24, 2016.

Chapter 12

[1] Photos taken from Ray Cottrell's personal library.

[2] Photos taken by Mandy Moss, April 2016.

[3] Photo taken from Cpt. Douglas Archibald's personal library.

[4] Information obtained via phone conversation with Ken McPeek, April 2016.

[5] http://www.wdrb.com/story/22769060/brandenburg-soldier-wins-order-of-st-maurice-award. Also held in Ray Cottrell's personal library.

[6] https://en.wikipedia.org/wiki/Saint_Maurice

[7] Quote taken from "De Brevitate Vitae" referred to as "On the Shortness of Life," a moral essay written by Seneca the Younger to his friend Paulinus.

[8] Story taken from oral conversations with Ray Cottrell Sr., February 2016.

[9] Story taken from video interview, 2016.

[10] From phone interview with Ray Cottrell Jr., March 2016.

[11] Taken from Ray Cottrell's personal library.

[12] "South to Naktong, North to the Yalu" Government Printing Office, compliments of the Center for Military History.

AUTHOR'S DEDICATION

To my son Robert J. Brooks II and my daughter Christina Marie Giovanetti. If you are happy doing what you do, you will never work a day in your life. While self-discipline is the hardest lesson you will ever learn, you really have only one job: be happy. Continue to improve yourselves and never ever stop learning. I love you both more than you may ever know. I pray that you and yours will always have enough.

CPSIA information can be obtained
at www.ICGtesting.com
Printed in the USA
LVOW03s1513180418
573963LV00002B/324/P